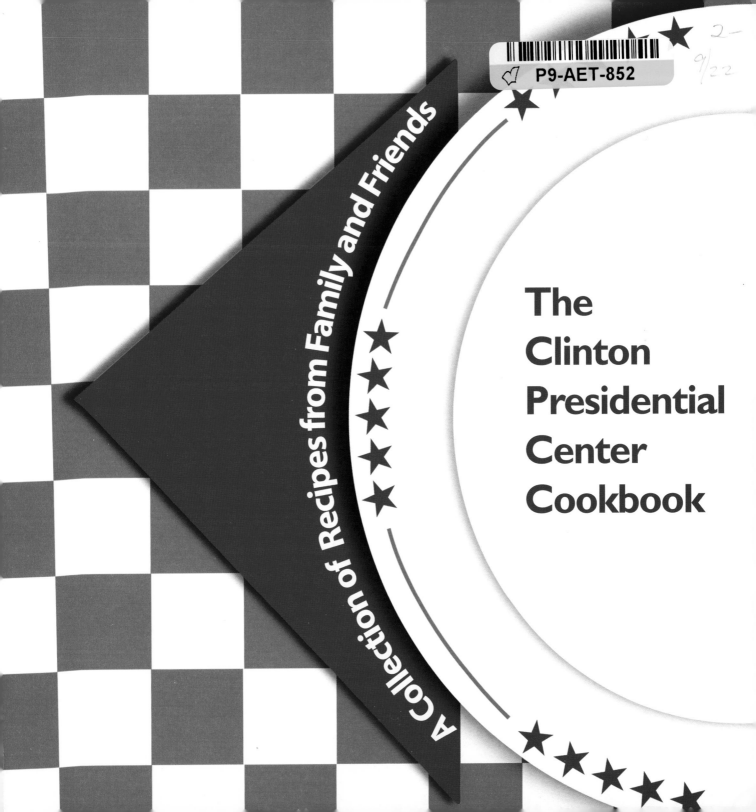

A Collection of Recipes from Family and Friends

The
Clinton
Presidential
Center
Cookbook

THE WILLIAM J. CLINTON PRESIDENTIAL FOUNDATION

P.O. Box 1104
Little Rock, AR 72203

Copyright © 2003
The William J. Clinton Presidential Foundation

ISBN: 0-9743016-0-4
Library of Congress Control Number: 2003109771

First Printing   August 2003   15,000 Copies

WIMMER
COOKBOOKS

ConsolidatedGraphics
1-800-548-2537

Polshek Partnership Architects

The staff of the William J. Clinton Presidential Foundation has really enjoyed putting this book together. We hope you will be pleased with the wide variety of recipes, stories and photographs.
The personalities in this cookbook range from Clinton family members, White House Staff and Cabinet, Clinton Foundation staff and volunteers, to lifelong friends and national and international celebrities.
We thank everyone for participating.

Editors: Shannon Butler and Nealon DeVore

We would like to give special thanks to Cindy Miller for her expert advice on cookbook production.

★ THE WILLIAM J. CLINTON PRESIDENTIAL FOUNDATION ★

The William J. Clinton Presidential Foundation supports both the construction of the William J. Clinton Presidential Center and Park—Library, Museum, Archives, School—as well as the policy work of President Clinton.

The William J. Clinton Presidential Library will be the 12th Presidential Library in the United States. It will consist of a museum highlighting the historic work of President Clinton's two terms in office and the Archives that will be the repository of President Clinton's official papers and other historical material related to the Clinton Administration. Together, the Museum and Archives will serve as the principal naitional and international resource on the eight years of the Clinton Presidency.

The education arm of the William J. Clinton Presidential Center will be the Clinton School of Public Service. Established as part of the University of Arkansas system, the Clinton School will offer a Master's degree in Public Service, certificate programs and collaborative programs and symposia with the Clinton Foundation, the Clinton Archives and other public service institutions.

The Clinton Policy Center will serve as a primary vehicle for President Clinton's ongoing public service mission. Carrying on the work of his Presidency, the Policy Center will focus its work in the following areas:

- *Economic empowerment of poor people*
- *Racial, ethnic, and religious reconciliation*
- *Health security, specifically combating AIDS*
- *Citizen Service*

The Clinton Policy Center will work through partnerships with like-minded idividuals, organizations, corporations and governments often serving as an incubator for new policies and programs.

The proceeds from the sale of this cookbook will benefit the William J. Clinton Presidential Foundation.

Top Left: Volunteers supervise as President Clinton decorates a cake at the DC Central Kitchen.

Top Right: President Clinton and First Lady Hillary Rodham Clinton prepare Thanksgiving Dinner for the homeless at Covenant Baptist Church in Washington, DC.

Above: President Clinton and First Lady Hillary Rodham Clinton work with Americorps volunteers to prepare food for the homeless at the DC Central Kitchen.

All Photos from Clinton Materials Project

★ WHITE HOUSE HOLIDAYS ★

Top Left: White House Pastry Chef Roland Mesnier presents Easter Brunch to the Clintons.

Top Right: President Clinton and First Lady Hillary Rodham Clinton participate in a menorah lighting ceremony in the Oval Office in celebration of Hanukkah.

Above: Each year the White House pastry chef, Roland Mesnier, creates an elaborate gingerbread house to be displayed in the White House for the Holiday Season.

★ FOOD, FRIENDS & FUN ★

Clinton Materials Project

Right: During the 1992 campaign, President Clinton and his staff frequented Doe's Eat Place in Little Rock, Arkansas. President Clinton is pictured here with Doe's staff.

Above: President Clinton celebrates his 50th birthday with the White House staff on the South Lawn.

Right: The Clintons and the Gores share a private moment together during the 1997 inaugural festivities.

Clinton Materials Project

Above: Chief of Staff John Podesta lets off steam in a hot air balloon ride just before one of the summer picnics that takes place on the South Lawn of the White House each year.

Top Right: Margaret Whillock, Ann McCoy, Missy Kincaid, and the late Diane Blair celebrate Missy's baby shower in the State Dining Room of the White House.

Right: As mentioned in her recipe, Nancy Hernreich Bowen loved to give engagement parties for other White House staffers. She is shown here in the East Room celebrating her own engagement with fiancé, Louis Bowen.

CELEBRATIONS ★

Left: President Clinton with Aviva and Dan Rosenthal at Dan's going away party in the White House.

Below: White House Social Secretary Capricia Marshall is treated like a queen for her birthday. First Lady Hillary Rodham Clinton and Cheryl Mills take part in the festivities.

All Photos from Clinton Materials Project

★ AND MORE WHITE HOUSE ACTIVITY ★

Left: The Fabulous Five (Bob Nash, Charles Duncan, Ben Johnson, Al Maldon, and Thurgood Marshall, Jr.) stroll along the West Wing Colonnade.

Right: Betty Currie celebrates her birthday with Justin Cooper, June Gayle Turner, Milli Alston and Janis Kearney.

Above: The Groundbreaking of the William J. Clinton Presidential Center took place on December 5, 2001. Following the ceremony, a barbeque lunch was provided by the Jennings Osborne Family. President Clinton is pictured here serving barbeque.

Right: Dr. David Alsobrook, Director of the Clinton Materials Project and his wife, Ellen, enjoy the food and festivities during the Groundbreaking ceremony.

Above: President Clinton, (back row, left to right) Little Rock Mayor Jim Dailey, City Manager Bruce Moore, and City Director Dean Kumpuris break ground at the ceremony.

★ TOPPING OUT CEREMONY ★

Left: The Topping Out Ceremony of the William J. Clinton Presidential Center took place on May 23, 2003. President Clinton addressed the crowd before the final beam, which had been signed by over five thousand people, was put into place.

Right: Skip Rutherford, President of the William J. Clinton Presidential Foundation, (far right) helps Mitzi and Jennings Osborne serve barbeque to thousands of guests during the Topping Out Fesitivities.

★ ★ ELVIS' FAVORITE ★ ★ GRILLED PEANUT BUTTER AND BANANA SANDWICH

President Clinton has always been a fan of Elvis and his music. Over the years, he has collected memorabilia and numerous records. The cookbook simply would not have been complete without this recipe!

PEANUT BUTTER AND BANANA SANDWICH

2	slices white bread	1	small banana, sliced
3	tablespoons peanut butter	2	tablespoons butter

Toast bread lightly and spread one slice with peanut butter. Place bananas on the other slice, then sandwich the two pieces together. Melt butter in small skillet and grill sandwich on each side until golden brown. Cut diagonally and serve hot.

This famous sandwich is now served daily at Elvis Presley's Memphis on Beale Street.

★ MUSICAL NOTES ★

An Interview with Oxford American -
Fifth Annual Music Issue.

OXFORD AMERICAN: Who was your musical hero as a child?

BILL CLINTON: Elvis.

What was your favorite song as a child?

"Don't Be Cruel." Later Stevie Wonder's "For Once In My Life."

Both you and your brother, Roger, are musical. Was there something about your upbringing that led to this?

We listened to a lot of music from a very early age, and our mother encouraged us.

How has being Southern affected your taste in music?

I like Southern music—and gospel, the blues.

Who is your favorite Southern musician?

B.B. King.

BILL CLINTON'S STATUS AS AMERICA'S FOREMOST AMATEUR SAXOPHONIST
has been noted and duly entered into the pop culture annals. But little else about Mr. Clinton's familiarity with music is known, by the public at least, and it was with the desire to find out more that we questioned Mr. Clinton on this subject. He was gracious enough to take some time while on a bus ride to Oxford (England) to answer our questions.

Jessie Renfroe
& Marc Smirnoff

Were you ever in a band in high school?

A jazz trio and a dance band.

What is your favorite example (on record) of saxophone playing?

Stan Getz's Brazilian music.

What is your favorite line from a song?

"I love you in a place where there's no space or time. / I love you, for in my life you are a friend of mine." Leon Russell, "A Song for You."

What song/piece can you play best?

"Summertime."

Is there a particular piece that you have trouble playing or have never been able to master?

"Take Five" — I could never improvise or cover it very well, no matter how many times I heard Paul Desmond do it.

Do you have a favorite musical moment from the White House?

There were so many—probably Jessye Norman's beautiful performance for the NATO leaders and Fleetwood Mac's reunion performance for my farewell party.

What is the best concert that you have ever been to outside of the ones you held in the White House?

Ray Charles. Constitution Hall, June 24, 1967. I saved the ticket stub for ten years.

What do musicians and politicians have in common?

A balance of order and creativity; discipline and passion.

What is the most memorable thing a musician has ever told you?

"Don't quit your day job."

What campaign songs did you consider before choosing "Don't Stop Thinking About Tomorrow"?

None! A young friend suggested it to me in 1991, and I knew he was right.

When was the last time you sang in public?

A few weeks ago with a band in Nigeria—"Georgia On My Mind."

What do you sing in the shower?

Songs I'd like to sing in public, but am afraid to do so.

There are widespread concerns about the lyrical content of a lot of rap music. What's your take on rap?

I find it interesting. I've tried to appreciate it, sometimes successfully.

What would people be surprised to know that you listen to?

Brötzmann, the tenor sax player, one of the greatest alive.

Is there an album that you could not live without?

The Gentle Side of John Coltrane.

In 1994 your brother, Roger, put out a CD called *Nothing Good Comes Easy.* **We loved the song "Brother, Brother" and in fact wanted it for one of our CDs, but Roger seemed to feel that we were making some kind of joke (which was not our intent; our editor thought it sounded like a really good Journey song). What do you think about that tune?**

I like it.

Do you and Chelsea listen to any of the same music?

Yes. The Beatles and Elton John.

What about you and Hillary?

Hillary and I love Carly Simon. Carole King, Judy Collins—all friends—and Joan Baez.

What is your and Hillary's song?

(Gershwin's) "My One and Only Love."

What is in your CD player now?

Virginia Rodrigues, a fabulous Brazilian singer.

The Virginia Clinton Kelley Birthday Club is a group of women who gathered together and celebrated Mrs. Kelley's birthdays with her. The group still meets every Friday for lunch and remembers Mrs. Kelley each year on her birthday by giving to, or working for, one of her charities.

CHEESE AND ONION SOUFFLÉ

2 (8-ounce) packages cream cheese, softened

1 cup Parmesan cheese
¼ cup mayonnaise

1 (10-ounce) package frozen chopped onions, thawed and drained

Preheat oven to 425°. In a large mixing bowl, combine cream cheese and remaining ingredients. Transfer mixture to baking dish and bake for 15 minutes. Serve with cheese-flavored tortilla chips.

Decrease amount of onion as desired.

Recipes

★ ABOUT THE RECIPES ★

Recipes have been edited for content, consistency, and clarity of ingredients and procedure where necessary. No claim is made as to the originality of each recipe included; they are simply among the favorite dishes of the contributors contacted for the production of the cookbook.

Recipes are presented in alphabetical order according to the contributor's last name as opposed to being in the specific categories as most traditional cookbooks. The following icons are presented alongside the recipe titles to help the reader quickly identify the kind of dish it is.

 APPETIZERS

 MAIN DISHES

 BEVERAGES

 SALADS

 BREADS

 SOUPS

 DESSERTS

 VEGETABLES AND SIDE DISHES

Lori's involvement with the Clintons, the White House, and, in fact, politics began the first time she heard Bill Clinton speak. She called the San Francisco campaign office the next day to volunteer. When the San Francisco office's campaign director received an appointment at the White House and offered Lori a position on her team, Lori packed up her life, moved across country, and never looked back. Her six and a half years at the White House and 18 months as a speechwriter at the Department of Education were treasured years in her life, and she looks forward to supporting the great work being done by the Clintons and the Foundation in the future.

 ## "THE" CHOCOLATE CAKE

CAKE

2	cups all-purpose flour	1	cup water	2	eggs
2	cups sugar	½	cup buttermilk	1	teaspoon vanilla
1	cup butter	1	teaspoon baking soda	¼	teaspoon cinnamon
4	tablespoons cocoa	½	teaspoon salt	1	cup pecan halves

Preheat oven to 350°. Combine flour and sugar in large mixing bowl. In small saucepan, melt butter over low heat; stir in cocoa and water. Add cocoa mixture to flour mixture, combining well. Beat in buttermilk and next 5 ingredients. Pour into prepared 9x13-inch baking pan. Bake for 25 to 28 minutes or until cake tester inserted into center comes out clean. Allow cake to cool. Pour warm Chocolate Icing over cake, spreading well to cover. Decorate with pecan halves.

CHOCOLATE ICING

1	(16-ounce) box confectioners' sugar	½	cup butter	¼	cup cocoa
		6	tablespoons milk	1	teaspoon vanilla

Pour sugar into large mixing bowl. In small saucepan, melt butter over low heat; stir in milk and cocoa. Add cocoa mixture to sugar and beat well. Add vanilla and continue to beat.

The warm icing will be of thin consistency, but will firm as it cools.

This recipe was a big family secret for many years, so much so, that I had to steal it from my grandmother's recipe box during a visit. Much to my surprise, the recipe was written in shorthand that I couldn't decipher. I had to confess my actions to get her to translate. The recipe was shared with my grandmother by her niece who swore her to secrecy. My grandmother has since passed away, but after learning about her unfortunate right-wing leaning politics, I can think of no better tribute than sharing the recipe in this venue. In addition, I used to make this cake a lot during my years at the White House. I was always asked for the recipe, but I never gave it out!

★ SECRETARY MADELEINE ALBRIGHT ★

Dr. Madeleine Korbel Albright served as the 64th Secretary of State of the United States from 1997 to 2001. She was the first woman Secretary of State and is the highest ranking woman in the history of the U.S. government. From 1993 to 1997, Dr. Albright served as the United States Permanent Representative to the United Nations and as a member of the President's Cabinet and National Security Council. In 1995, she led the U.S. delegation to the UN's Fourth World Conference on Women in Beijing, China. Dr. Albright is the founder of The Albright Group LLC, a global strategy firm. She was born in Prague, Czechoslovakia, and immigrated to America with her family after Communists took control of the country in 1948. She is the mother of three daughters and has six grandchildren.

 ## CZECH SAUERKRAUT-ZELI

5-6 bacon slices	Caraway seeds	1 large baking potato, peeled and
1 onion, chopped	3 teaspoons sugar	shredded
1 pound sauerkraut		

In large skillet, cook bacon until crisp. Remove bacon from skillet; drain on paper towels set aside. Sauté onion in bacon drippings until tender; set aside. In large saucepan, cook sauerkraut over medium heat for 15 to 20 minutes. Stir in onion and caraway seeds; mix in sugar and potato. Bring to a light boil, stirring frequently to keep from sticking. Stir in bacon or serve in individual dishes and garnish with reserved bacon.

Potato may be left out if you are watching the carbs!

Bacon drippings may be substituted with 2 tablespoons shortening.

Raised by a Czechoslovak mother, who loved to cook what she had grown up with, this is one of my favorite dishes. I was thrilled to have the opportunity to share it with First Lady Hillary Rodham Clinton when we visited the Czech Republic together in July of 1996. After a long walk through the capital city of Prague, we stopped at a great authentic restaurant. When the waiters brought out the small side portion of zeli, I insisted on more so she could get a real sense of the dish. The chef then went wild and huge amounts of the stuff were piled in front of us. It was evident after the second bite that this was not going to be a favorite of Hillary's. After that, I am convinced she lost confidence in my judgment of food.

★ MUHAMMAD ALI ★

Heralded as the "Athlete of the Century" by Sports Illustrated, Muhammad Ali is undoubtedly one of the greatest sportsmen of all time. He now spends a great deal of his time in humanitarian efforts at home and abroad in the developing world. Whether it's teaching tolerance and understanding, feeding the hungry, following the tenets of his religion, or reaching out to children in need, Muhammad Ali is devoted to making the world a better place for all people. No athlete has ever contributed more to the life of his country, or the world, than Muhammad Ali.

 ## MUHAMMAD ALI'S FAVORITE BREAD PUDDING RECIPE

15 French bread slices, cut into 1-inch cubes	3 eggs	½ teaspoon nutmeg
¼ cup raisins	3 egg yolks	1 cup heavy cream
3 tablespoons butter, cut into pats	½ cup sugar	1 cup milk
	½ teaspoon cinnamon	

Preheat oven to 350°. Arrange half of bread cubes along bottom of buttered 2-quart baking dish. Top with raisins and butter pats. Place remaining bread cubes on top and set aside. In large mixing bowl, whisk together eggs, egg yolks, sugar, cinnamon, and nutmeg until well blended. In medium saucepan, bring cream and milk to a simmer. Add hot cream mixture very slowly to egg mixture, so that it will not curdle. Pour over bread cubes and let stand 20 minutes in order to saturate bread. Place baking dish into roasting pan; add enough water to roasting pan to come halfway up sides of baking dish. Bake for 35 to 40 minutes or until custard sets. Serve warm with maple syrup.

★ DR. MALINI ALLES ★

Dr. Malini Alles, a psychologist and social entrepreneur, started **Stree: Global Investments in Women** in May of 2001. Stree is a non-profit foundation dedicated to improving women's health in disadvantaged communities worldwide. Dr. Alles also serves on the Board of Trustees of the William J. Clinton Presidential Foundation.

 ## SPICY CRAB

4	crabs		Salt to taste	1	cup water
3	onions	2	tablespoons chili paste	1	tablespoon cumin
10	garlic cloves	1	tablespoon sugar	½	teaspoon turmeric
3	serrano chiles	1	teaspoon tamarind	2	teaspoons curry powder

Cut crabs into 4 pieces and clean. Place on grill and cook until lightly brown. Place onions, garlic, chili paste, and tamarind in food processor; process until fine. Place mixture in saucepan over medium heat; cook until oil surfaces. Add cumin, turmeric, and curry powder, stirring well to combine. Fold in grilled crab to mixture and cook over medium heat 15 minutes or until mixture thickens and crab darkens.

I made this recipe up when I was in college. It was always a hit with the young graduate guys. I would cook meals for about 7 of them daily. It helped me polish my cooking skills!

★ DR. DAVID ALSOBROOK ★

Dr. David Alsobrook, Director of the Clinton Presidential Materials Project in Little Rock, was born in Eufaula, Alabama, and grew up in Mobile, Alabama. He participated in the movement of Presidential materials from the White House at the end of the Carter, Bush, and Clinton Administrations. He previously served at the Carter and Bush Presidential Libraries. He and his wife Ellen have two children and one grandson.

 **BRUNSWICK STEW**

2½ pounds chicken
3½ pounds pork roast
3 (14½-ounce) cans tomatoes
2 (14-ounce) cans okra
1 (8-ounce) can tomato paste

2 (14¾-ounce) cans cream-style corn
3 pounds potatoes, cooked and mashed
3 onions, finely chopped

½ cup butter
Dash of Worcestershire sauce
Cayenne pepper to taste
Salt to taste
Dash of garlic powder (optional)

In Dutch oven, stew chicken and pork over medium-high heat until tender. Remove meats from Dutch oven, reserving broth, and debone; discard bones. Return meats to Dutch oven; add tomatoes, tomato paste, onions, cayenne pepper and salt. Cover and simmer over low heat 3 hours. Add potatoes, okra, butter, corn, Worcestershire sauce and garlic powder. Simmer 30 minutes, stirring occasionally.

Yield: 8 to 12 servings

This is my mother's recipe and has been in our family for many years. Brunswick Stew is a traditional Deep South dish, which is often served with barbeque.

★ CLARA R. APODACA ★

Clara R. Apodaca, former First Lady of New Mexico, served in the Clinton Administration from 1993 to January 2001. From 1989 to 1993, she was General Assistant to Chairman Ron Brown at the Democratic National Committee. Prior to her moving to Washington, DC, she served as Cabinet Secretary for the New Mexico Office of Cultural Affairs. She is the mother of five children and has six grandchildren.

 ## Biscochitos (Mexican Cookies)

2 cups lard or solid shortening	4 cups all-purpose flour	2 teaspoons ground anise seed
1½ cups sugar, divided	½ teaspoon salt	1 teaspoon cinnamon
1 cup orange juice	1 teaspoon baking powder	

Preheat oven to 400°. In large mixing bowl, cream lard and ½ cup sugar, combining well. Add orange juice and let stand. In mixing bowl, sift together flour, salt, baking powder, and ground anise seed. Combine with lard mixture. Knead more flour into dough until it forms a ball and is not sticky. Roll out onto waxed paper to ⅛ to ¼-inch thickness. Cut into diamond shapes, using knife or pastry wheel. Bake for 12 minutes or until light brown. In shallow dish, combine remaining sugar and cinnamon; dip hot cookies in sugar mixture and cool.

Orange juice may be substituted with same amount of wine.

 *This traditional family cookie recipe was handed down to former First Lady of New Mexico Clara Apodaca by her mother, grandmother, and great-grandmother and is served at all festive occasions. It is a favorite holiday treat and is quite frequently referred to as the "Mexican Wedding Cookie" among New Mexicans.*

Ralph Appelbaum Associates serves as the exhibit designer for the Clinton Presidential Center. Ralph and his team have produced over 120 museums and exhibitions around the world for 25 years. His renowned work, which includes the United States Holocaust Memorial Museum, the Newseum, and the American Museum of Natural History, have won every major design award.

 **MINETRY'S MIRACLE**

1 pound butter	1 scant cup bourbon	1 cup chopped pecans
2 cups sugar	4 (1-ounce) squares unsweetened	24 double ladyfingers, split
12 eggs, separated	chocolate, melted	1½ cups heavy cream, whipped and
48 amaretti	1 teaspoon vanilla	sweetened to taste with
		confectioners' sugar

In large mixing bowl, cream together butter and sugar until light and fluffy. Beat egg yolks until light in color; beat into creamed mixture. Place amaretti in bourbon; let stand until saturated. Beat chocolate into creamed mixture. Add vanilla and pecans; set aside. Beat egg whites until stiff, but not dry; fold into mixture. Line a 10-inch springform pan around sides and bottom with split ladyfingers. Layer half of soaked amaretti in bottom of lined pan, then half chocolate mixture; repeat. Chill overnight. Remove sides of pan and top with whipped cream.

Yield: 12 servings

This long secret, Southern recipe from pecan and bourbon country was rediscovered while I was a Peace Corps Volunteer in the mid 1960s in the Peruvian Andes. When I got back to the States, I tried to make it and found it to be incredibly sumptuous and easy to make. It is the ultimate refrigerator cake, requiring no baking, and is an American cousin to the French "charlotte". It is so impressive that it should be saved for a special occasion or the inauguration of our next Democratic President!

★ LOREEN ARBUS ★

Loreen Arbus, President of Loreen Arbus Productions Inc., is the first woman in the United States to head programming for a national television network (both Showtime and Cable Health Network/Lifetime). She is a prolific writer of episodic scripts and has written six books. Additionally, she has been a contributing editor to *Los Angeles* and *Life* magazines. Loreen is also a foremost Argentine Tango dancer.

 ## NANA'S NOODLE PUDDING

3 egg yolks	2 cups sour cream	1 teaspoon vanilla
½ cup sugar	1 package egg noodles, cooked and	2 tablespoons butter, cut into pats
1 (8-ounce) package cream cheese, softened	drained	

Preheat oven to 325°. In medium mixing bowl, stir together egg yolks and sugar until white. Add cream cheese, combining well. Add sour cream and vanilla, combining thoroughly. Fold in noodles, stirring carefully. Pour into buttered 12x5-inch baking dish. Dot with butter. Bake for 1 hour.

My father's mother was a benevolent matriarch who definitely ruled the roost. She was the only grandmother I ever knew, and we affectionately called her "Nana". She lived to the age of 94, and up until the year she died, she would read the Wall Street Journal daily and discuss the market with my dad. Besides having an excellent head for business, Nana was an excellent cook. This particular recipe is of Russian-Jewish origin, and Nana served it as a dinner side dish with beef brisket. It may also be served as a dessert.

The Arnolds, who reside in Texarkana, Texas, are long-time friends and supporters of President and Senator Clinton.

 **COCA-COLA CAKE**

CAKE

2 cups all-purpose flour	2 eggs, beaten	2 tablespoons cocoa powder
2 cups sugar	2 teaspoons baking soda	1 cup Coca-Cola
1 cup butter, softened	1 teaspoon vanilla	1½ cups miniature marshmallows
½ cup buttermilk		

Preheat oven to 350°. In large mixing bowl, combine flour and next 8 ingredients, beating well with electric mixer. Gently fold in marshmallows. Pour into prepared 9x13-inch baking pan. Frost when cooled.

FROSTING

½ cup butter, softened	1 (16-ounce) box confectioners' sugar	1 cup chopped pecans
3 tablespoons cocoa powder	6 tablespoons Coca-Cola	

In medium mixing bowl, combine butter, cocoa powder, sugar and cola; mix until creamy. Fold in pecans.

This is the BEST chocolate cake in the world, so if you're into chocolate, you'll love this. Don't let its name deceive you! It was given to me about 25 years ago by one of the great cooks at my church in Texarkana, Arkansas. This sweet lady has long since passed away, but I never bake this cake without remembering her.

★ LIZA ASHLEY ★

Liza Ashley served as the cook (or as then-Governor David Pryor termed it, the "food production manager") at the Arkansas Governor's Mansion for seven governors, including Governor Bill Clinton. Liza was a part of each governor's family and has many recipes and stories to share about each of them.

GARLIC GRITS

1 cup grits, uncooked	¼ pound Cheddar cheese, shredded	3 dashes of Worcestershire sauce
1 (6-ounce) tube garlic cheese, cut into pieces	½ cup butter	3 egg whites, stiffly beaten

Cook grits according to package directions. Add cheeses, butter, and Worcestershire sauce; set aside. Just before baking, fold in egg whites. Bake at 350° for 30 minutes.

This is a great recipe to serve at buffets and a wonderful alternative to potatoes or rice with roast beef.

BEEF TENDERS

6 pounds beef tenders	Coarsely ground black pepper to taste
1 (16-ounce) bottle Italian salad dressing	

Marinate meat in salad dressing 4 to 5 hours, turning occasionally. Sprinkle with pepper. Grill to desired doneness.

Beef Tenders were one of President Clinton's favorites when Governor of Arkansas. I served them often at formal dinners. They will melt in your mouth!

A native of Kansas, Lori played a critical role in the 1992 Clinton campaign in the state, which produced the best showing for a Democratic Presidential nominee since 1964. She then served on the Transition Team's correspondence unit, and worked for the correspondence unit of the First Lady. She spent most of the Clinton Administration at the Department of Energy, helping enact the first compensation package for atomic workers who were made ill by their work for the government. Now living in Brooklyn, New York, and aiding progressive non profit groups, she is still fighting for community, opportunity, and responsibility. As a third-generation Lebanese-American, Lori loves cooking her grandmother's recipes from the "old country".

 **KIBBI NAYYE**

HUSHWA

2	tablespoons butter	2	tablespoons pine nuts	Salt and pepper to taste
1	pound chili-grind lean round steak		Cinnamon to taste	

In large skillet, melt butter over medium-high heat. Sauté round steak and pine nuts, adding cinnamon, salt, and pepper to taste. Set aside and keep warm.

KIBBI

1-2	cups finely ground bulgur wheat	1	sweet onion, cut into chunks	Marjoram to taste
1	pound lean round steak, cut into chunks	½	cup butter, melted	Salt and pepper to taste
			Cinnamon to taste	

Place wheat in bowl and cover with water. Soak until plump, approximately 10 minutes. In food processor, process round steak and onion, being careful not to over process. Drain wheat and add to steak mixture, mixing well. Add butter, cinnamon, marjoram, salt, and pepper. Serve raw, topped with small amount of Hushwa, and with thin Lavash bread or tortillas.

Raw Kibbi must be refrigerated immediately and must be eaten within two days of preparation.

This is an old recipe from my Lebanese father's side of the family. Many Lebanese immigrants settled in Wichita, Kansas, in the early 1900s, including my grandparents, who met and married in Kansas City. This recipe, eaten raw, is the ultimate comfort food for us.

★ DOUG BAND ★

Doug Band began working for the Clinton Administration as an intern in the White House Counsel's office after graduating from the University of Florida. In 1999 he became a special assistant to the President and shortly thereafter, a deputy assistant to the President and finally the President's aide in 2000. Doug stayed with the President after graduating from Georgetown Law School in 2001 and has been Counselor to him ever since.

 ## MYRN'S CHOCOLATE OR BANANA CHEESE PIE

BANANA FILLING

1 ounce crème de banana liqueur	3 (3-ounce) packages banana instant pudding mix	1 jar toddler bananas
2 (8-ounce) packages low fat or non fat cream cheese	2½ cups skim milk	Banana slices

In large mixing bowl, cream liqueur and cream cheese with electric mixer on medium speed. In separate bowl, combine pudding mix and milk. Gradually add to cream cheese mixture and beat until smooth. Place banana slices in bottom of crust and cover with baby food. Pour cream cheese mixture into pie crusts. Chill several hours before serving.

CHOCOLATE FILLING

1 ounce crème de cocoa	2 (8-ounce) packages low fat or non fat cream cheese	2 cups skim milk
		2 (3-ounce) packages chocolate instant pudding mix

In large mixing bowl, cream liqueur and cream cheese with electric mixer on medium speed. In separate bowl, combine pudding mix and milk. Gradually add to cream cheese mixture and beat until smooth. Pour into pie crusts. Chill several hours before servings.

CRUST

16 pecan sandies	6 tablespoons butter, softened	Nuts (optional)

Preheat oven to 350°. In food processor, process pecan sandies and butter in batches until crumbly. Add nuts if desired. Transfer mixture to baking sheet. Bake for 10 to 12 minutes. Remove from oven, stir, and press immediately into two (9 or 10-inch) pie pans.

Yield: 2 pies

This is a family recipe that has been a tradition in my family for many years. Our family makes a great effort to be together for Thanksgiving, and these pies are present every year. The recipe evolved from a visit to a very famous Tampa, Florida, restaurant, perhaps twenty years ago. My mother asked a waiter for the recipe, and he happily gave it to her. She started making the recipe and giving it to friends. A mutual friend of the restaurant owner let him know about this, and the owner promptly changed the restaurant's recipe to meld with their edict of using only natural ingredients. My mother has modified the recipe to be more heart healthy, but adheres to the basic original recipe.

★ ROBERT B. BARNETT ★

A partner at Williams & Connolly LLP, Mr. Barnett is considered one of the premier authors' representatives in the world. His clients have included Bill Clinton, Hillary Rodham Clinton, Katharine Graham, Bob Woodward, Art Buchwald, Queen Noor, and numerous senators and public figures. He has worked on six national presidential campaigns, focusing on debate preparation. During the 1992 Clinton/Gore campaign, Barnett practiced debating with Bill Clinton more than twenty times. He was named one of "Washington's Fifty Best Lawyers" by Washingtonian Magazine as well as one of the one hundred most powerful people in entertainment by Entertainment Weekly Magazine.

THE BEST TOMATO SOUP IN THE HISTORY OF THE WORLD

¾ cup butter, divided
2 tablespoons olive oil
1 onion, sliced
2 fresh thyme sprigs
   (or ½ teaspoon dried thyme)

4 fresh basil leaves
   (or ½ teaspoon dried basil)
Salt and pepper to taste
3½ pounds tomatoes, peeled and chopped

3 tablespoons tomato paste
¼ cup all-purpose flour
3¾ cups chicken broth
1 teaspoon sugar
1 cup heavy cream

In Dutch oven, melt ½ cup butter over medium-high heat. Add oil, onion, thyme, basil, salt and pepper. Sauté onion until golden brown. Add tomatoes and tomato paste, stirring constantly, 10 minutes. In large mixing bowl, combine flour and 1 cup broth and mix well. Add remaining broth, stirring until flour is smooth. Add flour mixture to tomato mixture; cook 30 minutes, stirring well. Add sugar and cream and stir 5 minutes. Add remaining ¼ cup butter, stirring until butter melts.

 SPANISH RICE

1 pound ground beef
1 cup chopped tomatoes
½ cup minced onion

½ cup chopped bell pepper
1 garlic clove, minced (optional)
1 tablespoon garlic salt

¼ teaspoon pepper
2 teaspoons chili powder
1 cup white rice, cooked

In large skillet, cook beef over medium-high heat, stirring occasionally to crumble, until brown; drain excess fat. Stir in tomatoes and next 5 ingredients. Simmer 30 to 45 minutes. Add rice to mixture; simmer 5 to 10 minutes, then serve.

Yield: 6 servings

★ ATTORNEY GENERAL MIKE BEEBE ★

On January 14, 2003, Mike Beebe was sworn in as the 51st Attorney General for the State of Arkansas, continuing to serve the public after having spent twenty years in the Arkansas General Assembly. Attorney General Beebe and his wife, the former Ginger Croom, have three adult children: David, Tammy, and Kyle.

MINI-CHOCOLATE-CHIP CHEESECAKE BALL

1 (8-ounce) package cream cheese, softened	¾ cup confectioners' sugar	¾ cup miniature semi-sweet chocolate chips
½ cup butter, softened	2 tablespoons brown sugar	¾ cup finely chopped pecans
	½ teaspoon vanilla	

In medium bowl, combine cream cheese and butter until smooth. Stir in sugars and vanilla; fold in chocolate chips. Cover with plastic wrap and chill 2 hours. Shape chilled mixture into a ball. Wrap with plastic wrap and chill 1 hour or overnight. Roll cheese ball in pecans before serving. Serve with chocolate graham crackers.

CORN AND WALNUT DIP

2 (8-ounce) packages cream cheese, softened	1 tablespoon chili powder	1 (8¾-ounce) can whole kernel corn, drained
¼ cup cooking oil	1 tablespoon cumin	1 cup chopped walnuts
¼ cup lime juice	½ teaspoon salt	1 onion, chopped
	Dash of pepper	

In large mixing bowl, combine cream cheese and next 6 ingredients; beat with electric mixer on medium speed until smooth. Fold in corn, walnuts, and onion and gently mix. Serve at room temperature with tortilla chips.

Ashley Bell served as an advance person for both the President and First Lady from the 1992 campaign through the Clinton Administration. Additionally, she worked as a consultant to the DNC and on numerous Administration projects, including the 53rd Inauguration and the Denver G-8 Summit.

 ## CHIPOTLE SAUTÉED SPINACH

1 tablespoon olive oil 2 garlic cloves, thinly sliced lengthwise	2 pounds spinach (about 2 large bunches), washed, stemmed, and drained	½ whole chipotle in adobo sauce, chopped or pureed Salt and pepper to taste

In large saucepan over medium-high heat, heat oil until hot, but not smoking. Add garlic and spinach and sauté, turning with tongs. Cook until spinach wilts, but is still bright green (about 2 to 3 minutes). Mix in chipotle just before removing from heat. Season with salt and pepper.

Serve as a side or under grilled chicken.

This is my version of a dish that I originally had in an Italian restaurant in San Miguel de Allende, Mexico. It's fast, easy, and has a great smoked flavor!

★ DON BINGHAM ★

Don Bingham is the Administrator of the Arkansas Governor's Mansion. He and Arkansas First Lady Janet Huckabee coordinated and directed the *Governor's Mansion Homecoming* in July of 2002, which brought together all seven living Arkansas governors, including President Clinton. One of the Governors who attended that special event, Frank White, passed away in May 2003.

 ## ARKANSAS HOT BROWN

½ cup butter	2 egg yolks, beaten	Sliced ham
3 tablespoons all-purpose flour	1 cup shredded American cheese	6 tomato slices
2 cups milk	1 cup shredded Colby cheese	6 bacon slices, cut in half and crisply
Hot sauce to taste	6 white bread slices, toasted	cooked
1 cup shredded Parmesan cheese	Sliced chicken or turkey	Paprika

Preheat oven to 400°. In 4-quart heavy saucepan, melt butter over medium heat. Mix in flour until smooth. Add milk slowly, stirring constantly until thickened. Add hot sauce and Parmesan cheese; remove from heat. Reserve ½ cup sauce and set aside remaining sauce. Combine egg yolks and ½ cup sauce, mixing well. Return mixture to remaining sauce, stirring constantly. Add American and Colby cheeses, stirring until cheese melts. Remove from heat. Place bread slices on individual heat resistant plates. Cover bread slices with chicken or turkey and ham. Cover each serving with sauce and top with tomato and bacon. Sprinkle with paprika. Bake for 10 to 15 minutes or until bubbly.

Yield: 6 servings

 ## CHICKEN À LA SCAMPI

1 bunch green onions, chopped	2 pounds boneless, skinless chicken breasts, cut into ½-inch pieces	2 tomatoes, coarsely chopped
1 teaspoon minced garlic		¼ cup freshly chopped parsley
¼ cup butter	1 teaspoon salt	Butter
¼ cup olive oil	½ teaspoon freshly ground black pepper	1 (12-ounce) package fettuccini, cooked al dente
Juice of 1 lemon		

In large skillet over medium-high heat, sauté onions and garlic in butter and olive oil until tender. Add lemon juice, chicken, salt and pepper. Cook, stirring constantly, 8 to 10 minutes, or until chicken is no longer pink. Add tomatoes and parsley; cover and cook 5 to 6 minutes, or until tomatoes are thoroughly heated. Serve over hot buttered fettuccini.

Yield: 4 to 5 servings

May also be served over rigatoni.

★ EUGÉNIE BISULCO ★

Eugénie Bisculo is currently Director of Correspondence and Advisor for Art and Collections to President Bill Clinton. During the Clinton Administration, she served first as the Assistant to the Director of the State Department's Art in Embassies Program and finally as Senior Writer in Oval Office Operations at the White House. She is the daughter of two wonderful cooks, Thomas and Geneviève Bisulco of Alco, Arkansas.

 ## MAMA EUGÉNIE'S ITALIAN MEATBALLS

3-6 pounds ground beef, turkey, pork, or combination
1-2 cups breadcrumbs or cracker crumbs
2 eggs, beaten
2 cups finely chopped onions
2 cups cooked rice

1 cup fresh parsley
½ cup dried herbs
2 tablespoons garlic powder
1 tablespoon fennel seeds
Salt and pepper to taste

Ketchup (optional)
Olive oil
Crushed tomatoes
Garlic
Basil

In large mixing bowl, combine meat with next 10 ingredients, blending well. Mixture should hold together when rolled between palms. Use firm circular motion between hands to form 2-inch meatballs. In large skillet over medium-high heat, brown meatballs in enough oil for frying, turning often. Drain on paper towels and set aside. In large saucepan over medium-high heat, combine crushed tomatoes, garlic, basil, and small amount of olive oil. Add meatballs to pasta sauce and simmer 2 to 8 hours.

Yield: 20 to 25 meatballs

The dried herbs may be a combination of oregano, basil, parsley, rosemary or other fresh herbs.
Quantities in this recipe are very flexible. Add or reduce the amount of spices according to your own taste.

★ BONO ★

According to President Clinton, Bono is a "21st century Renaissance Man", whose passion for music is matched, if not exceeded, by his passion for justice, human rights, and empowerment of the poor. Bono's efforts to combat the burgeoning AIDS pandemic, particularly in Africa, have helped focus the world's attention on one of the most significant challenges of our time. He has a keen awareness of global interdependence and knows that what happens in developing nations affects all nations. President Clinton is proud to be his friend, and prouder still that he is such a great friend to the world's poor and afflicted, for whom he has labored so hard and so well.

BLACK VELVET

1 part champagne
1 part Guinness stout

Half-fill champagne flute with Guinness. Top up with champagne and stir. The whole is not greater than the sum of the parts, but the hangover is...

Yield: 1 serving

Great Irishmen like Joyce, Beckett, and Oscar Wilde moved to Paris for good reason, but apart from that, they wanted to intellectually colonize the French speaking, French impressed world... they pulled it off... and the Black Velvet is why...

★ ERSKINE BOWLES ★

Erskine Bowles has a wealth of experience in both public and private sectors of the economy. He served as President Clinton's Chief of Staff from November of 1996 until November of 1998. As Chief of Staff, he was widely credited with being the architect of the 1997 bi-partisan balanced budget agreement. Erskine also served the Administration as Assistant to the President, Deputy Chief of Staff, and Administrator for the U.S. Small Business Administration. Erskine has served on numerous boards of directors for public companies while also remaining quite active in community service. He and his wife Crandall reside in Charlotte, North Carolina, and are the proud parents of three adult children.

 **HOT CHOCOLATE SAUCE**

1 ounce baker's unsweetened chocolate	1/3 cup boiling water	1/2 teaspoon vanilla
1 tablespoon butter	1 cup sugar	Pinch of salt
	2 tablespoons white corn syrup	

In small saucepan over very low heat, melt chocolate; stir in butter. When both are melted, add boiling water. Return to a boil and add sugar and corn syrup. Boil about 5 minutes, stirring constantly. Add vanilla and salt. For a thicker sauce, boil a bit longer; to thin, add hot water a teaspoon at a time until reaching desired consistency.

Sauce may be kept in same saucepan, covered, and placed in refrigerator until ready to reheat. The sauce will keep quite a while.

★ SAM AND JEAN BOYCE ★

Sam and Jean Boyce have been active supporters of the Clintons since President Clinton's days as Governor. They were a part of the Arkansas Travelers in the '92 and '96 campaigns. Jean represented Arkansas as a delegate to the '92 Democratic National Convention, and Sam represented Arkansas at the '96 Convention. Sam continues to practice law in Newport, Arkansas, while Jean watches over their three grandchildren.

 ## SWEET POTATOES ALEXANDER

1½ cups butter
½ cup sugar
½ cup orange juice
3 ounces Grand Marnier (optional)

1 cup sliced apples
2 cups cooked and sliced sweet potatoes

1 cup sliced peaches
2 bananas, sliced
2 ounces roasted almonds

Preheat oven to 350°. In medium saucepan over low heat, melt butter; add sugar, stirring until sugar dissolves. Add orange juice and bring to a boil. Remove from heat and add Grand Marnier. Spread sauce in bottom of baking dish. Layer apples, sweet potatoes, peaches, and bananas in baking dish. Top with almonds. Bake for 25 minutes.

This makes a great dish to serve company.

 ## YELLOW SQUASH CASSEROLE

2 cups squash, cooked and drained
1 (2-ounce) jar pimiento, drained
2 eggs, beaten

1¼ cups milk
2-3 tablespoons butter, melted
1 cup shredded processed cheese

Grated onion
18 crackers, crushed

Preheat oven to 350°. In large prepared casserole, gently combine squash and next 6 ingredients. Top with cracker crumbs and bake for 30 minutes.

Yield: 6 servings

★ REPRESENTATIVE JAY BRADFORD ★

Jay Bradford currently serves as State Representative for Arkansas District 18, located in Jefferson County, a seat he has held since 1999. Previously, Bradford served as a State Senator from Arkansas' Ninth District for sixteen years from 1983 to 1999. He has been an active member of the Pine Bluff business and political community since 1962. He is the founder and chairman of the board of First Arkansas Insurance, Arkansas' largest home-owned property and casualty insurance agency. The Arkansas Democrat-Gazette has named him one of the "10 Best Legislators in Arkansas".

REPRESENTATIVE JAY BRADFORD'S SEAFOOD CHOWDER

¼	cup butter	4	cups milk	2	tablespoons freshly chopped parsley
4	onions, sliced	1	cup white wine		Hot sauce to taste
2	cups boiling water	2	cups shredded Cheddar cheese		Worcestershire sauce to taste
6	medium uncooked potatoes, cubed	1	pound cooked, peeled shrimp		Seasoning salt to taste
1	tablespoon garlic salt	1	pound cooked scallops		Gumbo filé powder
1	teaspoon pepper	2	tablespoons chopped pimiento		

In Dutch oven over medium-high heat, melt butter; sauté onions until tender. Add water, potatoes, salt, and pepper. Cover and simmer until cooked (about 30 minutes). Do not drain. In large saucepan over medium heat, cook milk, wine, and cheese until cheese melts, being careful not to boil. Add to potato mixture. Add shrimp and remaining ingredients to Dutch oven, gently stirring. Serve warm.

Yield: 8 servings

Representative Bradford won the "Souperman Contest" benefiting the CASA Women's Shelter in Pine Bluff, Arkansas, with this recipe.

★ ZAC BRADLEY ★

Zac Bradley matured through adolescence during the Clinton Presidency. A loyal Clinton supporter, Bradley served as an intern for the William J. Clinton Presidential Foundation in Little Rock. A political science major, he will graduate from Yale University in the spring of 2006.

TACO SOUP

1   pound lean ground beef, browned and drained
1   (15-ounce) can black beans, drained
1   (16-ounce) can red beans, drained
1   (15¼-ounce) can whole kernel corn, drained
1   (10-ounce) can diced tomatoes and chilies
1   (10-ounce) can tomato soup
1   cup water
1   package taco seasoning
    Shredded cheese

In Dutch oven over medium heat, combine beef and next 7 ingredients. Reduce heat and simmer 20 minutes. Serve in individual bowls topped with cheese.

Christie Brinkley was raised in Harrisonville, Missouri and began modeling at the age of fourteen. In addition to being one of the world's most successful supermodels, she is also a politically active Democrat. In 2000, she served as a delegate from New York State for the Democratic National Convention in Los Angeles, California.

 ## BETTY K'S SESAME TOFU

TOFU

1 (14-ounce) package Chinese style firm tofu	2 tablespoons dark sesame oil	2 tablespoons toasted sesame seeds
Sesame Marinade	Brown rice, cooked	Freshly chopped cilantro

Cut tofu into ½-inch thick squares and blot well with paper towels. Pour half of Sesame Marinade into pie plate. Add tofu to pie plate; pour remaining marinade over tofu. Cover and let stand for 1 hour or longer. Drain tofu, reserving marinade for later use. In large skillet over medium-high heat, cook tofu in sesame oil until firm and browned. Add reserved marinade to skillet and cook until marinade is hot and bubbling. Serve over hot brown rice and garnish with sesame seeds and cilantro.

SESAME MARINADE

2 tablespoons sesame oil	5 tablespoons balsamic vinegar	2 tablespoons finely chopped green onions
1 tablespoons dark sesame oil	1-1½ tablespoons sugar	
¼ cup soy sauce		4 tablespoons freshly chopped cilantro

In large bowl, combine oils and remaining ingredients, stirring until sugar dissolves. Taste and adjust to desired sweetness.

Yield: 3 to 4 servings

Before she became our fabulous cook, Miss Betty heard that the new First Family (the Clintons) was looking for a chef for the White House. She applied for the job. Unfortunately, the Clintons had already selected their chef, but Betty still treasures her letter from the Clinton White House thanking her for her interest in serving her President. She also holds on to some delicious recipes! This is one she shared with me, so I could make a healthy meal for my family on her days off. The President's loss was our (weight) gain!

★ DR. HORACE WOODY BROCK ★

"Woody" Brock is President and Founder of Strategic Economic Decisions, Inc. He met President Clinton through mutual college class-mates and continues to support the Clintons and the work of the William J. Clinton Presidential Foundation.

 ## FEDERAL LEMON SPONGE PUDDING CAKE

4　tablespoons butter, softened
¼　cup, plus 2 tablespoons sugar
4　eggs, separated

¼　cup all-purpose flour
¾　cup milk
½　cup lemon juice

Zest of 1 lemon
Pinch of salt
Confectioners' sugar, for dusting

Preheat oven to 325°. In large mixing bowl, cream together butter and ¼ cup sugar with electric mixer. Add egg yolks one at a time, beating well after each addition. With mixer on low speed, beat in flour, milk, lemon juice, and zest. Set aside and clean mixing beaters. In separate mixing bowl, beat egg whites with pinch of salt and remaining 2 tablespoons sugar, until soft peaks form. Stir one-quarter of egg whites into lemon batter. Gently fold in remaining egg whites. Spoon batter into prepared 1½-quart baking dish. Place baking dish into large roasting pan. Carefully pour hot water into roasting pan until water comes halfway up sides of baking pan. Bake for 45 to 50 minutes or until top of cake has set. Allow to cool 20 minutes. Carefully lift dish from roasting pan. Spoon cake into 4 individual serving bowls. Sprinkle with confectioners' sugar and serve immediately.

Yield: 4 servings

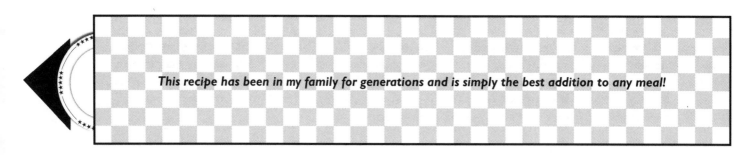

This recipe has been in my family for generations and is simply the best addition to any meal!

★ SHEILA AND RICHARD BRONFMAN ★

Sheila Bronfman met Bill Clinton in 1977, worked in his campaign for Governor, and became a friend soon thereafter. Governor Clinton officiated at Sheila and Richard's wedding. She coordinated the Arkansas Travelers in both Presidential campaigns and continues to support the Clintons by volunteering for the William J. Clinton Presidential Foundation.

 **BROCCOLI CASSEROLE**

1 (8-ounce) package shredded sharp Cheddar cheese, divided
2 (10-ounce) packages frozen chopped broccoli, thawed
1 (6.9-ounce) package wild rice, cooked according to package directions
1 (10¾-ounce) can cream of mushroom soup
½ cup milk
2 (8-ounce) cans mushrooms, drained
1 onion, chopped
½ cup butter, cut into pats

Preheat oven to 375°. In large prepared casserole dish, combine half of cheese and next 6 ingredients. Dot with butter and sprinkle with remaining cheese. Seal tightly with foil and bake for 30 to 45 minutes.

Yield: 8 servings

This casserole may be prepared the day before serving. It may also be frozen and cooked at a later date.

I got this recipe from a friend twenty-five years ago. I have been making it for Thanksgiving every year. It is a family favorite and many other friends now share the recipe.

★ MARILYN AND GREG BROWN ★

Greg Brown is currently the Chairman and CEO of The Union Bank. He served as Treasurer for the Democratic Party of Arkansas during President Clinton's first campaign. His wife, Marilyn, worked for Senator David Pryor for ten years, first in the Governor's Mansion, then in Senator Pryor's Little Rock office. They now reside in Benton, Arkansas.

 ## GOVERNOR'S MANSION RICE PILAF (USING ARKANSAS GROWN RICE)

½ cup butter, melted
1 onion, chopped

2 cups uncooked rice
2 (10.5-ounce) cans beef consommé

1 (10¾-ounce) can cream of mushroom soup

Preheat oven to 350°. In large saucepan over medium-high heat, melt butter. Add onion and rice and sauté until brown. Add consommé and soup; bring to a boil. Pour into prepared baking dish; cover and bake for 15 minutes. Stir dish to keep rice from settling to bottom. Bake additional 15 minutes.

Serve with beef or pork tenderloin or chicken.

This is a recipe I submitted for Liza Ashley's cookbook, Thirty Years at the Mansion. While I was manager of the Arkansas Governor's Mansion during David Pryor's term, the recipe was published in Governor Frances Cherry's chapter of the cookbook. Of course, Liza cooked this for then-Governor and Mrs. Clinton.

★ CAROL BROWNER ★

Appointed by President Clinton in January 1993, and unanimously confirmed by the U.S. Senate, Carol M. Browner served as Administrator of the U.S. Environmental Protection Agency (EPA) for eight years. She currently serves as Chair of the National Audubon Society, one of the country's oldest environmental organizations. Ms. Browner is also a founding member of The Albright Group, LLC, a global strategy firm that is committed to building public-private partnerships to address the most pressing challenges facing people in communities around the globe.

 ## MICHAEL BROWNER'S NO KNEAD IRISH BROWN BREAD

4	cups whole wheat flour	½	cup bran	2-2½	cups water
2	cups unbleached white flour	½	cup rolled oats	½	cup butter, softened
½	cup rye flour	1	tablespoon salt	⅓	cup molasses or honey
½	cup buckwheat flour	3	(¼-ounce) packages yeast	2	eggs, lightly beaten

Preheat oven to 450°. In large mixing bowl, combine flours, bran, oats, salt, and yeast, blending well. In large saucepan over medium heat, combine water, butter, and molasses; bring mixture to 120° to 130° (check temperature with candy thermometer). Using a spoon, add eggs and enough molasses mixture to flour mixture to make a wet, sticky dough. Spoon dough into 2 prepared bread pans. Cover with paper towels and allow dough to rise until just above sides of pans. Remove paper towels and bake for 50 minutes to 1 hour. To avoid over browning, cover tops of pans with foil for the last 10 to 12 minutes of baking.

One of my fondest memories of the Clinton Administration was joining the President on his final foreign trip—a visit to Ireland and England. For me, it was in some ways a trip home. My father was born and raised in Ireland; he came to the United States as a young man with only a limited education. After active combat in the Korean War, he used his veteran's benefits to attend college and become a professor. Now retired, he spends many an hour baking bread. This is one of my favorite recipes.

★ GIO BRUNO ★

Gio Bruno is a native of Little Rock, Arkansas. Raised in his family's Italian restaurant business (Bruno's Little Italy), he worked there in various chef and manager roles until his early thirties when he began his second career in advertising. Gio also has been the lead singer for the local band "The GroanUps" since 1986. "The GroanUps" performed for Governor Clinton at his 1987 and 1991 inaugural celebrations and his 1996 presidential victory party in Little Rock. He became part of the extended Clinton family when he married Marie Clinton in 1990. He is the proud father of four children.

 ## GIO'S PASTA SALAD

PASTA SALAD

1 pound elbow macaroni or multi-colored rotini, cooked and drained
½ cup frozen peas, thawed, rinsed, and drained
½ cup chopped celery
½ cup chopped red onion
1 (3.5-ounce) jar chopped pimientos, drained
2 cups shredded mozzarella cheese
1 teaspoon mustard
1 teaspoon coarsely ground black pepper
1 heaping tablespoon parsley flakes
2 teaspoons salt
½ cup mayonnaise
1 cup sweet and sour salad dressing
Sliced black olives, for garnish

In large bowl, combine pasta and next 5 ingredients, tossing well. In small bowl, combine mustard and next 5 ingredients, blending well. Pour mustard mixture over pasta salad, tossing well to coat. Chill several hours or overnight. Garnish with olives before serving.

Sweet and sour salad dressing is similar to cole slaw dressing.

My father, Jimmy, started Bruno's Little Italy Restaurant in the 1940s. My two brothers, Jay and Vince, and I began working with our father in the business as early as elementary school. Although our family sold the business after our father's death in the mid-1980s, Bruno's today remains a very popular restaurant, well-known for Neapolitan-style pizza and other authentic Italian dishes. Vince continues the family tradition in the kitchen as the head chef. President and Mrs. Clinton were among Bruno's patrons while they lived in Little Rock.

TUNA SAUCE FOR PASTA

¾ cup cooking oil
½-1 teaspoon chopped garlic
½ cup tomato sauce
½ teaspoon salt
  Pinch of coarsely ground black
    pepper

Pinch of crushed red pepper
Pinch of dried parsley
Pinch of basil
Pinch of ground thyme
1 teaspoon anchovy paste
2 (6-ounce) cans tuna packed in oil

1 tablespoon chopped pine nuts
¼ cup sliced black olives
  Linguine, cooked al dente
  Shredded Parmesan or Romano
    cheese
  Dried parsley, for garnish

In large skillet over medium heat, heat oil; add garlic and cook until slightly brown. Lower heat and stir in tomato sauce. Add salt and next 5 ingredients, stirring well. Simmer over low heat; stir in anchovy paste. Add undrained tuna, using a wooden spoon to gently stir (to keep tuna from flaking). Simmer until hot throughout. Before serving, stir in pine nuts and olives. Serve over linguine; sprinkle with cheese and parsley.

Yield: 2 to 3 servings

★ MARIE CLINTON BRUNO ★

Marie Clinton Bruno, Butch and Roy Clinton, Jr.'s oldest daughter, is a native of Fayetteville, Arkansas. (Roy Jr. is President Clinton's first cousin.) She is married to Gio Bruno. Marie worked as a volunteer in all of the Clinton campaigns, slowing down in the 1992 and 1996 presidential campaigns following her marriage to Gio and her new role as stepmother to his three children. Their son was born in January 1991. She is the Communications Manager for the Arkansas Department of Workforce Education and, between her work and her blended family, still supports her cousin by volunteering for the William J. Clinton Presidential Foundation.

 ## CHICKEN CORDON BRUNO

1   (8-ounce) package Neufchâtel cream cheese, softened
½   cup shredded Parmesan cheese
3   tablespoons butter, softened
1   tablespoon dried basil

1   (8-ounce) can mushrooms, undrained
½   cup white wine
½   cup white balsamic vinegar
2   tablespoons lemon juice

2   tablespoons olive oil or canola oil
4   boneless, skinless chicken breasts
4   thin ham slices
Shredded mozzarella cheese

Preheat oven to 325°. In medium mixing bowl, combine cheeses, butter, and basil; set aside. In large mixing bowl, combine mushrooms and juice, wine, vinegar, lemon juice, and oil. Mix well and set aside. Place waxed paper on flat working surface. Pound each chicken breast on waxed paper with mallet to ⅓-inch thickness. Top each chicken breast with ham slice. Spoon cheese mixture onto ham slice, spreading evenly across each piece. Roll each chicken breast up, jelly roll fashion, securing with toothpicks. Dip chicken in mushroom mixture 20 seconds. Remove from mushroom mixture and place into prepared 9-inch casserole dish. Bake for 20 minutes, basting chicken at least twice with mushroom mixture. Sprinkle with mozzarella cheese and baste again. Bake for additional 20 minutes or until chicken is no longer pink in center, basting at least one more time.

Yield: 4 servings

★ DOUG AND JULIE BUFORD ★

Doug and Julie Buford reside in Little Rock, Arkansas, where Doug is an attorney for Wright, Lindsey, & Jennings. Bill Clinton worked with Doug at Wright, Lindsey, & Jennings after his first term as governor. Their children, Molly Buford and Shannon Butler, both worked in the Clinton Administration.

CHOCOLATE TRUFFLE CAKE WITH BOURBON SAUCE AND RASPBERRY COULIS

CAKE

- 2 (8-ounce) packages semisweet chocolate squares
- ½ cup unsalted butter
- 1½ teaspoons all-purpose flour
- 1½ teaspoons sugar
- 1 teaspoon hot water
- 4 eggs, separated

Preheat oven to 425°. Grease bottom of 8-inch springform pan. Melt chocolate and butter in double boiler. Add flour, sugar, and water and blend well. Add egg yolks, one at a time, beating well after each addition. In separate bowl, beat egg whites until stiff, but not dry. Fold chocolate mixture into egg whites. Pour batter into pan and bake for 15 minutes. (Cake will look uncooked in center.) Cool completely and chill or freeze. Spoon Bourbon Sauce on dessert plate, place slice of cake on top, and decorate plate with dots of Raspberry Coulis.

BOURBON SAUCE

- 2 eggs, beaten
- ¾ cup half-and-half
- 2 tablespoons sugar
- 2 tablespoons bourbon (optional)

In medium saucepan over medium heat, combine eggs, half-and-half, and sugar, whisking constantly for 5 minutes or until mixture thickens. Remove from heat and stir in bourbon.

RASPBERRY COULIS

- 2½ pints raspberries
- ½ cup confectioners' sugar

Puree raspberries and confectioners' sugar in blender until smooth and strain. Cover and chill.

Yield: 8 servings

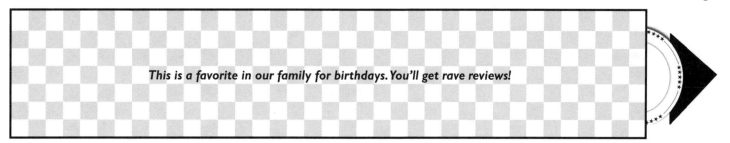

This is a favorite in our family for birthdays. You'll get rave reviews!

★ MOLLY BUFORD ★

Molly Buford worked in the Office of the First Lady as a Scheduler. In addition, she was the Associate Director of Advance for both the President and First Lady. She then worked under Secretary Bill Daley at the Department of Commerce as the Director of Scheduling and Advance. At the end of the Administration, she continued to work for Secretary Daley on the Gore/Lieberman campaign in Nashville, Tennessee.

 ## SKILLET CHOCOLATE PIE

1	cup milk	1	cup sugar	2	tablespoons butter
3	tablespoons cocoa	3	egg yolks, beaten	1	baked pie shell
3	tablespoons all-purpose flour	1	teaspoon vanilla		

In glass jar with top, combine milk, cocoa, and flour, mixing thoroughly. Pour mixture into skillet, stirring in sugar and egg yolks. Cook over medium heat, stirring constantly, until mixture is of pie consistency. Gently stir in vanilla and butter. Pour into pie shell and chill until set.

Yield: 8 servings

Filling may be doubled for a thicker pie.

★ SENATOR DALE BUMPERS AND BETTY BUMPERS ★

Dale Bumpers was elected to the Senate in 1974 and served four terms as a Democratic Senator from Arkansas. He previously served two terms as Governor of Arkansas. He recently pulished his memoir, *The Best Lawyer in a One-Lawyer Town*. As First Lady of Arkansas, Betty Bumpers developed a highly acclaimed national program for immunizing children. The Bumpers divide their time between Washington and Little Rock.

 **DALE'S CRAB SOUP**

6	tablespoons butter	8	cups fat-free milk	I	pound lump backfin crab
2	large celery stalks, finely chopped	2	cups half-and-half		Salt and pepper to taste
I	onion, finely chopped	I	garlic clove, minced		Hot sauce to taste

In medium skillet over medium heat, melt butter. Sauté celery and onion until tender. In large saucepan, stir together milk and half-and-half and heat gently, but do not boil. When warm, add celery, onion, and garlic to milk mixture. Carefully stir in crabmeat and adjust seasonings to taste.

This is good as a first course soup or as a main course with salad and oyster crackers.

We serve the soup as a family meal... it has become a tradition in our home because Dale makes it. We also serve the soup at parties with friends.

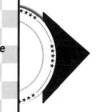

★ SHANNON BUTLER ★

Shannon Butler worked for the Administration from 2000 to 2001. She was the Special Assistant to the Director of Presidential Scheduling and then became the Assistant Director of Presidential Scheduling. At the end of the Administration, she worked for the Transition office as the Deputy Director of Presidential Scheduling. She currently lives in Little Rock and works for the William J. Clinton Presidential Foundation as the Associate Director.

 ## CHEESY DIP

1 (16-ounce) package pasteurized cheese, cubed	2 (14-ounce) cans diced tomatoes with green chiles	¼ teaspoon dry mustard
	2 teaspoons paprika	1 teaspoon chili powder
		½ teaspoon garlic salt
		1 teaspoon cumin

Place cheese cubes and tomatoes in microwave proof bowl. Microwave on medium to high setting until cheese melts, stirring occasionally. Stir in paprika and remaining ingredients. Serve with tortilla chips.

I avoid the kitchen whenever possible, however, this recipe is easy and good. Great appetizer for cookouts!

★ MARY CHRIS AND CHRIS BURROW ★

Chris Burrow is a member of the program management team for the William J. Clinton Presidential Center and Park. He and his wife Mary Chris have been long-time supporters of the Clintons.

 ## "BEST EVER BRISKET"

1 (10-pound) beef brisket	Dry Rub	Horseradish Sauce

Preheat oven to 200°. Prepare grill for searing brisket. Rub two-thirds of Dry Rub on fat side of brisket and remaining one-third of Dry Rub on other side. Place brisket directly over hot coals for 15 minutes on each side or until brisket is charred black. Remove from grill and wrap in foil. Transfer to oven and bake for 8 hours. Slice and serve with Horseradish Sauce.

DRY RUB
2	tablespoons cumin	2	tablespoons salt	2	tablespoons cornstarch
2	tablespoons garlic powder	2	tablespoons chili powder	1	tablespoons black pepper

In small bowl, combine spices and blend thoroughly.

HORSERADISH SAUCE
4	tablespoons prepared horseradish	½	cup sour cream	1	teaspoon sugar
½	cup mayonnaise		Juice of 1 lemon		

In medium mixing bowl, combine ingredients and mix well.

Yield: 6 to 8 servings

This is so good, you rarely make it to the table before it is eaten! It also makes great sandwiches with rolls and Horseradish Sauce.

★ ANGIE BYUN, ESQ. ★

Angie Byun worked in the White House in 1996 and again in 1999. She continues to support the William J. Clinton Presidential Foundation.

 ## GINGER LEMON COOKIES

½ cup butter	1 ⅓ cups all-purpose flour	⅓ cup thinly diced crystallized ginger candy
1 cup sugar, divided	½ teaspoon baking soda	
1 egg, beaten	½ teaspoon salt	36 pieces crystallized ginger candy (for decorating cookies)
2 tablespoons lemon zest		

Preheat oven to 350°. Mix butter and ¾ cup sugar until fluffy. Add egg and mix well. Stir in lemon zest. Combine flour, baking soda, salt and diced crystallized ginger candy. Add to butter mixture and blend well. Drop batter by tablespoon, about 2 inches apart, onto cookie sheet. Bake for 6 minutes. Sprinkle cookies with ¼ cup sugar and press one piece of the candy into the center of each cookie. (Cookies will be soft.) Return cookies to oven, rotating baking sheets for even browning. Bake an additional 7 minutes or until golden brown.

Yield: 3 dozen cookies

This is my sister, Julie Byun's, Asian-inspired recipe. It's a great cookie for those days when you want something light and refreshing but not too sweet. They are wonderful with afternoon tea or as a quick pick-me-up at the office. The combination of lemon and ginger makes for a truly scrumptious treat! These cookies were a hit when my sister served them recently at the launch party of her own design company, Box in Bloom. She placed a bag of these delectable delights into a small ribbon-laced box topped with a handmade crêpe paper flower. They were a treat for everyone! I hope you will enjoy her recipe as much as my family, friends and I have.

★ KARIM CAMEL-TOUEG ★

Karim Camel-Toueg is the co-founder of Contrack International, Inc., a U.S. international construction company. He has been the President and CEO of Contrack for more than seventeen years and is a member of the board of directors of Orascom Construction Industry. Karim is a supporter of the William J. Clinton Presidential Foundation. He currently lives in Northern Virginia with his wife Jennifer and son Alexander.

FABULOUS FILET

1 (9-pound) whole filet, trimmed (at room temperature)	1 tablespoon pepper	3-4 bay leaves
2-3 garlic cloves, peeled and halved	2 tablespoons unsalted butter	2 cups button mushrooms, sliced
½ cup, plus 2 tablespoons Dijon mustard	1½ onions, thinly sliced	2 tablespoons Worcestershire sauce
	2 cups red wine	1 tablespoon steak sauce

Preheat oven to 375°. With sharp knife, make several cuts into filet on all sides. Place garlic clove half in each incision. Rub ½ cup Dijon mustard generously over filet and sprinkle with pepper. Place roasting pan that may be used on stove top and in oven on stove top over medium-high heat and melt butter. Place filet in roasting pan and sauté until light brown (about 10 minutes). Add onion and continue to sauté until onion caramelizes. Whisk together wine and 2 tablespoons Dijon mustard. Pour wine mixture over filet and add bay leaves. Place roasting pan in oven. Baste and turn filet every 15 to 20 minutes. Check doneness by inserting meat thermometer into center of filet. About 10 minutes before finishing filet, add mushrooms, Worcestershire sauce, and steak sauce to roasting pan. Stir and continue cooking about 8 to 10 minutes.

Yield: 10 to 12 servings

Serve with steamed vegetables, roasted rosemary potatoes, and a mixed green salad.

★ LIB AND SANDRA CARLISLE ★

Lib Carlisle was the Chairman of the Democratic Party of Arkansas while President Clinton was Governor. Lib was an Arkansas Traveler in the Presidential campaigns, and he and his wife both attended President Clinton's first Inauguration. His wife, Sandra, volunteered in the White House.

CORNBREAD

1	cup white cornmeal	1	teaspoons salt	1½	cups buttermilk
½	cup all-purpose flour	1	egg, lightly beaten	2	tablespoons shortening, melted
2	teaspoons baking powder				

Preheat oven to 400°. In large mixing bowl, combine cornmeal, flour, baking powder, and salt, blending thoroughly. Add egg and buttermilk, mixing well. Stir in melted shortening and pour mixture into hot greased skillet. Bake 20 to 25 minutes or until top is golden brown.

This recipe was given to me by my mother, Mrs. J. E. Walls, from the Tomberlin Community in England, Arkansas. Our family has enjoyed it for over 20 years.

★ NANCY CARTER ★

Nancy Carter owned and operated Robert Half of Long Island and Accountemps, specializing in the placement of financial and information technology executives, but sold her company in 1990. Nancy resides in Palm Beach, Florida, where she is involved in charitable causes and exhibit planning for a new science museum. She is a supporter of the William J. Clinton Presidential Foundation.

VERY LIGHT CAESAR SALAD DRESSING (NO EGGS OR MAYONNAISE)

¼	cup extra virgin olive oil	Juice of 1 lemon	Salt to taste	
2	garlic cloves, peeled and lightly crushed	Anchovy paste to taste	Hot sauce to taste	

Place oil, garlic, lemon juice and anchovy paste (start with less than 1 teaspoon and add more if desired) in wooden bowl. Combine ingredients by rubbing mixture against sides of bowl with the back of a wooden spoon. Stir until mixture becomes cloudy and garlic flavor is pressed into dressing. Remove garlic cloves and season with salt and hot sauce.

Toss chopped raw and cooked vegetables with dressing before adding lettuce, raw spinach, or field greens.

Warm vegetables as well as chilled vegetables are delicious with this dressing. Various fruits also combine nicely with the dressing. Be creative and enjoy!

★ NANCY CARTER ★

 ## Donny's Favorite Banana Bread

2 cups all-purpose flour	⅓ cup sour cream	2 eggs
1 teaspoon baking powder	1 cup sugar	1½ cups very ripe banana slices
½ teaspoon salt	½ cup unsalted butter	½ cup semi-sweet chocolate chips
1 teaspoon baking soda		

Preheat oven to 350°. Grease loaf pan thoroughly with butter. Place precut baking paper on bottom of loaf pan and grease as well. In medium mixing bowl, combine flour, baking powder, and salt; set aside. In small mixing bowl, combine sour cream and baking soda, whisking until frothy; set aside. In large mixing bowl, cream together butter and sugar. Add eggs separately, beating well after each addition. Add flour mixture and sour cream mixture to butter mixture alternately a little at a time and mix well. Gently fold in bananas and chocolate chips. Pour batter into loaf pan and bake for 1 hour or until cake tester inserted into center comes out clean. Allow to cool and turn out onto wire rack.

This bread may be sliced, individually wrapped, and frozen. Just warm before serving!

★ BOB CARVER ★

Bob Carver was the Democratic County Coordinator for Polk County, Arkansas. He worked in many of Bill Clinton's campaigns and continues to support the Clintons.

 ## Spicy Chili

1 onion, finely chopped	2 teaspoons paprika	2 teaspoons salt
Cooking oil	2 teaspoons chili powder	1 teaspoons pepper
2 pounds lean ground chuck, browned	1 teaspoon cumin	2 (15½-ounce) cans kidney beans, drained (optional)
2 (8-ounce) cans tomato sauce and 2 cans water	1 teaspoon oregano	

In Dutch oven over medium-high heat, sauté onion in small amount of cooking oil. Add ground chuck, tomato sauce, water, and seasonings. Simmer 1 hour over low heat. Add beans and heat thoroughly.

★ JAMES CARVILLE ★

James Carville is America's best-known political consultant. His long list of electoral successes evidence a knack for steering overlooked campaigns to unexpected landslide victories and for remaking political underdogs into upset winners. Carville guided Bill Clinton to the Presidency in 1992. In 1993, he was honored as Campaign Manager of the Year by the Association of Political Consultants for his leadership of Clinton's fearsome and intense "War Room" at campaign headquarters in Little Rock. He is also an author, speaker, restaurateur, and talk show host. Carville resides in Virginia with his wife and two daughters.

 ## CHICKEN JAMBALAYA

3 large hens, cut into pieces	3 pounds onions, chopped	Hot sauce to taste
Salt and pepper to taste	1 garlic clove, chopped	9 cups uncooked rice
Cooking oil	Garlic salt to taste	

Season chicken with salt and pepper. Deep fry in Dutch oven in hot cooking oil until golden brown. Transfer chicken to platter lined with paper towels. Drain oil from Dutch oven, leaving enough to sauté onions and garlic. Sauté vegetables until tender. Return chicken to Dutch oven and add 20 cups water; bring to a boil. Add salt, pepper, garlic salt, and hot sauce to taste. Stir in rice, cover, and reduce heat. Stir twice during cooking. Cook until water is absorbed and chicken is tender.

Yield: 24 servings

This recipe may be used with a combination of the meat from 2 hens and 2 pounds smoked sausage.

This is my favorite dish from my mother's cookbook.

★ JAYNI AND CHEVY CHASE ★

Chevy Chase is one of the greatest comedians of his generation. After achieving immediate popularity following the first season of Saturday Night Live in 1975, Chase went on to star in many movies, including Caddy Shack, National Lampoon's Vacation, and Fletch. Chase and his wife Jayni are friends of the Clintons and supporters of the William J. Clinton Foundation.

 ## CAULIFLOWER SOUP WITH CROUTONS

SOUP

1 large cauliflower	3 cups vegetable or chicken stock	Pinch of nutmeg
¼ cup butter	Pinch of white pepper	¼ cup heavy cream (optional)
1 onion, chopped		

Blanch cauliflower in boiling, salted water for 3 minutes, rinse under cold water, and drain. Break cauliflower into pieces and set aside. In Dutch oven over medium heat, melt butter and sauté onion until tender. Add cauliflower and briefly sauté. Add stock, white pepper, and nutmeg; simmer 15 minutes. Allow to cool. Process mixture in food processor in batches so that no solids are in soup. Return soup to Dutch oven and heat thoroughly. Adjust seasonings and stir in cream if desired. Top with croutons.

CROUTONS

1 bagel
Olive oil

Cut bagel into small cubes. In small skillet over medium heat, sauté bagel cubes in oil, turning frequently, until golden. Drain and serve with soup.

★ PAM CICETTI ★

Pam Cicetti worked in the First Lady's West Wing Office for the length of the Clinton Administration and currently works in her Senate office.

 ## CHOCOLATE-HAZELNUT BISCOTTI

¼ cup unsalted butter, softened
¾ cup sugar
2 eggs
1 teaspoon orange oil or flavoring

2 cups, plus 2 tablespoons all-purpose unbleached flour
¼ teaspoon salt
¾ teaspoon baking powder

½ cup chopped bittersweet chocolate
½ cup chopped toasted skinned hazelnuts

Preheat oven to 350°. In large mixing bowl, cream butter with electric mixer on medium speed until light and fluffy. Beat in sugar until well blended. Beat in eggs one at a time and add orange oil. In separate bowl, combine flour, salt, and baking powder and mix well. Gradually add flour mixture to creamed mixture. Fold in chocolate and hazelnuts. Divide dough in half or into thirds and shape into logs. Place on baking sheet lined with parchment. Bake for 25 minutes or until golden brown. Remove from oven and cool on wire rack 15 minutes. Slice logs on the diagonal about ¾-inch wide. Return to oven and bake for additional 5 to 6 minutes on each side. Cool on wire rack.

Unlike other biscotti, these are great for dunking in everything (coffee, tea, and milk) but wine.

For over eight years, Pam baked dozens and dozens of biscotti for the White House staff. One of her proudest moments followed the big 1995 budget fight. She was on the stairs between the first and second floors of the West Wing and was stopped by then-White House Chief of Staff and fellow Italian-American, Leon Panetta, who said, "Are you the one who made the biscotti?" He was grateful for a break from the budget fight and for a reminder of his heritage and the wonderful treats his mother used to make.

★ CLARENCE CLEMONS ★

Clarence Clemons is most widely known for his unmistakable saxophone sound, which for more than two decades, has lofted Bruce Springsteen's E Street Band to, as some have deemed it, the greatest rock and roll band in the world. In addition to the E Street Band, Clemons has performed with his own band The Red Bank Rockers and The Jerry Garcia Band, The Grateful Dead, and Ringo Starr's All Star Band. He has also recorded with Aretha Franklin, Paul Young, Great White, Alvin Lee, Roy Orbison, and Patti LaBelle. In addition to music, he adds to his acting resume by appearing on television in CBS's Nash Bridges and on the big screen in Fatal Instinct and other films.

 ## BIG MAN OYSTER STEW

2	bacon slices	3-4	sprigs fresh dill, divided		Salt and pepper to taste
1	yellow onion, finely chopped	2	garlic cloves, crushed and chopped	2	tablespoons butter
1	yellow onion, cut into thin rings	1	pint shucked select oysters		Shot of very dry sherry (optional)
3	green onions, cut into 1-inch strips	2	cups whole milk		

In deep iron skillet over medium-high heat, cook bacon until crisp. Remove bacon to paper towel lined plate to drain. Sauté onion, green onion, 2 sprigs dill, and garlic in bacon drippings 3 to 4 minutes. Add oysters and milk and simmer slowly 10 to 15 minutes. Season with salt and pepper to taste. Add butter, stirring until melted. Add sherry before serving if desired.

 ## VEAL CHOPS CLEMENZA

2-4	veal chops, rinsed and patted dry	1	(12-ounce) can chopped tomatoes	¼	cup green pitted Sicilian olives, chopped
	Pepper to taste	1	(15-ounce) can tomato sauce	¼	cup small pitted dried olives, chopped
	All-purpose flour	2	sprigs fresh thyme		
2	tablespoons olive oil	½	teaspoon oregano or 2 sprigs fresh oregano	¼	cup black or green olives, chopped
1	large sweet onion, chopped				Salt and pepper to taste
2	garlic cloves, crushed and chopped	1	cup red wine		
2	anchovy fillets				

On large flat surface, season veal chops with pepper and dust generously with flour on both sides. In large, deep iron skillet, heat oil over medium-high heat. Add veal chops and brown 3 to 4 minutes on each side. Reduce heat to medium and add onion and garlic. Cover and slowly cook 20 minutes, turning chops once. Remove lid and add remaining ingredients. Slowly cook 30 to 40 minutes.

To alleviate saltiness in anchovies, soak in cold water for 30 minutes, then drain and pat dry with a paper towel.

★ PRESIDENT BILL CLINTON ★

Founder, William J. Clinton Presidential Foundation; Co-Chair with Nelson Mandela, International AIDS Trust; Co-Chair with Senator Robert Dole, Families of Freedom Fund; President of the United States 1993-2001; Governor of Arkansas 1979-1981, 1983-1992.

William Jefferson Clinton was elected President of the United States in 1992, and again in 1996-the first Democratic president to be awarded a second term in six decades. Under his leadership, the United States enjoyed the strongest economy in a generation and the longest economic expansion in U.S. history. President Clinton's core values of building community, creating opportunity, and demanding responsibility resulted in unprecedented progress for America, including moving the nation from record deficits to record surpluses; the creation of over 22 million jobs-more than any other administration; low levels of unemployment, poverty, and crime; and the highest homeownership and college enrollment rates in history.

 ## PRESIDENT BILL CLINTON'S FAVORITE CHICKEN ENCHILADAS

2 (4-ounce) cans chopped green chilies, drained	2 cups chopped onion	2 cups sour cream
1 garlic clove, minced	2 teaspoons salt, divided	2 cup shredded Cheddar cheese
Cooking oil	½ teaspoon oregano	⅓ cup cooking oil
1 (28-ounce) can tomatoes	3 cups shredded, cooked chicken	15 corn or flour tortillas

In large skillet over medium-high heat, sauté chilies and garlic in small amount of oil. Drain tomatoes, reserving ½ cup liquid. Break up tomatoes and add to skillet. Add onion, 1 teaspoon salt, oregano, and reserved liquid. Simmer, uncovered, until thickened (about 30 minutes). Remove from heat, transfer to bowl, and set aside. In large mixing bowl, combine chicken, sour cream, cheese, and remaining 1 teaspoon salt. In same skillet over medium-high heat, heat ⅓ cup oil. Dip tortillas in oil until they become limp; drain well on paper towels. Fill tortillas with chicken mixture; roll up and arrange side by side, seam side down, in 9x13x2-inch baking dish. Pour tomato mixture over enchiladas. Bake at 350° for 20 minutes or until heated thoroughly.

Yield: 15 enchiladas

President Clinton's recipe originated from his days as Governor of Arkansas. The Arkansas Governor's Mansion's cook, Liza Ashley, would often prepare this recipe for the Clintons during their time in the Mansion.

★ SENATOR HILLARY RODHAM CLINTON ★

During the eight years that Hillary Rodham Clinton served as First Lady, she championed issues affecting women, children and families that have been her lifelong interest. As the nation prepared to celebrate the birth of a new millennium, she created the program Save America's Treasures to focus national attention on the need to preserve the sites, artifacts and records that define our national character. She carried a message of hope to women and girls in remote corners of the world and worked to ensure that all of the people in our nation would realize the benefits of the prosperity experienced by the United States during her husband's presidency. In 2001, she became the first First Lady elected to the United States Senate and the first woman elected statewide in New York State. In the Senate she continues to fight for economic and national security, health care, education and the environment. Senator Clinton is the first New Yorker to serve on the Senate Armed Services Committee and also serves on the Senate Committees on Environment and Public Works; and Health, Education, Labor and Pensions. In addition, she chairs the Democratic Steering and Coordination Committee.

HILLARY RODHAM CLINTON'S CHOCOLATE CHIP COOKIES

1½ cups all-purpose flour	1 cup firmly packed light brown sugar	2 cups rolled oats, uncooked
1 teaspoon salt	½ cup granulated sugar	1 (12-ounce) package semi-sweet
1 teaspoon baking soda	1 teaspoon vanilla	chocolate chips
1 cup shortening	2 eggs	

Preheat oven to 350°. In mixing bowl, combine flour, salt, and baking soda. In large mixing bowl, beat together shortening, sugars, and vanilla with electric mixer on medium speed until creamy. Add eggs and beat until light and fluffy. Gradually beat in flour mixture and rolled oats. Stir in chocolate chips. Drop dough by rounded teaspoonfuls onto prepared baking sheets. Bake for 8 to 10 minutes or until golden brown. Cool on wire racks 2 minutes.

Family Circle made headlines in 1992 when its editors decided to do a "Bipartisan Bake-Off" between the Presidential candidates' wives. Barbara Bush and Senator Clinton were both asked by the magazine to submit cookie recipes. Once the recipes were published, readers were then encouraged to bake the two cookies, put aside their partisan loyalties, and decide who had the better cookie. The response was overwhelming, and Senator Clinton won the bake-off with this recipe. Family Circle then ran a second "Cookie Cook-Off" in 1996 between Senator Clinton and Senator Elizabeth Dole. Senator Clinton's cookies won again.

★ A CLINTON FAMILY CELEBRATION ★

President Clinton and First Lady Hillary Rodham Clinton joined his aunt, Janet Clinton, and some of the other members of the family during a celebration of "Aunt Janet's" 86th birthday on September 27, 1997.

Back row, left to right: Dick Kelley (who met Bill and Hillary at the airport and came along "for the ride"), Gio Bruno; Virginia Heath; Richard Bruno; Roy Clinton III; Patricia Clinton (expecting her and Roy III's son, Cole, who was born in December 1997); Hunter Edwards; Roy Clinton, Jr.; Hillary Clinton, Bill Clinton, Dan Clinton, Liz Clinton Little, Joan Clinton, Gene Little, Bill and Marie Miegel (Janet's brother and sister-in-law), Jay Clinton.

Front row, left to right: Genny Bruno, Dominic Bruno, Stacey Burks Briggs, Butch Clinton, Janet Clinton, Marie Clinton Bruno, Sissy Clinton, and David "Bo" Clinton.

Very front on the right: Jack Bruno, Theresa Clinton Edwards, and Hayden Edwards.

Roy Jr., Dan, Bo, and Liz are Janet's children who grew up with President Clinton.

★ JANET CLINTON ★

Janet Elizabeth Miegel Clinton has lived in Hot Springs, Arkansas, since she was born in September 1911. She is the widow of Roy Clinton, Sr., President Clinton's uncle. Together they owned Clinton's Antiques, which began in the living room of their home on Quapaw Avenue in the 1950s. Janet has four children, nine grandchildren, and eight great-grandchildren, and is thrilled to be able to see her nephew when he returns home to Arkansas to visit.

 ## AUNT JANET'S ICE BOX ROLLS

2 rounded tablespoons shortening	1 egg, beaten	6 cups all-purpose flour
¼ cup sugar	2 cups lukewarm water	Cooking oil
1 tablespoon salt	1 (¼-ounce) package yeast	Butter, melted

In large mixing bowl, cream shortening and sugar with electric mixer on medium speed. Add salt and egg and mix well. Dissolve yeast in lukewarm water. Add to mixture. Add flour until dough is stiff enough to handle. Turn out dough on flat surface and knead. Coat bowl well with cooking oil and return dough to bowl. Turn dough several times, taking care to coat dough well. Cover bowl with towel. If serving rolls the same day, allow dough to rise. If serving rolls the next day, chill dough. Punch down dough and knead again. Roll out dough on flat surface to ½-inch thickness. Cut dough with biscuit cutter. Dip rolls in melted butter and place in pan. If serving rolls the same day, cover, and allow to rise (about 2 to 3 hours). If serving rolls the next day, cover, and chill. When ready to bake, preheat oven to 400°. Bake about 15 minutes or until done.

Aunt Janet suggests using 2 packages of yeast in the winter.

Leftover dough may be refrigerated for up to 10 days in a covered greased bowl.

★ ROY JR. AND BUTCH CLINTON ★

Butch Clinton is a native of Memphis, Tennessee. She met her future husband, Roy Clinton, Jr. during her years at the University of Arkansas at Fayetteville. Roy is President Clinton's first cousin. Roy and Butch married in 1957 and have called Fayetteville home ever since, with two of their three children and four of their five grandsons living nearby. In the early 1970s, Butch's dinner table (and many others in Northwest Arkansas) was occasionally visited by a hungry young law professor and candidate for Congress! Both Butch and Roy have been actively involved in the Fayetteville and Northwest Arkansas communities, especially for the Washington Regional Medical Center, where Butch is a Hospice volunteer and Roy is a board member.

 ## Yun Yun's Chicken Parmesan

1 garlic clove, minced	1 cup shredded Parmesan cheese	1 fryer, cut into pieces or 6 chicken
¼ cup butter	Dash of pepper	breasts, rinsed and patted dry
1 cup seasoned breadcrumbs		1 (10.5-ounce) can chicken broth

Preheat oven to 350°. In small skillet over medium heat, sauté garlic in butter. In shallow dish combine breadcrumbs, cheese, and pepper. Dip chicken in butter, then roll in breadcrumb mixture. Place chicken in prepared casserole dish. Bake, uncovered, for 30 minutes. Reduce heat to 300°, cover, and bake for 30 additional minutes.

Yield: 6 servings

My mother, Yun Yun, is the late Hattie Marie Lilly of Memphis and Pickwick Lake, Tennessee.

★ ROY JR. AND BUTCH CLINTON ★

 **FRUIT COCKTAIL PIE**

1 (14-ounce) can sweetened condensed milk	⅓ cup lemon juice 1 (15¼-ounce) can fruit cocktail, drained	1 cup coarsely chopped pecans 1 Graham Cracker Crust

In large mixing bowl, combine milk and lemon juice. Gently fold in fruit cocktail and pecans. Pour into Graham Cracker Crust and chill 24 hours before serving.

GRAHAM CRACKER CRUST

22 graham cracker squares, crushed   2 tablespoons sugar   6 tablespoons butter, melted

Preheat oven to 350°. In large mixing bowl, combine graham cracker crumbs and sugar; add butter. Press mixture into pie pan and bake 8 minutes. Cool before adding filling.

★ BETTY J. COLES ★

Born in Louisiana, Betty J. Coles is the retired Deputy Superintendent of Brooklyn, New York, schools. She is also the former Chair of the Marin County Democrats in Northern California. Currently a resident in Westchester, New York, she is highly active in the Delta Sigma Theta Sorority.

 **PECAN PRALINES**

1 cup sugar ½ cup buttermilk 1 tablespoon butter	½ teaspoon baking soda Pinch of salt	¾ cup chopped pecans ½ teaspoon vanilla

In large saucepan over low heat, combine sugar, buttermilk, butter, baking soda, and salt. Stir constantly until mixture begins to thicken (about 20 to 25 minutes). Add pecans and vanilla, continuing to stir until thick. Very quickly drop by tablespoons onto greased waxed paper. Cool until firm before removing from waxed paper.

★ BEVERLY CONEY ★

Beverly Coney was an appointee in the Clinton Administration from 1993 to 1999, serving the first term at the Department of State and the second term at the Department of Education. She helped establish the Clinton for President campaign office in Chicago during the Illinois primary in 1991 through 1992 and served as Volunteer Coordinator. As a student at the University of Arkansas and a member of the Young Democrats club, Beverly worked on President Clinton's first gubernatorial race in 1978 and in his subsequent re-election campaigns. She has been a friend and loyal supporter for 25 years.

 ## CRANBERRY SALAD

1 quart fresh cranberries, rinsed and drained	2 small oranges, peeled and sectioned	2 cups sugar
4 small apples, peeled and cored	1 cup crushed pineapple, drained	2 packages cranberry flavored gelatin
		½ cup chopped pecans (optional)

Grind fruits and place in large bowl. Add sugar, stirring until dissolved. Prepare gelatin according to package directions. Pour over fruit mixture, stirring well. Stir in nuts if desired. Chill 4 hours or until firm.

This tasty recipe came from my grandma, Rachel Fryer, who voted Democratic for the first time in 1992 (at age 85) for Bill Clinton!

★ SARA M. COSTIN ★

Sara Costin worked in the 1996 re-election campaign as the Northeast Political Director. Afterwards, she was the Northeast Director for the Inauguration. During President Clinton's second term, she was a political appointee in the Department of Health and Human Services.

 ## HUNGARIAN SALAMI

1	(12-ounce) beef salami loaf	½	cup apricot jam	2	tablespoons dark mustard
½-¾	cup brown sugar				

Pierce holes throughout salami loaf with fork. In small mixing bowl, combine brown sugar, jam, and mustard. Taste and adjust seasonings. Roll salami in mixture, making sure to completely cover and penetrate salami. Bake in toaster oven at 300° about 45 minutes. Allow to cool 10 to 15 minutes. Cut approximately 1½-inch thick slices, then quarter. Pierce quarters with toothpicks and serve.

My grandmother makes this incredible appetizer whenever she has friends and/or family over. My mother and I now continue the tradition. For such an easy recipe, the cook gets rave reviews. I've entered it in "work cook-offs" and have won every single time in the appetizer category! Thanks, Grandma Lee!

★ BETH GLADDEN COULSON AND MIKE COULSON ★

Beth Gladden Coulson is an attorney and was appointed to the Arkansas Court of Appeals by Governor Clinton where she served from 1986 to 1988. Her husband, Mike Coulson, is the president of the Coulson Oil Company. They are both long time supporters and friends of the Clintons.

 ## APPLE PIE IN PAPER BAG

3 large Granny Smith apples, peeled and thinly sliced
½ cup sugar (or sugar substitute equivalent)
2 tablespoons all-purpose flour

2 tablespoons lemon juice
2 tablespoons cinnamon
1 (15-ounce) package refrigerated pie crusts

½ cup sugar
½ cup all-purpose flour
½ cup butter, melted

Preheat oven to 350°. In large mixing bowl, toss apples with ½ cup sugar. Add 2 tablespoons flour, lemon juice, cinnamon; toss well to coat. Press one pie pastry into pie pan. Pour apple mixture into pie pan. Top with remaining pie pastry and seal edges together. Pierce top of pie. In small mixing bowl, thoroughly combine remaining ingredients and pour over pie. Place pie in brown paper grocery bag; fold top over twice and staple. Bake for 1 hour.

Yield: 6 to 8 servings

 ## BLISSFUL BANANA PIE

1 cup crushed vanilla wafers
½ cup chopped pecans
⅓ cup butter, melted

1 cup chocolate chips
2 cups milk, divided
2-3 bananas, peeled and thinly sliced

1 (3-ounce) package banana flavored instant pudding mix
1 (8-ounce) carton frozen whipped topping

In small mixing bowl, combine crushed wafers, pecans, and butter. Press into 9x9-inch baking pan. Bake at 350° for 5 minutes. In small saucepan over medium heat, melt chocolate chips with ½ cup milk, stirring well. Pour into crust. Arrange banana slices on top of chocolate mixture. In medium mixing bowl, combine pudding mix and 1½ cups milk, mixing well. Chill until slightly set; stir in frozen whipped topping and pour over bananas. Chill until ready to serve.

Yield: 9 servings

Paulette Craig is employed with Cranford Johnson Robinson Woods in Little Rock, Arkansas. In her current position as Public Policy Coordinator, she assists executive vice president, Skip Rutherford, in the day-to-day operations of the Public Policy Consultancy, as well as closely working with the William J. Clinton Presidential Foundation. From 1990 to 1996, she served under the gubernatorial administrations of Jim Guy Tucker and Bill Clinton as Special Assistant.

 ## ICEBOX LEMON PIE

1 (11-ounce) package vanilla wafers	2 (14-ounce) cans sweetened condensed milk	1 teaspoon lemon zest
3 eggs, separated		Juice of 3-4 lemons
		¾-1 cup sugar

Line bottom and side of pie plate with vanilla wafers. Crush 15 wafers and sprinkle over whole wafers and set aside. Place egg whites in small bowl and chill. In large mixing bowl, combine egg yolks and milk and mix thoroughly. Add zest, stirring well. Add lemon juice, stirring quickly until thickened (about 1 minute). Pour into pie dish, smoothing out and spreading evenly. In large mixing bowl, beat egg whites with electric mixer on medium speed until stiff peaks form; gradually beat in sugar. Spread meringue on top of pie. Place in oven to brown meringue, taking care not to overcook. Remove from oven and cool. Chill at least 2 hours. Serve cold and enjoy!

Yield: 8 servings

Paulette has won several awards for her Icebox Lemon Pie, a family favorite recipe, that she received many years ago from her dear friend, Wanda Porter, who passed away in 1995, at age 40, from complications of Lupus.

★ FRANCES AND WAYNE CRANFORD ★

Wayne Cranford is the chairman and co-founder of Cranford Johnson Robinson Woods and is involved in managing communications programs for the agency's clients as well as developing new business for the agency. In addition to his professional responsibilities, Wayne and his wife Frances devote considerable time and energy to civic, charity, and community organizations.

SPICY CHICKEN SALAD

¼ cup corn oil
2 tablespoons apple cider vinegar
Salt to taste
¼ teaspoon cayenne pepper

6 cups cooked, cubed chicken breasts
1½ cups chopped celery
¼ cup sliced, pitted ripe olives

2 tablespoons chopped capers, rinsed and drained
¾ cup mayonnaise
Carrot curls, for garnish
Beet slices, for garnish

In small mixing bowl, combine oil, vinegar, salt, and cayenne pepper. In large mixing bowl, combine chicken, celery, olives, and capers. Pour oil mixture over chicken mixture, tossing well to coat. Chill 2 hours to allow flavors to blend. Toss with mayonnaise just before serving. Garnish with carrot curls and beet slices if desired.

Yield: 6 to 8 servings

★ PATTY CRINER ★

Patty Criner sat next to Bill Clinton in the first grade. She has been a family friend since then and served Governor Clinton as Scheduler and Press Secretary in his first term.

CHICKEN DIVAN OR CHICKEN SOFA

2 (10-ounce) packages frozen chopped broccoli
2 cups chopped boiled chicken

2 (10¾-ounce) cans cream of chicken soup
1 cup mayonnaise

1 teaspoon lemon juice
½ teaspoon curry powder
½ cup shredded sharp American cheese

Preheat oven to 350°. In medium saucepan over medium-high heat, cook broccoli in salted water until tender; drain. Arrange broccoli in prepared baking dish. Cover with chicken. In mixing bowl, combine soup, mayonnaise, lemon juice, and curry powder. Pour over chicken. Sprinkle with cheese. Bake for 25 to 30 minutes or until thoroughly heated.

Yield: 6 to 8 servings

This chicken dish may be prepared ahead and refrigerated.

★ SECRETARY ANDREW CUOMO ★

Andrew Cuomo is the former Secretary of Housing and Urban Development during the Clinton Administration. At HUD, he won awards from Harvard for his innovation and success in passing major legislation. He served as campaign manager for his father, Mario M. Cuomo, in his successful 1982 race for Governor of New York. He has three daughters, Mariah, Cara, and Michaela.

 **NOUGAT TIRAMISU**

2 cups double-strength decaffeinated espresso	3 cups heavy cream	20-25 ladyfinger cookies
1 cup Simple Syrup	1 cup finely chopped dark chocolate	Chopped chocolate, for garnish
⅓ cup, plus 2 teaspoons Amaretto di Saronno liqueur	1 cup coarsely crushed Toffee Nougat	Finely crushed Toffee Nougat, for garnish

In large mixing bowl, combine espresso, Simple Syrup, and ⅓ cup liqueur; set aside. In separate large mixing bowl, whisk heavy cream until stiff peaks form. Gently fold in 1 cup dark chocolate, 1 cup Toffee Nougat, and 2 teaspoons liqueur. Dip ladyfingers into espresso mixture and place into bottom of serving dish. Pour cream mixture over ladyfingers, spreading evenly with spatula. Chill several hours before serving. Sprinkle with chopped chocolate and crushed Toffee Nougat for garnish.

SIMPLE SYRUP
1 cup water	1 cup sugar

In small saucepan over medium heat, combine water and sugar. Boil until sugar dissolves, stirring frequently, and allow to cool.

TOFFEE NOUGAT
1 cup sugar	1 cup water
1 tablespoons light corn syrup	1 cup sliced almonds

In large, heavy saucepan over medium heat, combine sugar, corn syrup and water, stirring slowly until sugar dissolves. (Use a pastry brush dipped in cold water to scrape down sides of saucepan.) Continue to cook until mixture turns light golden brown, gently shaking saucepan across burner to prevent hot spots. When small puffs of smoke begin to rise, carefully remove from heat. Working quickly, use rubber spatula to fold in almonds, then pour onto baking sheet. Cool completely. Place in plastic zip-top bag and coarsely crush with bottom of saucepan.

Toffee Nougat will keep for up to a month when stored in airtight container at room temperature.

Tiramisu is one of my favorite desserts, rich and creamy. It's the perfect comfort food for a sweet tooth.

★ BETTY CURRIE ★

Betty Currie was President Clinton's personal secretary for his entire term of office. Betty is best known for her special attachment to Socks, the Clinton family's cat, who was never far from Betty's office in the White House and now resides with her in Maryland.

 CRÈME CELESTE

1½ teaspoons unflavored gelatin	½ cup sugar	1 (10-ounce) package frozen
3 tablespoons cold water	1 cup sour cream	raspberries, thawed
1 cup heavy cream	1 teaspoon vanilla	1-3 tablespoons Grand Marnier

In small bowl, soften gelatin in cold water. In medium saucepan over medium heat, combine cream and sugar, stirring until sugar dissolves. Stir in gelatin mixture, stirring until gelatin dissolves. Remove from heat. Stir in sour cream and vanilla. Pour into prepared mold or bowl. Chill until firm (about 4 hours). In small mixing bowl, combine raspberries and Grand Marnier. Pour over gelatin mold before turning out or pour over individual servings.

A simple, tasty dessert with great presentation! This recipe is in memory of my youngest sister, Celeste.

DOG BISCUITS

2 cups whole wheat flour	¾ cup cornmeal	4 beef bouillon cubes
2 cups all-purpose flour	4 tablespoons cooking oil	2 cups boiling water

Preheat oven to 300°. In large mixing bowl, combine flours, cornmeal, and cooking oil; mix well. In medium bowl, dissolve bouillon cubes in water. Add to flour mixture, mixing until stiff dough forms. Roll out onto floured surface and cut out shapes with cookie cutter or open end of glass. Transfer biscuits to baking sheet and bake for 30 minutes. Let stand overnight. Store in airtight container.

Add garlic, crisp bacon strips, bacon drippings, or your dog's favorite flavor. Betty always used bacon bits then basted with bacon drippings while the biscuits baked.

This recipe is in memory of Buddy, President Clinton's dog. I hope your pet enjoys this recipe!

★ NEALON DEVORE ★

Nealon DeVore is presently a senior at the University of Central Arkansas, where he will graduate in May 2004 with a degree in political science and French. He serves as an intern in the William J. Clinton Presidential Foundation's Little Rock office and devoted much time, along with Associate Director Shannon Butler, to this cookbook.

 **LAYERED NACHO DIP**

1 (16-ounce) can refried beans	1 (8-ounce) container sour cream	1 bunch green onions, chopped
1 (1¼-ounce) package taco seasoning mix	1 (4-ounce) can chopped olives	1 (4-ounce) can chopped green chilies
1 (16-ounce) container avocado dip	2 tomatoes, chopped	2 cups shredded Monterey Jack cheese

In mixing bowl, combine beans and taco mix. Spread in a 12x8x2-inch dish. Layer remaining ingredients in order listed. Serve with corn chips.

Ever since I can remember, my mother has made this dip for every function that we have had with our extended family. It is wonderful and not at all holiday-specific, as we have enjoyed it at Christmas, Thanksgiving and Easter, not to mention every birthday party, anniversary celebration and family reunion. Everyone crowds around the island in the center of my mother's kitchen, or my Aunt Katy's, and has to have "just one more bite" before being dismissed to the dining room for the actual meal that has been prepared. Even though the dip dish is usually scraped clean by then, there is always room for dinner because there is often way too many of us and way too little of this delicious appetizer!

★ M. JANE DICKEY ★

Jane Dickey resides in Little Rock where she is a member of the Rose Law Firm and specializes in municipal bond law. Issues of local government are one of her prime interests. She was instrumental in the creation of Central Arkansas Water and was that organization's first Chair. She is a past president of Little Rock's Downtown Partnership which focuses its efforts on urban development of Little Rock's downtown and River Market district. She is an attorney for the William J. Clinton Presidential Foundation.

SOUTHERN SPOON BREAD (CORNBREAD SOUFFLÉ)

1 cup yellow cornmeal	1 teaspoon baking powder	3 egg whites, stiffly beaten
3 cups milk, divided	2 tablespoons butter, melted	Butter
1 teaspoon salt	3 egg yolks, beaten	

Preheat oven to 325°. In medium saucepan over medium heat, combine cornmeal and 2 cups milk. Cook until thickened, then remove from heat. Stir in salt, baking powder, butter, and remaining 1 cup milk, mixing well. Add egg yolks and mix well. Fold in egg whites, gently stirring. Pour into prepared 2-quart baking dish. Bake for 1 hour. Dot with butter while warm

Yield: 6 servings

This is my grandmother's, Sallie Dickey, recipe for "spoon bread", a great favorite in our Altheimer household, especially for Sunday dinner.

★ LYNDA DIXON ★

Lynda Dixon is Director of Volunteers and Exhibits for the William J. Clinton Presidential Foundation. She was Governor Bill Clinton's personal secretary until he went to Washington in 1993. During the Clinton Administration, she served as Presidential and White House Liaison, then as the Executive Director of the Arkansas office.

 ## CARROT AND RAISIN CITRUS SALAD

2 cups shredded carrots	¼ cup light brown sugar	Juice of 1 lemon
½ cup raisins	Juice of 2 oranges	Salt to taste

In large serving bowl, combine carrots, raisins, and brown sugar. Pour juices over carrot mixture and season with salt. Chill several hours or overnight.

 ## SAUSAGE AU GRATIN

10 medium potatoes, peeled and cut into chunks	1 (8-ounce) carton sour cream	1 package smoked cocktail sausages, halved
1 (8-ounce) jar pasteurized processed cheese spread	2 tablespoons parsley flakes	
	2 tablespoons onion flakes	

In large saucepan, cover potatoes with water. Boil until potatoes are done, drain, and set aside. Combine cheese spread, sour cream, parsley flakes, and onion flakes and mix well. Fold in sausages. Add to potatoes and toss gently. Transfer to casserole and bake, uncovered, at 350° for 30 minutes.

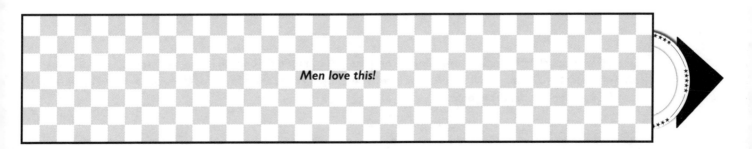

Men love this!

★ DOE'S EAT PLACE ★

Doe's Eat Place, located on the corner of Markham and Ringo in downtown Little Rock, was one of President Clinton's favorite places to eat during his days as Governor. It was also a gathering place for the campaign staffers during the '92 race. It is known worldwide for its hot tamales and huge steaks. It is frequented all the time by out-of-town visitors who enjoy viewing the pictures and memorabilia that Doe's has collected over time.

 ## DOE'S CHILI

15 pounds ground beef, browned	1 tablespoon cumin	1½ cups chopped onions
1 tablespoon salt	5 tablespoons chili powder	4 cups tomato paste
1 tablespoon cayenne pepper	1 tablespoon chopped garlic	4 cups crushed tomatoes

In 5-gallon stockpot over medium-high heat, combine ingredients. Bring to a boil; reduce heat and simmer several hours. *Will feed approximately 30 to 50 people... depending upon their appetites!*

Doe's Chili is most often poured over Doe's world-famous tamales. Of course, it can be eaten alone. Customers always request this recipe, but it is never given out. The Clinton Foundation should feel special since we're allowing it to be published in the cookbook!

★ JOHN EMERSON AND KIMBERLY MARTEAU ★

John ran the Clinton Campaign in California in '92, coordinated the Economic Conference during the transition. While in the White House, he served as Deputy Assistant to the President for Presidential Personnel and then Intergovernmental Affairs. Kimberly was Director of Public Affairs at USIA during the first Clinton term. While in Washington, John and Kimberly had three children. When they moved back to Los Angeles, John became president of the wealth management division of the international investment management firm, the Capital Group.

 ## STEVIE'S FRENCH TOAST

1	large loaf French bread, sliced 1-inch thick	⅓	cup sugar		¼	teaspoon cinnamon	
2	tablespoons unsalted butter, melted	3	cups milk			Confectioners' sugar	
4	eggs	1	cup heavy cream			Fresh berries	
2	egg yolks	1-1½	tablespoons vanilla			Maple syrup (optional)	
		¼	teaspoon nutmeg				

Preheat oven to 350°. Brush both sides of bread with butter. Place slices in bottom of 9x13-inch baking pan. In large mixing bowl, beat together eggs and egg yolks. Add sugar and next five ingredients, mixing well. Pour over bread. Place baking pan in larger pan (or roasting pan). Add enough water to larger pan to come halfway up sides of baking pan. Bake for 45 to 50 minutes or until light and fluffy. Remove from oven and let stand 10 to 15 minutes. Dust with confectioners' sugar and top with fresh berries. Drizzle with maple syrup if desired.

Stevie is a friend of a friend who has created an original and easy way to serve a delicious brunch dish. We just love this recipe!

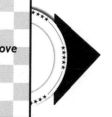

★ MADELINE EMRICH AND TIMOTHY EMRICH ★

Timothy W. Emrich served three years in the White House between 1998 and 2001, including stints as Deputy Directory of Presidential Scheduling and Presidential Scheduler, Director of Presidential Scheduling Correspondence, and Presidential Scheduling Coordinator. Throughout 2001, Timothy served as Account Manager for President Clinton at the Harry Walker Agency in New York. Madeline Emrich is Timothy's mother.

 ## GOURMET SHRIMP ROLL

1 (8-ounce) package cream cheese, softened

1 (4½-ounce) can deveined shrimp, drained and rinsed

1½ teaspoons minced onion

1 teaspoon lemon juice

1 teaspoon Worcestershire sauce

½ cup chopped walnuts, pecans, or cashews

In large mixing bowl, combine cream cheese, shrimp, onion, lemon juice, and Worcestershire sauce. Place mixture in food processor and pulse until thoroughly processed. Chill until lightly set. Spoon mixture out onto plastic wrap and shape into ball or log. Roll in nuts, gently pressing nuts into sides. Wrap in plastic wrap and chill several hours. Serve on cheese board surrounded by crackers.

This recipe may also be served in serving dish (without nuts) as a spread.

This recipe was given to our family along with a generous sample over 25 years ago. No holiday get-together is complete without it. Some in our family eat it on toasted bagels Christmas morning. In fact, I served this each year at the Scheduling and Advance Holiday Party. The best part is remembering the dear friend who gave it to us and all the happy memories our families have shared these many years. Our friendship still continues.

Mark Erwin is the President of Erwin Capital, Inc., a family-owned investment company located in Charlotte, North Carolina. President Clinton appointed Erwin to serve as United States Ambassador to the Republic of Mauritius, the Republic of the Seychelles, and the Federal Islamic Republic of Comoros from 1999 to 2001. From 1997 until 1999 Ambassador Erwin served as a Presidential appointee to the Board of Directors of the Overseas Private Investment Corporation. His wife Joan is a homemaker and was the consummate hostess as an Ambassador's spouse, being quite popular with the diplomatic community. She is working on her own cookbook of family and friends' recipes. They have two daughters.

 ## SWEET POTATO CASSEROLE

3 cups cooked, mashed sweet potatoes (about 7 sweet potatoes)	½ cup butter, softened	1 (5-ounce) can evaporated milk
	½ cup sugar	1 teaspoon vanilla
	½ cup brown sugar	¼ teaspoon nutmeg

Preheat oven to 450°. In large mixing bowl, combine sweet potatoes and remaining ingredients, mixing well. Pour into prepared casserole dish and spread with Brown Sugar Topping. Bake for 15 minutes.

BROWN SUGAR TOPPING

1 cup brown sugar	½ cup chopped pecans
½ cup butter, softened	2 cups crushed corn flakes

In large mixing bowl, combine brown sugar, butter, pecans, and corn flakes; mix well.

I always serve this recipe at Thanksgiving and Christmas. It freezes well, so it's nice to prepare ahead of time. My mother, Lottie Payne, from Tennessee gave me this recipe. She was a wonderful cook until Alzheimer's disease took away her ability to cook.

★ KAREN FINNEY ★

Karen Finney worked on the 1992 Clinton/Gore campaign as an advance person and was part of the transition advance team in Little Rock. From there, she went to Washington, DC, in December of 1992 to help with the physical move into the White House and served as Deputy Press Secretary for Mrs. Clinton from January 1993 through April 1997. She became Deputy Director of Scheduling for the President until April of 1998. Finney also served as Press Secretary during Mrs. Clinton's Senate race. She currently works at Scholastic Inc. as Director of Business Development and Strategy.

 ## FINNEY'S DECADENT SOUTHERN PECAN PIE

FILLING

3 eggs, lightly beaten	¼ teaspoon salt	1½-2 cups pecan halves or chopped
1 cup light corn syrup	1 teaspoon vanilla	pecans
1 cup brown sugar	½ cup butter, melted	Frozen whipped topping

Preheat oven to 450°. In large mixing bowl, combine eggs and remaining ingredients. Pour into crust. Bake for 10 minutes. Reduce heat to 350° and bake for 40 minutes to 1 hour or until filling firms and crust begins to brown. Remove from oven and allow to cool. Top individual slices with frozen whipped topping.

CRUST

2 cups whole wheat pastry flour	1 teaspoon salt	⅔ cup shortening

Sift flour and salt into large mixing bowl. Cut in shortening with two knives until pea-sized lumps begin to form. Add small amount of very cold water (no more than ½ cup) and mix in until dough can be formed into a ball. (Be careful not to touch dough more than necessary, as it will soften dough, making it difficult to roll out.) Roll out dough onto floured surface with floured rolling pin. Transfer to 9-inch pie plate. Trim and flute edges.

Yield: 6 to 8 servings

If pie appears to be browning too quickly, reduce heat to 325°, as filling will not set if cooked too quickly.

This is a recipe that my mom has been making for years, and it is truly spectacular. During the 1992 Clinton transition in Little Rock, I called my mother on Thanksgiving and convinced her to Delta Dash me a pie. She thought I was crazy! Fortunately, we were able to go home for Christmas, and she made one for me then. Holidays are just not the same for me without it.

A recounting of the accomplished career of Jimmie Lou Fisher, from her start in Greene County in 1971 to her retirement as State Treasurer of Arkansas in 2003, would take pages. She has also served in the Democratic Party of Arkansas and on the Democratic National Committee. In 2002, she answered her party's call to run for Governor in Arkansas. Gracious in loss, she proved once again her reputation of being one of the most beloved politicians in the state.

JACK CHEESE, CHICKEN, AND RICE CASSEROLE

2 (10¾-ounce) cans cream of mushroom soup

1 (10¾-ounce) can cream of chicken soup or chicken broth

1 (8-ounce) package hot pepper Jack cheese, cubed and melted

Salt and pepper to taste

4 boneless skinless chicken breasts, cooked and cubed

1½ cups cooked rice

Preheat oven to 375°. In microwaveable bowl, combine soups and cheese. Season with salt and pepper and heat until thoroughly combined. Stir in chicken and rice. Pour mixture into prepared casserole dish and cover. Bake for 30 to 45 minutes.

Canned chicken may be substituted for chicken breasts. Use regular cooking rice-not the "instant" or quick-cooking kind!

As much Arkansas chicken and Arkansas rice that Bill Clinton and I have had the pleasure of eating over the past 30 years, this is a new and unique way to keep chicken and rice interesting.

Easy Strawberry Pie

3	tablespoons cornstarch	1	cup sugar
½	cup water	2	cups crushed strawberries
1	tablespoon lemon juice	2	cups sliced strawberries
⅛	teaspoon salt		

1	(9-inch) pie shell, baked
	Frozen whipped topping
	Strawberry halves, for garnish

In large saucepan, combine cornstarch and water, blending until smooth. Add juice, salt, sugar, and crushed strawberries. Cook over low heat, stirring constantly until mixture thickens (about 5 minutes); allow to cool. Add sliced strawberries and pour into pie shell. Chill until set. Spread frozen whipped topping over pie and garnish with strawberry halves.

Yield: 6 to 8 servings

Next to Hope watermelon, Bald Knob strawberries are a favorite summertime dessert. This recipe is easy and delicious-you'd better make two!

Rick Fleetwood is a community activist living in Little Rock, Arkansas. He is a long-time supporter of the Clintons.

 ## Cajun Baked Catfish

| 6 (6-ounce) catfish fillets | Cajun seasoning | ½ cup cornmeal |

Preheat oven to 400°. Coat both sides of fillet with Cajun seasoning. Roll in cornmeal. Place fillets on baking sheet sprayed with nonstick cooking spray. Lightly coat fillets with cooking spray. Place baking sheet on bottom shelf of oven. Bake for 20 minutes. Reduce heat to 350° and bake for additional 5 minutes or until crust is golden and fillets flake easily.

Yield: 6 servings

 ## New Potato Salad in Mustard Vinaigrette

2 pounds small red new potatoes, washed	¼ cup extra virgin olive oil	1 tablespoon freshly chopped parsley
¼ cup red wine vinegar	1 tablespoon Dijon mustard	1 teaspoon salt
	3 tablespoons freshly chopped chives	Freshly ground black pepper to taste

In large saucepan, cover potatoes with cold water. Cook over medium-high heat and bring to a boil. Reduce heat to low, cover, and simmer 15 to 20 minutes or until tender. Drain potatoes and set aside until cool enough to touch. Combine vinegar and remaining ingredients in glass jar. Seal tightly with lid and shake well. Quarter potatoes and place in large bowl. Pour vinaigrette over warm potatoes, tossing well to coat. Serve warm or cover and chill.

Yield: 4 to 6 servings

★ JOE AND CAROLYN FLEISCHER ★

Born and raised in Brooklyn, New York, Joe Fleischer met his wife of thirty-five years at the City College of New York. Carolyn is likewise a born and bred New Yorker. Joe received his architectural degree from the City College and then joined Jim Polshek in what was, at the time, a two-person architectural practice. The rest is history, including his role as Partner-in-Charge of the Clinton Presidential Center project. Carolyn and Joe have two sons, one daughter-in-law, and currently live in Montclair, New Jersey.

 ## JUBILANT CHEESECAKE

FILLING

3 (8-ounce) packages cream cheese, softened	3 eggs	1 tablespoon orange juice
1 cup sugar	¾ cup sour cream	½ pound frozen strawberries
	1 teaspoon vanilla	

Preheat oven to 350°. In large mixing bowl, cream together cream cheese and sugar with electric mixer on medium speed. Add eggs, one at a time, beating well after each addition. Add sour cream, vanilla and orange juice and beat 30 seconds with electric mixer. Pour into crust. Bake for 45 minutes or until set. Allow strawberries to defrost; spoon berries and juice over individual slices just before serving.

CRUST

1½ cups graham cracker crumbs	⅓ cup butter, melted	3 tablespoons sugar

In medium mixing bowl, combine ingredients, mixing well. Press onto bottom of springform pan. Bake at 350° for 10 minutes.

Yield: 8 to 10 servings

★ ZINA GARRISON ★

Tennis legend Zina Garrison remains one of the world's most respected sports celebrities. Her amazing tennis career ended in 1997 when she announced her retirement. She represented the United States in the 1988 Olympics, returning from Seoul with a Bronze Medal in Singles and a Gold Medal in Doubles. Garrison's 1989 performance earned her the Singles titles at the Virginia Slims of Chicago, California and Newport, three Doubles titles with partner Katrina Adams, and the Mixed Doubles title at Wimbledon with partner Sherwood Stewart. Zina Garrison always cooked for herself and the other tennis players when she competed at Wimbledon.

 ## MATCH POINT MOZZARELLA SALAD

1 (7-ounce) package baby spinach, washed	1 (4½-ounce) package mozzarella cheese, cubed	½ cup extra virgin olive oil
1 (8-ounce) package cherry tomatoes, halved	2 teaspoons balsamic vinegar	Salt and pepper to taste

Remove stalks from spinach and discard. Place spinach in large bowl. Add tomato halves and mozzarella cubes. In small mixing bowl, combine vinegar and oil, whisking well. Season with salt and pepper to taste. Pour over spinach, tossing well to coat. Serve immediately or chill until ready to serve.

Yield: 4 servings

 ## GRAND SLAM SPINACH

1 garlic clove, minced	2 tablespoon butter	2 pounds fresh smooth-leaf spinach, rinsed and patted dry
1 tablespoon olive oil		

In small skillet over medium heat, sauté garlic in oil; set aside. In large skillet over medium heat, melt butter. Add spinach and increase heat to medium-high. Toss spinach until cooked (about 5 minutes). Add garlic mixture and toss well. Season with salt and pepper to taste.

Yield: 4 servings

★ GASTON'S WHITE RIVER RESORT ★

Gaston's White River Resort, located in Lakeview, Arkansas, began in 1958 when Jim Gaston purchased twenty acres on the White River with six cottages and six boats. Today, the nationally recognized resort covers four hundred acres, rents seventy-nine cottages, and docks over seventy boats.

 ## GRILLED BONELESS STUFFED TROUT

1	rainbow trout	Juice of ½ lemon
	Stuffing	Olive oil

Stuff trout with hot stuffing; sprinkle with lemon juice. Truss with toothpicks and rub outside with olive oil. Grill for 3 minutes on each side or until flesh becomes white.

STUFFING

2	tablespoons butter	2	teaspoons chopped chives	1	teaspoon Anisette or Pernod
½	cup sliced mushrooms, sautéed	½	cup chopped onions		Chopped parsley
½	cup baby shrimp	1	teaspoon chopped bell pepper		Salt and pepper to taste

In large skillet over medium-high heat, melt butter. Sauté mushrooms and next 4 ingredients until onions are golden. Add Anisette or Pernod and parsley. Season with salt and pepper to taste.

Yield: 2 servings

Anisette and Pernod are both licorice-flavored liqueurs.

Mark D. Gearan is presently President of Hobart and William Smith Colleges. During the 1992 campaign, he served as Campaign Manager for Al Gore's Vice Presidential campaign. He was the Deputy Director of the Transition. During the Administration, he served in the White House as Assistant to the President and Deputy Chief of Staff as well as Director of Communications. President Clinton later appointed Gearan as Director of the Peace Corps, a post he held from 1995 to 1999.

 ## SLIM GOURMET BOEUF BOURGUIGNON

3	pounds lean, well-trimmed beef round, cubed	
1	onion, finely chopped	
2	garlic cloves, minced	
2	cups dry Burgundy	

1	bay leaf
1	pound small carrots, washed and peeled
16	small pearl onions, peeled
½	pound small fresh mushrooms

⅓	cup cold water
1	tablespoon all-purpose flour
1	tablespoon cornstarch
	Salt and pepper to taste

In Dutch oven over high heat or large electric skillet, brown beef cubes on all sides. Add onion, garlic, Burgundy, and bay leaf. Cover and simmer about 2 hours or until tender. (More wine may need to be added.) Skim fat while cooking. Add carrots; cover and cook 20 minutes. Add pearl onions and mushrooms; cover and cook 10 minutes. In small mixing bowl, combine water, flour, and cornstarch, mixing well. Stir into simmering sauce. Season with salt and pepper to taste. Remove bay leaf before serving.

Yield: 8 servings

This is a lower fat version of the French classic. This recipe is especially good on a cold winter evening. We usually serve it with noodles and French bread.

★ JOSH GIBSON ★

Josh Gibson served as a White House Intern in the summer of 1993, specifically working on the Department of Labor Reinvention Team of Vice President Gore's Nation Performance Review. Since then, he has gone on to receive a Master of Public Policy degree from the John F. Kennedy School of Government at Harvard University. In 2000, he was elected an Advisory Neighborhood Commissioner in the Adams Morgan neighborhood of Washington, DC.

 ## GRANDMA DOTTY'S CHEESE PIE

2 (8-ounce) packages cream cheese, softened
2 large eggs
1 teaspoon vanilla
¾ cup sugar
2-3 tablespoons butter, melted
25 shortbread cookies, finely crushed

Preheat oven to 350°. In large mixing bowl, combine cream cheese, eggs, vanilla, and sugar. Beat with an electric mixer on medium speed until smooth; set aside. In small mixing bowl, combine butter and crushed cookies. Press mixture on bottom and up sides of pie plate. Pour cream cheese mixture into crust. Bake for 20 minutes. Allow to cool, then chill overnight.

Yield: 8 to 10 servings

Add fresh fruit, fruit toppings, or whipping cream before serving.

This is the best cheesecake you'll ever have! Eating this dessert calls to mind memories of happy visits to see my grandparents, particularly summer trips to their cottage in Old Lynne, Connecticut. "Grandma Dotty's Cheese Pie" once sold for $80 in a charity auction at the Kennedy School of Government at Harvard University.

★ SECRETARY DAN GLICKMAN ★

Dan Glickman served as the Secretary of Agriculture from March 1995 until January 2001. Before his appointment to that position, he represented Kansas' Fourth Congressional District for eighteen years. He currently serves as the Director of the Institute of Politics located at the John F. Kennedy School of Government.

 BAR-B-QUE BRISKET OF BEEF

1	onion, sliced	1	pound mushrooms, sliced		Seasoning salt to taste (optional)
1	large brisket	1	(1¼-ounce) package dry onion soup mix	1	bottle hickory smoke flavored barbecue sauce
12-18	small red potatoes, washed		Salt and pepper to taste (optional)		
1	(12-ounce) package baby carrots, peeled and sliced				

Preheat oven to 325°. Place onion in bottom of roasting pan. Place brisket on top. Arrange potatoes, carrots, and mushrooms around brisket. Sprinkle onion soup mix over brisket. Season with salt, pepper, and seasoning salt if desired. Cover and bake for 5 hours. Remove from oven and allow to cool; thinly slice brisket. Return slices to roasting pan with vegetables and juices. Pour barbecue sauce into roasting pan. Bake for additional 45 minutes to 1 hour, being careful not to overcook. Cover brisket again if cooking too quickly.

Yield: 6 servings

★ SECRETARY HERSHEL W. GOBER ★

Originally from Monticello, Arkansas, Hershel Gober served in the Clinton Administration as the Acting Secretary and Deputy Secretary of the Department of Veterans Affairs from 1993 to 2001. He was the Arkansas State Director of Veterans Affairs from 1988 to 1993 and the Director of Arkansas Veterans Child Welfare from 1985 to 1988. He served two tours in Vietnam and is a retired Army Major.

 ## POT ROAST

1 (4-pound) beef chuck roast Cooking oil	1 (10¾-ounce) can cream of mushroom soup	1 teaspoon basil
2 cups red wine	1 onion, chopped	4-5 medium potatoes, peeled and cut into chunks
2 cups water	1 bay leaf, crushed	6-8 carrots, peeled and cut into 1-inch chunks
1 (1¼-ounce) package dry onion soup mix	3 garlic cloves, chopped	
	1 teaspoon thyme	

In large skillet over medium-high heat, brown roast in oil on all sides; transfer to crockpot. Pour wine and water into crockpot. Add onion soup mix and next 6 ingredients. Cover and cook approximately 5 hours. Add potatoes and carrots. Cover and cook at 350° for 3 hours, 30 minutes or until vegetables are tender.

★ WHOOPI GOLDBERG ★

Whoopi Goldberg, a New York City native, is a comedienne and actress. She is also a friend of the Clintons. She was responsible for bringing the crowd to its feet as the host of the *Very Special Christmas* program, an event benefiting the Special Olympics held on the South Lawn of the White House in 1998.

MALIBU BEACH BUFFET

On the way home from the studio, have your driver stop at Bristol Farms. Run in to deli counter. Select two or three favorite dishes... Pasta al Pesto, Veal Piccata, Chicken Bombay, maybe some chocolate chip cookies—couldn't hurt! On your way through the kitchen, grab napkins, paper plates, and plasticware. Rush to the window to catch the sunset. Um-um good!

Yield: Ideally serves two!

★ PAUL GOLDENBERG ★

Paul Goldenberg is owner of Paul's TV, The King of Bigscreen retail business, in Southern California. He is a lifelong Democrat and supporter of the Clintons. This recipe by his Aunt Betty Klein (age 86) has been a family favorite for years.

 ## AUNT BETTY'S STUFFED CABBAGE ROLLS

2	pounds ground beef	2	onions, finely chopped	I	can tomato sauce
5	garlic cloves, minced	I	large head cabbage	I	can sauerkraut
					Brown sugar

Preheat oven to 350°. In large saucepan over medium-high heat, bring cabbage to a boil. Cook 5 minutes or until leaves are soft and pliable enough to roll. In large mixing bowl, combine beef, garlic, and onion. Divide mixture into 8 equal portions. Wrap meat mixture with cabbage leaf. Repeat process 7 more times. Place rolls in baking dish. Cover with tomato sauce and sauerkraut. Top with brown sugar. Bake for I hour.

Yield: 8 servings

I am fortunate enough to have two great friends, Bill and Hillary Clinton. I'm sure they would both love Aunt Betty's Stuffed Cabbage Rolls, and Aunt Betty would feel honored to be in the cookbook.

★ DR. MARY L. GOOD ★

Dr. Mary Good was the Undersecretary for Technology in the Department of Commerce during President Clinton's first term. During the term of Presidents Carter and Reagan, Dr. Good served on the National Science Board and chaired it from 1988 to 1991. She is currently the Dean of the CyberCollege at the University of Arkansas at Little Rock.

 ## DATE-NUT ROLL

2	cups sugar	1	(8-ounce) package pitted dates,	1	teaspoon vanilla
1	cup milk		chopped	2	tablespoons butter
				1	cup chopped pecans

In small saucepan over medium-high heat, combine sugar and milk. Bring to a boil and cook to firm ball stage. (When a small amount of mixture is dropped into very cold water, it forms a firm but pliable ball.) Add dates, stirring until dates melt. Add vanilla and butter, stirring frequently. Remove from heat; add pecans and stir until stiffened. Spread candy mixture onto wet tea towel. Roll jelly roll fashion and chill until firm. Slice into rounds.

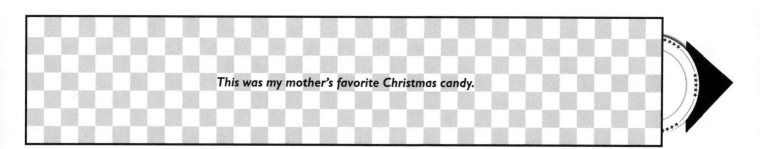

This was my mother's favorite Christmas candy.

★ VICE PRESIDENT AL GORE AND TIPPER GORE ★

Former Vice President Al Gore is Vice Chairman of Metropolitan West Financial, LLC, and a member of the Firm's executive leadership team. For the past two years, he has also served as Senior Advisor to Google, Inc. In March 2003, he was elected to the Board of Directors of Apple Computers, Inc. Al Gore's political career began when he was elected to the U.S. House of Representatives in 1976 where he served eight years representing the then Fourth District of Tennessee. He was elected to the U.S. Senate in 1984 and was re-elected in 1990, becoming the first candidate in modern history-Republican or Democratic-to win all 95 of Tennessee's counties. Al Gore was inaugurated as the 45th Vice President of the United States on January 20, 1993.

Tipper Gore is a world renown leader and activist. As an advocate for families, women, and children, she is actively involved in issues related to mental health, education, and the plight of homeless people everywhere. Her commitment to eradicating the stigma associated with mental illness placed her in the unique position to serve as the Mental Health Policy Advisor to President Clinton. In June 1999, she chaired the first-ever White House Conference on Mental Health. Mrs. Gore co-founded and chaired in 1986 Families for the Homeless, a non-partisan partnership of families that raises public awareness of homeless issues.

Al and Tipper Gore were married in 1970. They have four children and two grandchildren.

TENNESSEE TREATS

2 cups firmly packed dark brown sugar	¼ cup boiling water	½ teaspoon salt
2 eggs	2 cups all-purpose flour	½ cup raisins
2 egg whites	½ teaspoon cinnamon	½ cup chopped dates
2 tablespoons honey	⅛ teaspoon allspice	½ cup coarsely chopped walnuts
1 teaspoon baking powder	⅛ teaspoon ground cloves	

Preheat oven to 350°. In large mixing bowl, combine sugar, eggs, and egg whites. Stir in honey. In small mixing bowl, add baking powder to water and mix well. Add to sugar mixture, stirring well to combine. In large mixing bowl, sift together flour, cinnamon, allspice, cloves, and salt. Add to sugar mixture and mix well. Fold in raisins, dates, and walnuts. Pour into prepared 8x12-inch baking pan. Bake for 30 to 40 minutes or until cake tester inserted in center comes out nearly dry. Cut into squares while warm.

Yield: 12 servings

★ VICE PRESIDENT AL GORE AND TIPPER GORE ★

 SPICED ROAST CHICKEN

1 (3½-pound) chicken	1 tablespoon butter	Thyme sprigs, for garnish
Mushroom Stuffing	⅔ cup Marsala	Watercress sprigs, for garnish
¼ cup water		

Preheat oven to 375°. Stuff chicken with Mushroom Stuffing and truss securely with cooking twine. Place in roasting pan, breast side down, and add water. Roast 45 minutes; turn chicken breast side up and dot with butter. Roast about 45 minutes or until meat thermometer inserted in thickest portion of thigh (being careful not to touch bone) registers 185°. Transfer chicken to serving platter and keep warm. Pour off and discard fat from roasting pan; add Marsala to remaining cooking juices, stirring to scrape browned bits. Boil over high heat 1 minute and reduce slightly; adjust seasons to taste. Remove skin and carve chicken. Garnish with thyme and watercress sprigs. Serve with Mushroom Stuffing, flavored meat juices, and seasonal vegetables.

MUSHROOM STUFFING

1 onion, finely chopped	4 ounces button or brown	¼ cup minced walnuts
2 tablespoons olive oil	mushrooms, chopped	2 teaspoons freshly chopped thyme
1 teaspoon garam masala	1 cup coarsely shredded parsnips	1 cup fresh white breadcrumbs
	1 cup coarsely shredded carrots	1 egg, beaten
		Salt and pepper to taste

In large saucepan over medium-high heat, sauté onion in olive oil for 2 minutes or until tender. Stir in garam masala and cook 1 minute. Add mushrooms, parsnips, and carrots; cook 5 minutes, stirring frequently. Remove from heat. Stir in walnuts and remaining ingredients.

Yield: 4 servings

★ KAY COLLETT GOSS ★

A former college professor, Kay C. Goss is the only woman to have served as Associate Director of the Federal Emergency Management Agency, being in charge of National Preparedness, Training, and Exercises Directorate in the Clinton Administration. She now serves on the Certified Emergency Manager Commission, housed at the Emergency Management Institution in Emmitsburg, Maryland, and the Arkansas Emergency Management Association.

 ## AN EMERGENCY MANAGER'S EARTHQUAKE CAKE

1½ cups nuts, chopped
1½ cups shredded coconut
1 (18-ounce) package German chocolate cake mix

1 (8-ounce) package cream cheese, melted
½ cup unsalted butter, melted

1 (16-ounce) package confections' sugar

Preheat oven to 350°. Sprinkle nuts on bottom of greased and floured 9x13-inch baking pan. Sprinkle coconut over nuts. Prepare cake mix according to package directions. Pour batter over coconut. In medium mixing bowl, combine cream cheese and butter. Stir in confectioners' sugar, whipping until smooth. Pour over cake batter. Bake for 40 to 50 minutes or until cake tester inserted in center comes out clean. Cake will crack (I mean "quake") on top.

It was my pleasure for twenty years to serve, first as Governor Clinton's Senior Assistant for Intergovernmental Relations and secondly, as President Clinton's Associate Director of the Federal Emergency Management Agency. In both positions, we prepared Arkansas State and the region for a potential earthquake as well as other natural and unnatural disasters. I grew up near Tontitown, a Sicilian village, in Northwest Arkansas, where this cake was a favorite, and it has been embellished and renamed by yours truly!

Sissy Griffin lives in Little Rock and volunteers weekly at the William J. Clinton Presidential Foundation. She is a loyal Democrat and has volunteered in many Presidential campaigns since the Kennedy years. She doesn't spend much time in the kitchen, so she uses this eggplant recipe quite often!

 ## BAKED EGGPLANT ROUNDS

I eggplant, unpeeled and sliced into ¾-inch thick rounds	Olive oil Garlic salt	Red pepper flakes

Preheat oven to 350°. Line baking sheet with aluminum foil and coat with cooking spray. Rub both sides of eggplant rounds with olive oil. Sprinkle lightly with garlic salt. Sprinkle very lightly with red pepper flakes. Place rounds on prepared baking sheet and bake for 15 to 20 minutes.

Quick and easy... no peeling, stuffing, or chopping... no pans to clean... my kind of cooking!

★ CATHERINE GRUNDEN ★

Catherine Grunden did advance work for President and Senator Clinton during the 1992 and 1996 campaigns. She served as Senior Advisor and Director of Scheduling for Secretary of Transportation Rodney Slater during the Clinton Administration.

SWISS ONION SOUP

1 (10¾-ounce) can cream of chicken soup	1 (10¾-ounce) can chicken broth	¼ soup can white wine
1 can French onion soup	¾ soup can whole milk	1 cup shredded mozzarella cheese

In large saucepan over medium-high heat, combine soups and broth. Add milk and wine, stirring well to blend. Simmer until thoroughly heated. Divide cheese evenly among 4 soup bowls. Pour soup over cheese and serve immediately.

Yield: 4 servings

★ BART HANDFORD ★

An automobile accident derailed Bart Handford's second attempt at college, but led to an opportunity to work in Little Rock on Bill Clinton's 1992 Presidential campaign. In January 1993, Bart moved to Washington, DC, and began work at the White House in the Office of Presidential Scheduling and Advance. In 1995, he moved to the U.S. Department of Agriculture to work in the Rural Development Agency and eventually was named Midwestern Regional Coordinator for Rural Development in 1998. While at USDA, Bart finished his undergraduate work and earned a bachelor's degree. He now works for a Washington, DC, non-profit group that funds social justice programs in Israel.

ARKANSAS CORNBREAD

Cooking oil	1 teaspoon salt	2 eggs, beaten
2 cups cornmeal	1 teaspoon baking soda	2 cups buttermilk

Preheat oven to 450°. Generously coat bottom and sides of 10-inch cast iron skillet with cooking oil. Heat skillet in oven 5 minutes or until hot. In large mixing bowl, combine cornmeal, salt, and baking soda. Add eggs and stir in buttermilk until smooth. Pour batter into hot skillet and bake for 18 to 20 minutes or until top is golden and cake tester inserted into center comes out clean. Allow to cool before cutting. Serve warm with butter.

This is the cornbread I grew up on, and I still make it regularly.

★ KIRK T. HANLIN ★

As one of the Lead White House advance staff, Kirk Hanlin oversaw Presidential events all over the world. He also oversaw many key events in the 1992 and 1996 campaigns, including the Arsenio Hall Show, the 1992 Democratic Convention, televised town hall meetings, some of the famous Bus Trips, and both election nights in Little Rock. In 1997, Hanlin became the President's Trip Director, thereby making over 1000 flights on Air Force One.

 ## KIRK HANLIN'S "AIR-FORCE-ONE" PEANUT BUTTER AND JELLY SANDWICH

2 slices fresh white bread	I jar grape jelly	I can soda, chilled
I jar peanut butter	I bag rippled potato chips	

Place bread slices on plate. Open peanut butter. Using knife, carefully spread peanut butter evenly on one bread slice, taking care not to tear bread. Clean peanut butter knife on inside of peanut butter jar. Using second knife, evenly spread jelly on second bread slice, again, taking care not to tear bread. Lift piece of bread with peanut butter and carefully cover piece of bread with jelly, taking care that sides are even. Flip sandwich so that jelly side is up, and use peanut butter knife to cut sandwich diagonally. Serve with potato chips and soda.

Yield: I serving

As President Clinton's Trip Director, I spent a lot of time on Air Force One. While the menus and food onboard were excellent, the crew always kept a stash of ingredients for my favorite meal onboard. On many occasions, the President and other members of the Senior staff would join me in this culinary delight. I hope you all like this recipe and can picture yourself on the world's most amazing aircraft sitting with the world's most powerful man enjoying this delightful meal!

★ CHRIS HEHMEYER ★

Chris manages a futures and options trading business in Chicago. He was born and raised in Memphis, where his yellow dog Democrat mother still lives. Chris's dad was the Press Secretary for the Truman Committee, and his mother was a secretary for then-Senator Truman. With these roots, Chris has come to be an active supporter of Dems from Mayor Daley to the former President.

 ## HEHMEYER'S EGG SANDWICH

1 tablespoon butter	Salt and pepper to taste	1 tablespoon mayonnaise
1 egg	1 English muffin, split and toasted	

In a small skillet over medium heat, melt butter. Break egg into skillet, making sure yolk is broken somewhat evenly. Shape egg to size of English muffin with spatula. Season with salt and pepper while egg cooks (about 1½ to 2 minutes) and flip. Spread English muffin with mayonnaise. Sprinkle egg with salt and pepper and place on muffin.

Yield: 1 serving

Add one slice of American cheese after flipping egg for Hehmeyer's Royal Egg Sandwich.

Served around-the-clock, but ideally between 12:00 AM and 2:00 AM with a glass of cold 2% milk!

Heifer International is a non-profit organization designed to eliminate hunger and poverty domestically and around the world. The organization's vision of securing self-reliant communities through donations of cows, goats, and other income-producing live-stock to impoverished families took shape in 1944. Since its beginnings, Heifer has given aid to 5 million in 128 countries around the world.

Heifer's unique practice of "Passing on the Gift", requiring recipients to give offspring of their animals to others in need, multiplies the effect of every gift to Heifer while making every recipient an equal partner in the fight against hunger and poverty. Heifer's dedication to achieving this vision and accomplishing its goal has initiated a legacy in central Arkansas that reaches around the globe.

Besides delivering the gifts of livestock, Heifer also trains the recipients in animal care and environmentally sound agricultural practices, so they are able to lift themselves from poverty to become self-reliant. Milk, eggs, wool, meat, draft power, and other benefits from the animals provide nutrition, money for education, better housing, better health care, and the resources to start small business enterprises.

Heifer International plans to construct a new Heifer International Center with offices and a learning center in Little Rock, Arkansas. The site, adjacent to the new Clinton Presidential Center and Park, will provide the organization a vibrant outlet to continue toward achieving its vision of ending world hunger. Heifer International and the Clinton Presidential Center share a common interest in the well-being and advancement of the less fortunate.

photo courtesy of Heifer International

While they were in Little Rock for a Global Team Meeting, the International Program Directors with Heifer International made time to visit their future neighbors at the William J. Clinton Presidental Center construction site.

PLEASE NOTE: The international recipes that follow from Heifer Project International programs around the world have been left in their original format to ensure authenticity.

★ HEIFER INTERNATIONAL-AFRICA PROGRAM ★

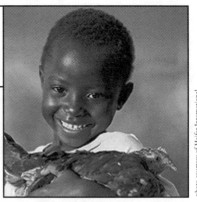

From Cameroon to Mozambique, Heifer International is building a vast bridge of hope across the African continent. For example, in Ghana, Heifer-supplied ducks are buoying family incomes hit hard by the collapse of the local fishing and shellfish industry. In Kenya, cows and draft oxen are helping families who care for children orphaned by AIDS. Heifer is also working with partner organizations to support educational efforts on how to stop the disease's spread. In Rwanda, still feeling the effects of genocide, Heifer cattle are helping provide a common economic interest-and common ground-for once-divided communities. While improving nutrition, income, and employment, Heifer is also helping build a stable peace.

RICH GROUNDNUT SOUP

½ pound skinned raw groundnuts	1 tablespoon butter or margarine	Salt and pepper to taste
1 onion, chopped	1 tablespoon all-purpose flour	4 tablespoons heavy cream
1 celery stalk, cut in thin slices	1 garlic clove, crushed	Coarsely ground peanuts
1 cup milk	3 cups water or stock	(optional)

Pound the nuts in a mortar or chop finely in a blender. Combine with the onion, celery, and milk and simmer 1 hour. Make a sauce with the butter or margarine, flour, garlic, and stock. Add to nut mixture and bring to a boil. Season with salt and pepper to taste. Stir in cream just before serving. Sprinkle with coarsely ground peanuts if desired.

★ HEIFER INTERNATIONAL-ASIA/SOUTH PACIFIC PROGRAM ★

From the embattled mountains of Afghanistan to the plains of Mongolia and the lush islands of the Philippines, Heifer's Asia/South Pacific Program is working to help families become self-reliant through increased incomes, improved health, and access to skills and education. We're helping Afghanistan recover from decades of war with new animals to replace lost livestock, trees to replenish windbreaks, and training to prevent further environmental damage. We're providing an animal management project in Mongolia, a recovery program for flood caused economic devastation in China, a livestock raising program for women in Nepal, and animal distribution and training in North Korea. With other projects in India, Indonesia, Laos, Thailand, Cambodia and Viet Nam-Heifer is working throughout the region to put an end to hunger and poverty.

 ## PORK (ADOBO)

2¼ pounds pork, cut into 1½x2-inch chunks
1 garlic head, pounded

4 teaspoons salt or toyo to taste
1 teaspoon freshly ground black pepper

1 tablespoon lard
2 cups water
½ cup vinegar

Place pork in saucepan. Add vinegar, garlic, pepper, salt or toyo, and water. Cover saucepan and cook slowly until meat is tender and broth has reduced to ¼ cup. Drain, separate pieces of garlic from pork and fry in lard until brown. Add pork and fry until brown. Add broth and simmer about 5 minutes. Serve hot.

★ HEIFER INTERNATIONAL-CENTRAL AND EASTERN EUROPEAN PROGRAM ★

As the Central/Easter European program enters its second decade, Heifer faces significant challenges. Since the fall of the Berlin Wall in 1989, the economic, technical, and social infrastructures of many nations in the region fell apart. The transition from central planning to market economies hasn't been easy. For example, in Albania, Heifer is providing saplings to aid in erosion control, training and micro-credit to help families improve their small farms and purchase livestock. In cooperation with the United Nations, Heifer is engaged in an innovative Peace Project that encourages farmers to swap weapons for Holstein and Jersey heifers. In Armenia, Kosovo, Lithuania, Poland, Romania, Hungary, Georgia, Moldova, Russia, Ukraine, Slovakia, and elsewhere in the region, Heifer and its project partners are making a difference.

APPLE FRITTERS (RACUSZKI)

2   eggs, separated
    Pinch of salt
1   tablespoon olive oil

1   cup all-purpose flour
¾   cup milk
1   pound tart apples, peeled and cut
    into ¼-inch slices

Cooking oil
Confectioners' sugar

Mix eggs, salt, olive oil, and flour in a blender. Add milk and mix well. Cover blender with a towel and let rest for 15 minutes. Whisk egg whites into a stiff foam, then gently fold into batter. Dip apple slices in the dough and fry in hot oil until light golden brown on both sides. Remove from oil and immediately sprinkle with powdered sugar. Serve hot.

★ HEIFER INTERNATIONAL-LATIN AMERICA/ CARIBBEAN PROGRAM ★

In Latin America and the Caribbean, Heifer gives cause for hope. Heifer is battling poor nutrition and inadequate access to land and water. And Heifer is reintroducing indigenous livestock-guinea pigs, alpacas, and llamas-and is working to diversify household small-animal raising and stabilize sustainable family farms. In Peru, Heifer is providing horses so families can develop eco-tourism operations. In Haiti, the poorest nation in the western hemisphere, Heifer is working to improve the standard of veterinary care, providing training for women in project planning and execution. In Guatemala, a Heifer Peace Project is assisting local people in the Ixil region to recover from the decades of political violence.

 ## STUFFED BELL PEPPERS (ROCOTO RELLENO)

PEPPERS

6 large bell peppers	5 tablespoons sugar, divided	Juice of 2 limes

Slice off tops of bell peppers and set aside. Remove seeds and membranes, rinse, and sprinkle ½ teaspoon sugar in each pepper; rub well. Rinse again and sprinkle with lime juice. Place peppers in a large pot and cover them with water, adding 1 teaspoon salt. Cover and bring to a boil. Add more water to cover and 1 tablespoon sugar.

MEAT STUFFING

¾ cup cooking oil	4 tablespoons powdered "panca" red peppers	Salt and pepper
3 large onions, chopped		½ tablespoon oregano
4 garlic cloves, chopped	1 pound ground beef	½ cup chopped peanuts, toasted
		3 hard-boiled eggs, chopped

Heat oil in skillet and sauté onion and garlic. Add powdered red pepper; cook several minutes and add meat. Season with salt and pepper. Sprinkle with oregano and peanuts. Remove from heat and stir in eggs. Stuff bell peppers with Meat Stuffing.

CASSEROLE

3 pounds potatoes, sliced	3 eggs	¾ cup cooking oil
6 slices cheese	3 cups milk	Salt and pepper to taste

Parboil potatoes; place them in casserole and top them with stuffed bell peppers. Top each with a slice of cheese. Cover with the bell pepper tops. Whisk eggs; add milk and cooking oil. Season with salt and pepper. Pour mixture over stuffed peppers in casserole. Bake at 375° for 45 minutes to 1 hour.

Yield: 6 servings

★ HEIFER INTERNATIONAL-NORTH AMERICA PROGRAM ★

photo courtesy of Heifer International

Heifer International is engaged in perhaps the most important work of our times-fighting deprivation and environmental decay in the developing world and in North America. Some 31 million hungry people live in the United States alone. From the Native American communities of the Canadian plains to the concrete canyons of Chicago and Mexico's southern mountains, Heifer's North American Program is dedicated to ending hunger and poverty. At the same time, the North Ameri can Program is building self-sufficiency and community among urban communities where poverty has spanned several generations. In Chicago, youths who might be otherwise recruited into gangs are learning marketing and production skills through Heifer-supported worm and fishing projects. In the poorest neighborhoods of New York and Philadelphia, residents have almost no access to fresh fruits and vegetables. In those cities and others, Heifer is active in assisting with community gardens. And in Mexico's Puebla state, families are benefiting from microcredit loans, training and the provision of mules, sheep, and worms.

SIMPLE TRADITIONAL SOUTHWESTERN GOAT CHEESE

1 gallon goat's milk	Salt to taste	Chopped onion (optional)
¼ cup vinegar	Dill, black pepper, or garlic	Chopped pecans (optional)

Slowly heat milk to 185°, using a stainless steel or enamel-ware pan (NOT aluminum). Add vinegar. Keep temperature at 185°, stirring constantly, for 10 to 15 minutes. A soft curd should form. Line a colander with cheesecloth. Pour the curd into the colander and sprinkle with salt. Tie the corners of the cloth together and hang it to drip for a few hours. Add seasonings, such as dill, pepper, or garlic. For a real treat, add onion or pecans. Chill several hours. Eat cheese immediately or keep in refrigerator for up to a week.

★ DON HENLEY ★

Don Henley is a member of The Eagles, which won four Grammy awards in its heyday. He started his very successful solo career in 1982, but took a hiatus during the 1990s to concentrate on his activism, especially with environmental issues. Don became a friend of the Clintons when he played for one of the last dinners at Camp David.

 ## CORN DOGS

½	cup all-purpose flour	1	egg, beaten		Wooden sticks or skewers
½	cup yellow cornmeal	1	tablespoon cooking oil		Cooking oil
1	teaspoon salt	12	hot dogs		American-style mustard
½	cup milk or buttermilk				

In large mixing bowl, combine flour, cornmeal, and salt. Add milk, egg, and 1 tablespoon oil, stirring until smooth. Insert skewers lengthwise into hot dogs. Dip hot dogs into batter and drain over bowl. Place in hot oil in deep skillet or electric skillet; cook 2 to 3 minutes or until golden brown, turning once. Remove from oil and drain. Enjoy with lots of mustard.

Yield: 12 servings

If a coarser, grainier batter is preferred, use more cornmeal and less flour. Also, hot dogs may be boiled briefly before battering. If batter gets too stiff, add small amount of water or milk. If batter is too thin, add more cornmeal or flour.

★ DON HENLEY ★

 ## Fresh Peach Cobbler

2 cups all-purpose flour	2 tablespoons sugar	¼ cup butter, cut into pats
⅛ teaspoon salt	¾ cup sugar, divided	Dash of nutmeg (optional)
¾ cup butter, cut into pats	7 large, ripe peaches, peeled and	
⅓ cup cold water	sliced	

In large mixing bowl, combine flour, salt, and ¾ cup butter. Cut with pastry blender (or food processor) until mixture has texture of cornmeal. Sprinkle cold water quickly over surface, mix with large spoon, and pull dough together lightly. Gently shape dough into ball with hands and divide into two slightly unequal portions. Place dough in two separate bowls, cover with a cloth, and chill 20 to 30 minutes. (Chill rolling pin as well for greater ease in rolling.) Remove dough about 15 to 20 minutes before rolling. Lightly flour rolling pin and board; roll out larger portion of dough into square shape. (To gauge size, place an 8x8x2-inch baking dish over rolled-out dough and allow an additional two-and-one-half inches to cover the sides and rim. Roll up dough onto pin and carefully unroll over baking dish. Gently press dough into bottom and sides of dish. Sprinkle dough with 2 tablespoons sugar and chill until ready to assemble. Remaining dough may be rolled out and chilled between two sheets of waxed paper. For a lattice top cobbler, simply roll out remaining dough and cut into eight strips. Remove dough from refrigerator approximately 1 hour, 30 minutes before serving. Preheat oven to 450°. Sprinkle half of ¾ cup sugar over bottom of crust; add peaches, placing last slices in a mound in the center. Sprinkle with remaining sugar and dot with ¼ cup butter. Weave four lattice strips across pie and four lengthwise (or place diagonally, although lengths and widths of strips may have to be altered). Moisten rim with cold water and press down lattice edges to seal. Set cobbler on middle oven rack and bake for 10 minutes. Reduce heat to 425° and bake for additional 35 minutes. Allow to cool for 30 minutes. Serve warm with vanilla ice cream or thick, fresh cream.

Yield: 12 servings

Peach cobbler or any peach pie is a seasonal dish. It is very important to use tree-ripened peaches. The peaches that are normally sold in supermarkets have not been allowed to fully ripen on the tree and are generally hard as rocks and have little or no flavor. A good, tree-ripened peach should be slightly soft to the touch and should smell like a peach. The flesh should be juicy as opposed to hard and dry. Check the local farmer's market or roadside stands during July and August.

Some people like a little nutmeg in their peach pie, but for my taste, they usually add too much, and it overwhelms the flavor of the peaches. Add nutmeg if you like, but use it sparingly!

★ NANCY HERNREICH-BOWEN ★

Nancy Hernreich Bowen began working for Bill Clinton during his 1976 campaign for Attorney General. She then ran his campaigns in Sebastian County in 1980, 1982, and 1984. In 1985, she went to work for him as his Scheduling Secretary in the Governor's office and held that position until 1993. At that time, she went to the White House with the Clintons. She worked in the Administration for the entire eight years serving as Director of Oval Office Operations.

 **BROWNIE HEARTS**

4 ounces unsweetened chocolate (4 squares)	2 cups sugar	1½ teaspoons vanilla
1½ cups butter	1 cup all-purpose flour	1 (12-ounce) package semi-sweet chocolate chips
4 eggs	½ teaspoon salt	

Preheat oven to 350°. Grease a 15½x11¼x1-inch baking pan and line with parchment. Melt chocolate squares and butter in microwave or in top of double boiler and cool. With a whisk, beat in eggs one at a time, mixing well after each addition. Add sugar and mix well. Fold in flour and salt. Add vanilla and chocolate chips. Spread mixture evenly in baking pan and bake for 20 to 25 minutes. Allow to cool completely to room temperature (several hours) before cutting into desired shapes with cookie or biscuit cutters.

I made these brownies for most of the engagement parties we had at my house for the brides in the Clinton Administration and also gave the recipe to young prospective brides to make for their sweethearts. I made them for parties for Lee Satterfield and Patrick Steele, for Anne Wally and Jim Hawley, for Andrew Friendly and Kelly Crawford, for Rebecca Cameron and Marvin Blount, to name a few. You can cut the brownies to any shape you want for special occasions or just in squares for every day.

 ## SPICED PARTY NUTS

½ teaspoon cumin	¼ teaspoon cayenne pepper	2 cups pecan halves
½ teaspoon chili powder	¼ teaspoon ground ginger	1 tablespoon coarse salt (optional)
½ teaspoon curry powder	¼ teaspoon cinnamon	Garlic salt (optional)
½ teaspoon garlic salt	2 tablespoons olive oil	

Preheat oven to 325°. In small mixing bowl, combine cumin and next 6 ingredients; set aside. In small nonstick skillet, heat oil over low heat. Add spice mixture and stir well. Simmer to allow flavors to combine (about 3 to 4 minutes). Place pecans in large mixing bowl. Add spice mixture and toss well. Spread pecans in single layer on baking sheet. Bake for 15 minutes, shaking pan several times. Remove baking sheet from oven. Using a rubber spatula, toss pecans with any spices and oil that have accumulated on the bottom of the pan. Sprinkle with salts. Let stand in cool place 2 hours. Store in airtight containers.

Yield: 2 cups

Keep pecan batches this size. They need plenty of tossing and drying room.

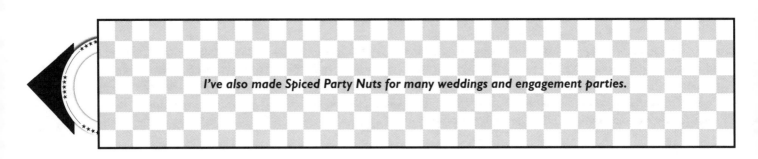

I've also made Spiced Party Nuts for many weddings and engagement parties.

★ KITTY HIGGINS ★

Kathryn "Kitty" Higgins is the Vice President for Public Policy at the National Trust for Historic Preservation. Before joining the National Trust in May 1999, Kitty was Deputy Secretary of the Department of Labor. Prior to her tenure at Labor, Kitty served in several positions both within the Clinton Administration and on Capitol Hill, including Assistant to the President and Secretary to the Cabinet, Chief of Staff to the Secretary of Labor, Chief of Staff to Congressman Sander Levin, and Minority Staff Director for the Senate Labor and Human Resources Committee.

 **IRISH STEW**

3	pounds lamb shoulder	1	garlic clove, peeled and crushed	2	finely shredded, peeled potatoes
4	cups cold water	1	teaspoon brown sugar	12	small whole onions, parboiled
1	onion, sliced	1	parsley sprig	6	potatoes, peeled and cut into chunks
	Celery greens	⅛	teaspoon thyme	1	tablespoon salt
½	(10½-ounce) can beef consommé	1	bay leaf	2	cups peas, cooked
	Cooking oil for browning	¼	teaspoon pepper	2	cups sliced carrots, cooked

Trim skin and bones from lamb; discard skin and reserve bones. Cut lamb into 2-inch pieces and set aside. Place bones in large saucepan. Add water, onion, and celery. Bring to a boil, then lower heat and simmer, uncovered, about 30 minutes. Strain over mesh strainer and reserve liquid. Combine liquid and consommé; set aside. In large skillet over medium-high heat, brown lamb in oil. Transfer to Dutch oven; add garlic and next 6 ingredients. Add consommé mixture. Cook slowly, uncovered, to reduce broth (about 1 hour, 30 minutes). Liquid will thicken slightly as potato shreds dissolve. Add whole onions, potato chunks, and salt. Cook 30 minutes. Serve in soup tureen with peas and carrots around edges.

Yield: 9 to 12 servings

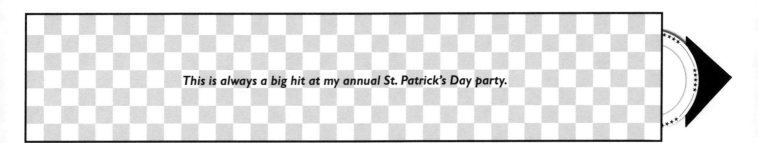

This is always a big hit at my annual St. Patrick's Day party.

★ KAKI HOCKERSMITH ★

Kaki Hockersmith was involved in many design and decorating projects at the White House, including the Blue Room, Oval Office, State Dining Room, the Grand Staircase and other projects in both the private residence and at Camp David. She currently resides in Little Rock, Arkansas, where she operates an active design firm named Kaki Hockersmith Interiors which has both local and national projects.

ACORN SQUASH SOUP

4 acorn squash	1 teaspoon salt	Dash of ground allspice
3 carrots, sliced	½-1 teaspoon black pepper	Dash of cayenne pepper
1 onion, sliced	2 (14½-ounce) cans chicken broth	1 cup half-and-half
⅓ cup water	½ cup sherry	1½ tablespoons sherry (optional)
2 tablespoons butter	½ teaspoon ground nutmeg	Kale leaves
1 tablespoon all-purpose flour	⅛ teaspoon paprika	Paprika

Cut squash in half lengthwise; remove and discard seeds. Place squash, cut side down, in broiler pan. Add hot water to pan to a depth of 1 inch. Bake at 350° for 30 minutes. Spoon pulp from squash to create a serving bowl, reserving pulp. Place carrots and onion in saucepan and cover with water. Bring to a boil; cover, reduce heat, and simmer 15 minutes or until vegetables are tender. Drain; combine vegetables with reserved pulp and ⅓ cup water in container of electric blender or food processor. Process 30 seconds or until mixture is smooth and set aside. In large Dutch oven over low heat, melt butter. Add flour, salt, and pepper, stirring until smooth. Cook 1 minute, stirring constantly. Gradually add pureed vegetable mixture, chicken broth, and next 5 ingredients; bring to a boil. Cover, reduce heat, and simmer 1 hour, stirring occasionally. Stir in half-and-half and 1½ tablespoons sherry if desired. Cook until heated thoroughly. If desired, serve in squash shells on a bed of kale. Sprinkle with paprika.

Yield: 8 servings

★ BOBBY AND LOIS HOPPER ★

Bobby Hopper met Bill Clinton in the early 1980s and helped him get reelected as Governor in 1983. The governor twice appointed Bobby to the Arkansas State Highway Commission, where he served two terms as Chairman. Bobby and Lois often hosted and entertained Governor Clinton in their Springdale, Arkansas, home when he was on the campaign trail.

 **PUMPKIN CREAM PIE**

1 cup sugar, divided	¼ teaspoon cloves	1 tablespoon butter
2 tablespoons cornstarch	½ teaspoon salt	1 baked pie shell
1 teaspoon cinnamon	1 (15-ounce) can pumpkin	Frozen whipped topping
½ teaspoon nutmeg	2 cups evaporated milk	Finely chopped nuts
½ teaspoon ginger	2 eggs, separated	

In large saucepan, combine ¾ cup sugar and next 6 ingredients. Stir in pumpkin and milk. Cook over medium heat until thickened, stirring constantly. Remove from heat and stir in egg yolks; cook 2 to 3 minutes. Add butter and set aside. In medium mixing bowl, beat egg whites until soft peaks form; gradually fold in sugar. Fold into pumpkin mixture. Pour into pie shell and chill until set. Top individual servings with frozen whipped topping and nuts.

★ CAROLYN HUBER ★

Carolyn Huber first met Hillary Rodham Clinton in May of 1976 when she came to the Rose Law Firm for an interview. She worked at the Rose Law Firm for two years. When Bill was elected Governor in 1978, Hillary asked her to run the Governor's Mansion. She worked at the Mansion for two years, from January 1979 to January 1981. During that period, she became close friends with the Clintons. Carolyn returned to Rose Law Firm in 1981, but left there again to follow the Clintons to Washington. She's been like family to them over these years.

 ## HEAVENLY SALAD

1 (28-ounce) can crushed pineapple	1 teaspoon lemon juice	1 cup shredded mild Cheddar cheese
1 (3-ounce) package lemon flavored gelatin	1 cup chopped pecans	1 cup heavy cream, whipped

Drain pineapple and reserve juice. Set pineapple aside. In large saucepan over medium-heat, dissolve gelatin in pineapple juice and lemon juice, stirring until dissolved. Remove from heat and allow to cool. Fold in pineapple, pecans, and cheese and chill until slightly firm. Fold in whipping cream and pour into greased mold. Chill overnight. Turn out onto platter before serving.

This is a recipe from a friend. I've had it for over 35 years. It's always a hit when I take it to a covered dish luncheon or serve it at home.

 **TEXAS SHEET CAKE**

CAKE

2	cups all-purpose flour	4	tablespoons cocoa	1	teaspoon baking soda
2	cups sugar	2	eggs, lightly beaten	1	teaspoon vanilla
1	cup butter	½	cup buttermilk	½	teaspoon cinnamon
1	cup water				

Preheat oven to 350°. In large mixing bowl, combine flour and sugar. In medium saucepan over medium-high heat, bring butter, water, and cocoa to a gentle boil. Remove from heat; add to flour mixture, stirring well. Add eggs and remaining ingredients. Beat thoroughly to combine. Pour into prepared baking pan. Bake for 20 to 25 minutes or until cake tester inserted in center comes out clean. Frost cake while still hot.

FROSTING

½	cup butter	4	tablespoons cocoa	1	teaspoon vanilla
6	tablespoons milk	1	(16-ounce) package confectioners' sugar	1	cup chopped nuts

In large saucepan over medium heat, cook butter, milk, and cocoa. Bring to a hard boil; remove from heat. Stir in sugar and vanilla, mixing well. Stir in nuts.

A cousin gave me this recipe over 35 years ago when I lived in Houston. It's a hit wherever I take it... and easy to make!

★ MICKEY IBARRA ★

Prior to being named an honorary mayor for the Salt Lake 2002 Winter Paralympic Games, Mickey Ibarra served in the Clinton Administration as an Assistant to the President and Director of Intergovernmental Affairs at the White House from 1997 to 2001. He is an accomplished public speaker and a member of the National Advisory Committee for the National Educational Leadership Initiative of the National Association of Latino Elected and Appointed Officials.

 ## BAKED PINEAPPLE STUFFING

½ cup butter, softened	4 eggs	5 slices white bread, cubed
1 cup sugar	1 (20-ounce) can crushed pineapple, drained	

Preheat oven to 350°. In large mixing bowl, cream together butter and sugar. Add eggs one at a time, beating well after each addition. Stir in pineapple. Fold in bread cubes. Pour into greased 1½-quart casserole. Bake, uncovered, for 1 hour.

Serve as a side dish with ham. My mom received this recipe from a friend in Hawaii. Every time you serve it, guests will ask you for the recipe!

Mrs. Jayawardena has a diploma in Sri Lankan cuisine and has won many awards there for her novel recipes of Sri Lankan origins. She is a chef who demonstrates foods from Eastern, Western, and Chinese cuisines and is well known for her cakes and pastries.

 **GRANDMA'S LOVE CAKE**

14 eggs, separated	1 pound chopped pumpkin preserve (optional)	1/4 ounce almond essence
2 pounds sugar	1 pound finely chopped almonds	1 teaspoon mixed spice
Zest of 1 lemon or lime	1 ounce vanilla essence	1/4 teaspoon nutmeg
1 cup butter	1/2 ounce rose essence	1/2 ounce brandy
1 pound semolina, roasted		1 wine glass bee's honey

Preheat oven to 120°. In medium mixing bowl, beat egg whites until stiff. In large mixing bowl, beat together egg yolks, sugar and zest until foamy. Fold in semolina, pumpkin, and almonds. Fold in egg whites. Add essences and remaining ingredients. Pour into prepared 15x12-inch baking pan. Bake for 2 to 3 hours or until well browned. (The cake should stand on its own and not stick to the oil paper.) When cool, store in a cool, dry place. Can be kept for up to one month.

An irresistible Christmas delicacy, unique to Sri-Lanka. An old Portuguese recipe, reminiscent of sixteenth, seventeenth, and eighteenth century Ceylon.

★ BEN JOHNSON ★

Ben Johnson was the primary liaison between the White House and the African American community. He is a former Assistant to the President and Director of the White House One America Office. He is one of thirty White House staff members who served the entire eight years of the Clinton Presidency and is currently the chairman of the One America Foundation.

 ## BARBECUE SAUCE

| 4 | (28-ounce) bottles barbecue sauce | 3 | tablespoons brown sugar | 1 | lemon, peeled and chopped |
| ½ | cup chopped onions | ½-1 | tablespoon vinegar | | |

In large saucepan over medium-high heat, combine sauces and remaining ingredients. Bring sauce to a low boil, stirring occasionally. Reduce heat and simmer 20 minutes, stirring frequently. Dip choice meat in sauce with tongs.

Elaine Johnson is Chairman of the Clinton Birthplace Foundation located in Hope, Arkansas. During President Clinton's days as Governor, she served as his County Coordinator.

 ## MAW MAW'S PRUNE CAKE

4 eggs, well beaten	1 teaspoon cinnamon	1 teaspoon baking soda
2 cups sugar	1 teaspoon ground cloves	1 cup cooked unsweetened prunes, mashed
1 cup cooking oil	1 teaspoon nutmeg	1 cup chopped pecans or walnuts
2 cups all-purpose flour	1 cup buttermilk	
½ teaspoon salt		

Preheat oven to 350°. In large mixing bowl, combine eggs and sugar, beating well with electric mixer on medium speed. Add oil, beating thoroughly, and set aside. In large mixing bowl, sift together flour, salt, cinnamon, cloves, and nutmeg. In small bowl, combine buttermilk and baking soda, stirring until baking soda dissolves. Add to flour mixture, mixing well. Combine egg mixture and flour mixture. Gradually beat in prunes. Fold in nuts. Pour into prepared baking pan. Bake for 45 minutes or until cake tester inserted in center comes out clean.

Yield: 12 servings

This is a great moist cake. My mother-in-law made this cake every Christmas. We called her "Maw Maw".

★ JORDAN JOHNSON ★

Jordan Johnson is employed by Cranford Johnson Robinson Woods, a regional full-service communications firm, and assists the William J. Clinton Presidential Foundation with its special projects and events.

 ## ARKANSAS DUCK GUMBO

1 (5-pound) duck	1 cup chopped celery	2 tablespoons chopped green onions
2 teaspoons, plus ¾ cup cooking oil	2 cups sliced assorted wild mushrooms	Salt and cayenne pepper
2 teaspoon Cajun seasoning	1 tablespoon minced garlic	8 cups chicken broth
¾ cup all-purpose flour	½ teaspoon dried thyme	1 cup water
2 cups chopped onion	3 bay leaves	2 cups cooked white rice
1 cup chopped bell pepper	1 cup beer	

Preheat oven to 400°. Rub duck with 2 teaspoons oil and season with Cajun seasoning. Place duck in roasting pan and bake, uncovered, for 45 minutes or until rare. Let stand until cool. Debone duck and set aside. In Dutch oven over medium heat, make a roux by slowly combining remaining ¾ cup oil and flour, stirring until smooth and thickened. Add onion, bell pepper, celery, and duck to roux; cook over medium heat about 10 minutes, stirring frequently. Add mushrooms and next 5 ingredients. Season with salt and cayenne pepper and cook 5 minutes. Add chicken broth and water and bring to a boil. Simmer at least 2 hours over low heat. Remove and discard bay leaves. Serve in individual bowls over rice.

Two (2 to 3-pound) ducks may be substituted for one large duck.

This duck gumbo recipe was originally developed and perfected by Brian Smith of Bryant, Arkansas and Charles Whiteside, III of Little Rock, Arkansas.

★ PAULINE JOHNSON-BROWN ★

For the past twenty-eight years, Pauline Johnson-Brown has worked both nationally and internationally developing and renovating residential property. She currently owns property in Little Rock, Arkansas; New York City; Washington, DC; Santa Fe, New Mexico; Los Angeles and Carmel, California; and Paris, France. She has one grown daughter, Lara Brown, who loves nothing more than "talking politics and making Cowboy Cookies with mom".

 ## "COWBOY COOKIES"

2	cups all-purpose flour	1	cup butter, melted	2	eggs, beaten
¼	cup oatmeal	¾	cup sugar	1	(11½-ounce) package chocolate chips
½	teaspoon salt	¾	cup firmly packed brown sugar	½	cup walnuts
1	teaspoon baking soda	2	teaspoons vanilla	½	cup raisins

Preheat oven to 375°. In large mixing bowl, combine flour, oatmeal, salt, and baking soda. In separate bowl, combine butter, sugars, and vanilla. When cool, add eggs, mixing well. Add butter mixture to flour mixture, blending thoroughly. Fold in chocolate chips, walnuts, and raisins. Drop by tablespoonfuls onto baking sheet. Bake for 12 minutes or until golden brown.

Yield: 36 cookies

Hearty version of chocolate chip cookies... great for taking on the trail!

★ PEGGY JONES ★

Peggy Jones was an executive assistant to the Pastor of Immanuel Baptist Church (President Clinton's home congregation) from 1969 until 1982. She has been a volunteer receptionist for the Clinton Foundation office, whenever needed, since her retirement.

 ## PEGGY'S BROWNIES

2 squares unsweetened baking chocolate	4 eggs, well beaten	1 cup coarsely chopped pecans (optional)
1 cup margarine	2 cups sugar	1 tablespoon vanilla
	1 cup self-rising flour	

Preheat oven to 325°. In small saucepan over low heat, melt chocolate and margarine; set aside. In large mixing bowl, combine eggs and sugar. Add chocolate mixture and mix well. Add flour and blend thoroughly. Stir in pecans and vanilla. Pour into prepared 9x12-inch baking pan. Bake for 20 minutes or until cake tester inserted in center comes out almost clean. Allow to cool and cut into squares.

Yield: 12 servings

Do not use real butter for this recipe.

I received this recipe from one of my neighbors when I lived in Amory, Mississippi, 40 years ago. I have had many compliments about my brownies, and people have even suggested that I bake them to sell! They are delicious!

★ QUINCY JONES ★

Quincy Jones helped to create the magnificent and amazing Millennium Evening at the White House by providing his incredible talent as a producer and creator. He also attended the Mandela dinner with Oprah Winfrey. He is a supporter of the Clintons and the William J. Clinton Presidential Foundation.

 ## CHICKEN SAUERKRAUT

8	chicken pieces	6	sweet cherry peppers, sliced	2	garlic cloves, minced	
	Salt and pepper to taste	1	cup chicken broth		Spike seasoning to taste (optional)	
6	potatoes, peeled and quartered	1	(32-ounce) jar sauerkraut, drained			
1	onion, sliced		and rinsed			

Season chicken with salt and pepper. Place in deep, heavy cast iron skillet. Layer with potatoes, onion, then peppers. Pour chicken broth over vegetables. Cover with sauerkraut. Add garlic and pepper. Bring to a boil over medium-high heat. Reduce heat; cover and simmer 45 minutes.

Yield: 8 servings

★ ANN JORDAN ★

Ann Jordan is originally from Tuskegee, Alabama and currently resides in Washington, DC where she works as a consultant to Broadwave, USA. She serves as the Chairman of the Board of the National Symphony Orchestra and sits on other boards including the Federal and Corporate Board of CitiGroup, Inc. and Johnson & Johnson. She is the Vice President of the William J. Clinton Presidential Foundation's Board of Directors.

POUND CAKE

1	cup butter, softened	1½	cups whipping cream	3	cups, plus 3 tablespoons all-purpose
2	cups sugar	4	teaspoons lemon extract		flour
6	eggs	3	tablespoons vanilla extract		

Preheat oven to 325°. In large mixing bowl, cream butter and sugar with electric mixer on medium speed. Add eggs one at a time, beating well after each addition. Add whipping cream and extracts. Add flour and mix thoroughly. Pour batter into oiled and floured Bundt pan or tube pan. Bake about 1 hour. Cake is done when cake tester inserted in center comes out clean.

This cake is delicious. I make about twenty of these cakes to give at Christmas by demand from friends.

★ ARAM AND KATHRYN KAILIAN ★

Aram H. Kailian worked for President Bill Clinton and Vice President Al Gore. He served in various capacities and interagency efforts focusing on Urban Policy, Empowerment Zones, and New Market Initiatives, spending the last three years of the Clinton Administration with the Office of the Vice President. He has also played lead roles in the last several campaign cycles with advance and troubleshooting at the DNC Conventions. Aram is an architect by training and is currently a practicing professional and construction management program and project consultant.

Kathryn I. Kailian is an aesthetician, electrologist, and consultant for historic preservation in Washington, DC. She is passionate about cooking and her husband of thirty years and shares his love of democratic politics.

 ## ARMENIAN RICE PILAF

1	cup thin noodles	1	cup rice	Freshly ground black pepper to
2	tablespoons butter	2	cups reduced sodium chicken broth	taste

In large skillet over medium-high heat, melt butter. Add noodles and brown. Add rice and mix. Add broth and pepper, cover, and tightly cover with lid. Bring to a boil; reduce heat immediately to low. Cook until rice is fluffy.

This recipe is "food from God", in that it is easy, delicious, and always comes out well. Armenian families eat it most nights, especially when children are around. It is simple enough for everyday meals, yet elegant enough for company.

★ RICHARD "DICK" KELLEY ★

Dick Kelley married Virginia Clinton Dwier on January 17, 1982. He is President Clinton's step-father.

 ## ITALIAN SPAGHETTI

1	pound ground beef	1	(6-ounce) can tomato paste	Salt and pepper to taste
2	onions, chopped	1	(4-ounce) can mushrooms, drained	1 (7-ounce) package spaghetti, cooked al dente
½	bell pepper, seeded and chopped	1	garlic clove, minced	Parmesan cheese
1	tablespoon butter	1	tablespoon Worcestershire sauce	
1	(20-ounce) can tomatoes	1	tablespoon chili powder	

In large skillet or Dutch oven over medium-high heat, cook ground beef, onion, and bell pepper in butter until slightly browned. Add tomatoes and next 5 ingredients. Season with salt and pepper to taste. Simmer over low heat 3 to 4 hours, stirring occasionally. Serve sauce over spaghetti and sprinkle with Parmesan cheese.

My wife Virginia loved spaghetti. We would eat it at least once a week at a local cafe called Rocky's. When the President was in Hot Springs, we always took him there. He loved spaghetti, too.

★ DAVID KENDALL ★

David E. Kendall is a lawyer at Williams & Connolly LLP in Washington, DC, who has represented the President and Senator Clinton as personal counsel from 1993 to the present. A native of Indiana, he graduated from Wabash College in 1966 and studied at Oxford on a Rhodes Scholarship from 1966 to 1968, leaving just before a now-famous Arkansas Rhodes Scholar arrived. He graduated from Yale Law School, clerked for Justice White at the Supreme Court of the United States, served in the U.S. Army, and worked as staff counsel at the NAACP Legal Defense and Educational Fund, Inc., before joining his present law firm in 1978. He and his wife have two sons and a daughter.

 ## GRANDMOTHER REAGAN'S SWEET ROLLS

2 (¼-ounce) packages dry yeast	4-4½ cups white bread flour, divided	1½ cups brown sugar, melted and divided
½ cup warm water	1 egg, lightly beaten	1 teaspoon cinnamon, divided
¾ cup milk, scalded	10 tablespoons butter, melted and divided	⅓ cup sugar
6 tablespoons sugar	2 teaspoons light corn syrup, divided	½ cup chopped pecans, divided (optional)
1 tablespoon salt		
5 tablespoons butter		

Dissolve yeast in warm water and set aside. In large mixing bowl, combine hot milk, 6 tablespoons sugar, salt, and 5 tablespoons butter. Allow mixture to cool to lukewarm. Add 2 cups flour and mix well. Add yeast and egg, mixing thoroughly. Stir in flour ½ cup at a time until soft dough forms. Turn dough onto flat, floured surface and knead in remaining flour. Place dough in greased bowl, turning once to coat. Cover and chill 6 hours or overnight. About two hours before serving, place 4 tablespoons butter in each of two 9x13-inch baking pans. Stir 1 teaspoon corn syrup into each pan. Sprinkle ¾ cup brown sugar over mixture in each pan. Knead and roll out half of dough onto flat, floured surface, forming a 10x15-inch rectangle. Brush dough with 1 tablespoon butter. Combine cinnamon and ⅓ cup sugar. Sprinkle dough with half of cinnamon-sugar mixture and half of pecans, if desired. Roll up dough in jelly roll fashion. Seal edges and slice into 15 even pieces. Place rolls in single layer in prepared baking pan. Repeat process with remaining dough. Cover baking pans with a light cloth. Let rise in warm place about 45 minutes to 1 hour or until doubled in size. Bake at 350° for 20 to 25 minutes. Invert each baking pan onto serving platter. Serve warm. *Yield: 30 rolls*

This recipe is from my mother's mother, Belle Reagan (1885-1975), who was not related to THAT Reagan, although she was a Republican (but never had a chance to vote for Bill Clinton). However, I consider this recipe "mine" because I have been a massive consumer of this recipe over the years and can verify that it is well taste-tested, but the "mine" might be just a teensy, weensy bit misleading, suggesting as it does, that I might be able to actually cook the recipe.

Sharon Kennedy was Special Assistant to the President and Deputy Social Secretary at the Clinton White House. She coordinated special events including state dinners, bill signings, and award ceremonies. Active in both Clinton Presidential campaigns, she was on the National Advance Staff in 1992 and served as Colorado State Press Secretary in 1996. She spent the early years of the Clinton Administration in Intergovernmental Affairs, where she was the liaison between the White House and a variety of governmental entities.

 ## MY MOTHER'S SIMPLY DELICIOUS CHEESECAKE

⅓ (14-ounce) package honey graham crackers, finely crushed

4 tablespoons butter, melted

3 (8-ounce) packages cream cheese, softened

5 eggs

3 teaspoons vanilla, divided

1½ cups sugar, divided

3 cups sour cream

½ cup sugar

Preheat oven to 350°. In small mixing bowl, combine crumbs and butter. Press mixture onto bottom of 9x13-inch baking pan. In large mixing bowl, cream the cream cheeses with electric mixer on medium speed. Add eggs one at a time, beating well after each addition. Add 1½ teaspoons vanilla and 1 cup sugar and beat well. Pour filling over crust. Bake for 45 to 50 minutes or until cake tester inserted in center comes out clean. Remove from oven and allow to cool 5 minutes. (The cake will set and crack.) In large mixing bowl, combine 1½ teaspoons vanilla, ½ cup sugar, and sour cream, mixing by hand with spoon. Pour over top of cooled cake, spreading evenly. Return to oven and bake for 5 minutes. Remove from oven and cool. Chill until ready to serve.

Yield: 12 servings

This cheesecake is simple to make and delicious to eat. No matter the time of year or family gathering, my mother was always asked to make her famous cheesecake to everyone's delight. Unfortunately for me, since I am no Roland Mesnier, the holidays are only once a year!

★ JENNIFER KLEIN AND TODD STERN ★

Jennifer Klein was a Special Assistant to the President for Domestic Policy and worked both on the Domestic Policy Council and First Lady's Office staffs. She focused on issues affecting children and families, including health care, child care, early childhood development, and women's issues. Since leaving the White House in 1999, Jennifer has spent much of her time with two products of the Clinton Administration—Jacob and Zachary Stern—and consults to non-profit organizations on children and families issues.

Todd Stern served as Assistant to the President and Staff Secretary, Assistant to the President for Special Projects, including global climate change, and Counselor to Secretary of the Treasury Lawrence Summers. In these capacities, he worked on a wide variety of domestic and international issues and also handled special assignments, such as contested nominations. After the Clinton Administration, Todd spent several months teaching at the Kennedy School and serving as a fellow at the German Marshall Fund before joining Wilmer, Cutler & Pickering, where he currently practices law. He is married to Jennifer Klein, whom he managed to meet in his spare time at the White House.

 ## PANCAKES

1½ cups sifted all-purpose flour	1¾ teaspoon double-acting baking powder	2½ tablespoons butter, melted
1 teaspoon salt	3 egg whites, lightly beaten	1-1¼ cups milk
1 teaspoon sugar		

In large mixing bowl, sift together flour, salt, sugar, and baking powder. Add egg whites, butter, and milk; mix thoroughly. Drop by spoonfuls onto hot lightly greased or nonstick griddle. When bubbles begin to form on top, flip pancake and continue cooking until lightly browned.

Low fat milk or soy milk may used in the recipe. If thinner pancakes are preferred, add more milk to batter.

Todd and I met, got married, and had our first child while working in the White House. We didn't have much time for relaxing breakfasts, but when we did, we often made these pancakes. Todd modified this recipe to make it lower in fat and calories, but still very delicious.

★ LORI KRAUSE ★

Lori Krause worked for the White House from "Day One" to January 20, 2001. She worked in the Volunteer Office, Presidential Correspondence, and the Gift Office. She also worked closely with the intern program and supervised correspondence interns for four years. At the end of the administration, she was Director of the Gift Office. She also worked with the Travel Office and did press advance domestically and internationally from October 1994 to 2000.

 **RUM BALLS**

3	cups finely crushed vanilla wafers (about 75)	1	cup finely chopped pecans or walnuts	½	cup light rum
2	cups confectioners' sugar	¼	cup cocoa	¼	cup light corn syrup
					Sugar or confectioners' sugar

In large mixing bowl, combine crumbs, 2 cups confectioners' sugar, nuts, and cocoa. Stir in rum and corn syrup, mixing well. Shape into 1-inch balls. Roll in sugar or confectioners' sugar. Cover and chill several days before serving.
Brandy or bourbon may be substituted for rum.

 **CRAB WEDGES**

6	tablespoons butter, softened	1½	teaspoons mayonnaise	8	ounces fresh lump crabmeat
1	(6-ounce) sharp processed cheese spread	½	teaspoon garlic salt	4	English muffins, split

In large mixing bowl, combine butter, cheese spread, mayonnaise, and garlic salt. Fold in crabmeat. Spread mixture on muffin halves. Cut into quarters. Place on baking sheet and broil until golden and bubbly.

Yield: 8 servings

Crab Wedges may be frozen if not serving immediately.

These are perfect for a cold winter day. Just pop out of the freezer, place under broiler, and it's the perfect snack!

★ DR. DEAN KUMPURIS AND MARY KUMPURIS ★

Dr. Dean Kumpuris and his wife Mary live and work in Little Rock, where they also raised their family. They have a daughter, Kate, who recently married Jonathan Vogel, and a son, Andrew, a college student. Dr. Kumpuris maintains a gastroenterology clinic with two other physicians while also staying extremely active in city business. He has been a driving force behind the River Market, involved in the Clinton Presidential Center and Park, and serves on the Little Rock City Board of Directors. Mary volunteers and works with various civic organizations including the Arkansas Commitment program that she and her husband founded.

 ## MARY'S NEW YEAR'S DAY GREEK BREAD

2   (1.25-ounce) packages dry yeast
1   tablespoon sugar
⅓   cup warm water
1   cup unsalted butter
½   cup sugar

1½ cups whole milk
2   teaspoons machlepi
½   teaspoon crushed masticha
6   eggs, divided

9-10 cups all-purpose flour, divided
1   tablespoon water
⅓   cup sesame seeds or sliced, blanched almonds

In small bowl, dissolve yeast and 1 tablespoon sugar in warm water. Cover and put in warm place 10 to 15 minutes or until yeast activates and becomes bubbly. In medium saucepan over medium-high heat, combine butter, sugar, milk, machlepi, and masticha. Cook until butter melts and sugar dissolves, stirring frequently. Remove from heat, allow to cool, and set aside. In mixing bowl, beat 4 eggs with electric mixer until foamy. In large mixing bowl, combine 2 cups flour, cooled butter mixture, yeast, and beaten eggs; stir thoroughly. Add 6 cups flour, one cup at a time, mixing well after each addition. While dough is still sticky add 1 unbeaten egg. Continue adding remaining flour until dough is soft, but no longer sticky. Knead about 10 minutes. Place dough in lightly greased bowl, cover with damp cloth, and let rise in warm place about 2 hours. When doubled in size, punch down dough and divide into two equal balls. Place dough ball in center of large springform pan. Wrap a quarter in aluminum foil and hide the coin in the dough. In small bowl, combine 1 well beaten egg with 1 tablespoon water. Brush wash over dough. Sprinkle generously with sesame seeds or almonds. Cover with damp cloth and let rise about 30 minutes. Bake at 350° for 40 to 45 minutes or until bread browns. Reduce heat to 250° and bake until bread sounds hollow when tapped. Repeat process with remaining ball of dough.

The spices, machlepi and masticha, found in specialty stores or gourmet shops, give the bread its unique flavor. Machlepi is ground seed from Syria. Masticha comes from the sap of the mastichodendro bush grown primarily on the Greek island of Chios and used in the production of gum.

On New Year's Day, the bread is cut and the person who has the coin in their piece of bread has good luck for the year. In our family, the first piece of bread is for the New Year, the second is for business, the third is for the home, the next for the parents. This is followed by the children and then any guests who are present.

Michael Lake worked at the White House from 2000 to 2001 as the Special Assistant for White House Operations.

 **MAGIC COOKIE BARS**

½ cup butter
1½ cups graham cracker crumbs
1 cup finely chopped pecans or walnuts (optional)

1 (12-ounce) package chocolate chips
½ (12-ounce) package butterscotch chips

1 (14-ounce) can sweetened condensed milk
1 cup shredded coconut

Preheat oven to 350°. Melt butter in 9x13-inch baking pan in oven. Cover bottom of baking pan with crumbs. Sprinkle evenly with nuts, chocolate chips, and butterscotch chips. Drizzle with milk. Sprinkle with coconut. Bake for 30 minutes or until golden brown.

Yield: 12 servings

This recipe has been handed down through my family and is one of our favorites. It is quick, simple, and a crowd pleaser. The recipe originated from a dear family friend, "Aunty Fran"-my mother's second grade teacher. I hope you and your loved ones will enjoy these as much as we have.

★ MAYOR DAVID LAURELL ★

After establishing his career as a television writer and producer in Florida and New Jersey, the Arkansas Educational Television Network brought David Laurell to Arkansas in 1985. It was during this time that Laurell met then-Governor Bill Clinton, who made a profound and lasting impression on him. Not long after, Laurell moved to Burbank, California, where he devoted a tremendous amount of time to the Clinton Presidential campaigns. In March of 2002, Laurell was elected Mayor of Burbank and credits Bill Clinton as his inspiration.

 ## MAX'S KAHLÚA CHIP COOKIES

2½ cups all-purpose flour
1 teaspoon baking soda
½ teaspoon salt
¼ cup Kahlúa
1 teaspoon instant coffee

1 cup unsalted butter, softened
¾ cup sugar
¾ cup firmly packed light brown sugar
2 eggs

1½ cups walnuts, coarsely chopped
1 cup semi-sweet chocolate chips
1 cup milk chocolate chips
A whole lot of love

Position rack in center of oven and preheat to 375°. Line two baking sheets with cooking parchment or aluminum foil. In medium mixing bowl, sift together flour, baking soda, and salt; set aside. In small mixing bowl, combine Kahlúa and coffee, stirring until coffee dissolves; set aside. In large mixing bowl, beat butter 30 to 40 seconds with electric mixer on low speed until creamy. Gradually add sugars and beat on medium speed 2 minutes or until light and fluffy. Beat in eggs and Kahlúa mixture. Add flour mixture, beating well. Fold in nuts and chocolate chips, stirring until well combined. Drop dough by heaping tablespoonfuls onto baking sheet, leaving 2 inches between cookies. Bake for 10 to 12 minutes or until lightly brown around edges. Cool on baking sheet 5 minutes. Transfer to wire racks to cool.

Yield: 60 cookies

 *In the mid-1980s, while living in Little Rock and working for the Arkansas Educational Television Network, I became a devoted lover of Southern cooking. I am still passionate about the "southern comforts" I was introduced to during my days as an Arkansan, but when it comes to cookies, there are none better than my wife Max's Kahlúa Chips. After a hard day at City Hall, I may be craving a big ol' mess of catfish, collard greens, red beans and rice, but after dinner, my cravings turn to Max's baked beauties. I hope you enjoy them as much as I do, and remember, love truly is the most important ingredient!*

Bruce Lee is the Founder, Chairman of the Board, and CEO of the UAW-Labor Employment and Training Corporation located in Long Beach, California. The UAW-LETC is a non-profit public benefit corporation which provides employment training and human resource services to the economically disadvantaged and dislocated workers. It also assists the private sector in training and retraining to meet the needs of their current and future workforce. Bruce is also an Executive Committee Member of the Democratic National Committee and a supporter of the William J. Clinton Presidential Foundation.

 ## CREAMED CORN AU GRATIN

1 pound frozen whole kernel corn	2 teaspoons sugar	1½ tablespoons all-purpose flour
1½ cups heavy cream	Pinch of white pepper	3 tablespoons Parmesan cheese
½ teaspoon salt	1½ tablespoons butter, melted	

In large saucepan over medium-high heat, combine corn, cream, salt, sugar, and white pepper. Bring to a boil; simmer 5 minutes. In mixing bowl, combine butter and flour, mixing well. Add to corn, stirring until thoroughly combined. Remove from heat. Transfer mixture to casserole. Sprinkle with and brown under broiler.

This was a collaborative effort of mine and my late wife. We tried to duplicate a similar dish served by one of our favorite restaurants. Ours is better!

★ LURA LEE ★

Originally from Tampa, Florida, Lura Lee worked in the Office of Presidential Letters and Messages in the fall of 1996, volunteered with the Christmas festivities, and drove in the San Diego motorcade in June of 2000. In addition to working full time, she is involved in the start-up of a southern California historical consulting company, BackInTime.com.

 ## TIRAMISU FOR ESPRESSO LOVERS

12 shots of espresso	3 tablespoons sugar	2 tablespoons milk
5 shots of chocolate liqueur, divided	6 eggs, separated	48 ladyfingers
½ shot of rum	2 (8-ounce) packages mascarpone	6 ounces cocoa, divided
2 shots of coffee liqueur	½ cup bittersweet chocolate chips	Frozen whipped topping, for garnish

In mixing bowl, combine espresso, 3 shots of chocolate liqueur, rum, and coffee liqueur; set aside. In small saucepan, combine egg yolks, 2 shots of remaining chocolate liqueur, and sugar, mixing well. Place saucepan in large saucepan filled with boiling water (to create a water bath). Heat about 3 minutes or until mixture is light and bubbly, stirring constantly. Remove from heat and add to mixing bowl with mascarpone, beating well with electric mixer on medium speed. In separate mixing bowl, beat egg whites with clean beaters until stiff peaks form. Fold egg whites into mascarpone mixture and set aside. In small saucepan, melt most chocolate chips (save some for garnish) with milk, stirring until chocolate melts. Dunk two-thirds of ladyfingers one at a time in chocolate and milk mixture. Layer one-third of ladyfingers along bottom of trifle bowl. Spread half of mascarpone mixture over ladyfingers. Sprinkle one-third of cocoa over mascarpone layer. Drizzle with one-third of remaining chocolate and milk mixture. Repeat process for second layer. Arrange remaining one-third of ladyfingers on top. Pour remaining chocolate and milk mixture over trifle, saturating ladyfingers. Lightly dust with remaining cocoa. Cover with plastic wrap and chill 12 hours. Garnish with frozen whipped topping and remaining chocolate chips before serving.

Yield: 12 servings

While working in a drafty part of the Old Executive Office Building, I often needed coffee to warm my hands. I drank so much coffee that I not only fell in love with the bean, but also became addicted. A little while after that, I started a coffee-centered hobby website with a few friends. This is one of my favorite coffee dessert recipes. I hope you like it!

★ DAVID LEOPOULOS ★

President Clinton and David met on the playground at Ramble School in Hot Springs, Arkansas, in the third grade and have been best friends ever since. They mainly ate peanut butter and banana sandwiches and peach ice cream in the early years-now they eat good ol' Arkansas BBQ. As a child, President Clinton loved to eat food prepared by David's mom and dad, and one of the best recipes was Greek Chicken and Pilaf. David wore the image shown here on a campaign button during both of President Clinton's campaigns.

GREEK CHICKEN

1	chicken, quartered, rinsed and patted dry	2	teaspoons salt	3	tablespoons butter, cut into pats
3	teaspoons paprika	3	teaspoons Greek seasoning		Juice of 1 lemon
		4	teaspoons oregano		

Sprinkle chicken with paprika, salt, Greek seasoning, and oregano. Place chicken on wire rack in broiling pan bottom side down. Sprinkle additional paprika, salt, Greek seasoning, and oregano. Dot chicken with butter. Drizzle with lemon juice. Broil until top of chicken is slightly crisp and rather brown. Transfer chicken baking pan and bake for 1 hour, 30 minutes at 325°. Serve with Pilaf (recipe to follow).

Yield: 4 servings

PILAF

1	onion, chopped	3	tablespoons olive oil	2	teaspoons Greek seasoning
2	garlic cloves, crushed	1	cup rice		Juice of 1 lemon
2	teaspoons oregano	1	teaspoon salt	2½	cups chicken broth

In large skillet over high heat, sauté onion, garlic, and oregano in olive oil until tender. Add rice and cook, stirring constantly, until rice is brown. Reduce heat to low. Add salt, Greek seasoning, and lemon juice, stirring well. Add chicken broth. Cover and cook 30 minutes or until rice is done. Remove from heat and serve immediately.

Yield: 4 servings

These recipes have been passed down for generations in Krokess, a small town outside Sparta, Greece, located in the Peloponnesus.

★ LINDA LEOPOULOS ★

Linda Leopoulos first met President Clinton on December 27, 1971. It was her wedding day, and she had no idea who the bearded man with long hair and a mustache was sitting in the back of the church. As it turned out, her husband-to-be (David) and Bill were old friends. Linda met President Clinton only briefly at the wedding reception without knowing how much her future would be touched through his friendship.

 ## CRUSTY POUND CAKE

1 cup butter, softened	1 tablespoon vanilla	3 cups all-purpose flour
3 cups sugar	1 teaspoon almond extract	½ teaspoon salt
6 eggs		

Preheat oven to 325°. In large mixing bowl, cream together butter and sugar with electric mixer on medium speed. Add eggs one at a time, beating well after each addition. Blend in vanilla and almond extract. In separate mixing bowl, sift together flour and salt. Add to creamed mixture. Mix until dry ingredients are just moistened, being careful not to overmix. Pour into greased and floured tube pan. Bake for 1 hour, 20 minutes. Allow cake to cool in pan 10 minutes before removing.

Yield: 16 servings

I have baked this yummy cake for late night get-togethers when President Clinton and childhood friends play cards and visit until almost daybreak.

Black Bottom Cups

1 (8-ounce) package cream cheese, softened	1½ cups all-purpose flour	1 cup water
1 egg	1 cup sugar	⅓ cup cooking oil
⅓ cup sugar	¼ cup unsweetened cocoa	1 tablespoon vinegar
⅛ teaspoon salt	1 teaspoon baking soda	1 teaspoon vanilla
1 (9-ounce) package semisweet chocolate chips	½ teaspoon salt	Chopped nuts (optional)

Preheat oven to 350°. In small mixing bowl, combine cream cheese, egg, ⅓ cup sugar, and ⅛ teaspoon salt, beating well with electric mixer on medium speed. Fold in chocolate chips and set aside. In large mixing bowl, sift together flour, 1 cup sugar, cocoa, baking soda, and ½ teaspoon salt. Add water, oil, vinegar, and vanilla and beat well. (Mixture will be thin.) Fill greased muffin cups half full with flour mixture. Top with heaping tablespoon of cream cheese mixture. Garnish with nuts if desired. Bake for 25 minutes. Allow to cool.

This is a fabulous recipe that is rich and easy. No frosting is needed. It's a chocolate lover's delight!

★ EUGENE AND BOBBYE LEVY ★

Rabbi Eugene Levy met then-Governor Clinton during the national board meeting of the NAACP in October 1987—just three months after moving to Little Rock from Tyler, Texas. As a result of that encounter, the Levys began to meet with the Clintons to discuss interfaith education issues. Through their friendship and connection with Mrs. Carolyn Staley, they became a special part of the "Friends of Bill" group. Rabbi Levy eventually worked on President Clinton's primary campaign and was invited to give the challenge at the pre-1993 Inaugural Interfaith Service.

 JAPANESE NOODLE COLE SLAW

2	(3-ounce) packages oriental flavored noodle mix		Salted sunflower seeds	¼-½	cup rice wine vinegar
1	(16-ounce) package cole slaw mix	3-4	tablespoons sesame seeds		Sugar to taste
		½-¾	cup cooking oil		

Crush noodles from mix and save flavor packets for later use. In large salad bowl, combine noodles, cole slaw mix, and seeds. In medium mixing bowl, whisk together flavor packets from noodle mix with oil, vinegar, and sugar; mix well. Toss cole slaw with dressing just before serving.

If salad is tossed with dressing too early, noodles become soggy.

 BAKED GOUDA

1	(8-ounce) package crescent rolls	1	small wheel Gouda, rind removed

Preheat oven to 375°. Wrap crescent roll dough around cheese, covering completely. Bake for 20 minutes or until bread browns and cheese softens in middle. Serve with grapes and apples.

★ CARL LEWIS ★

Carl Lewis a nine-time Olympic Gold Medalist in track and field, including four straight gold medal performances in the long jump in the 1984, 1988, 1992, and 1996 Olympics. He made Olympic history when he became the second person to win the same event in four straight Olympics. He was inducted into the U.S. Olympic Hall of Fame in 1985. He retired in 1997 and is currently pursuing an acting career.

 LEWIS HOLIDAY TURKEY

1 (18 to 22-pound) turkey, rinsed and patted dry	1 tablespoon cayenne pepper	1 red bell pepper, seeded and chopped
¼ cup mayonnaise	1 tablespoon paprika	2 onions, chopped
½ cup Dijon mustard	1 tablespoon thyme	1 celery stalk, chopped
1 tablespoon pepper	1 tablespoon marjoram	1 garlic clove, minced
1 tablespoon sage	1 tablespoon turmeric	1 apple, halved
1 tablespoon poultry seasoning	Dash of salt	1 lemon, halved
1 tablespoon curry powder	6 bay leaves	2 cups water
1 tablespoon lemon pepper	1 green bell pepper, seeded and chopped	

Remove neck, gizzard, and liver from turkey cavity and set aside. Coat turkey with mayonnaise and Dijon. In small mixing bowl, combine pepper and next 10 ingredients. Coat turkey thoroughly with spice mixture. Press bay leaves onto turkey. Combine bell peppers, onion, celery, and garlic in small bowl. Cover turkey with half of vegetable mixture. Fill cavity with remaining vegetables, apple, lemon, and water. Place turkey in large roasting pan and cover with two layers of aluminum foil then cover with the lid. Bake at 350° for 3 hours. Remove and discard bay leaves before serving. Place neck, gizzard, and liver in 8 cups water and bring to a boil; cook until tender. Drain and reserve stock for dressing and gravy.

★ BRUCE LINDSEY ★

Bruce R. Lindsey has been a long-time advisor to former President Bill Clinton. During the eight years of the Clinton Administration, he served as an Assistant to the President, Deputy White House Counsel, and Senior Advisor. During 1993, Mr. Lindsey was also Director of the Office of Presidential Personnel where he supervised the selection and approval of political appointees in the Cabinet departments and on Presidential boards and commissions. In the White House Counsel's Office, he handled judicial selection issues, clemency requests, and investigative matters. During the 1992 Presidential campaign, he served as the National Campaign Director. In his various positions, Mr. Lindsey has been described as the Administration's "master strategist" on a variety of high profile issues, including tobacco settlement negotiations, products liability reform, security law reform, international aviation issues, labor law issues, and the baseball strike settlement discussions. He currently resides in Little Rock, Arkansas, where he is "Of Counsel" to the Wright, Lindsey & Jennings law firm and a consultant to the William J. Clinton Presidential Foundation.

 ## CHICKEN AND RICE CASSEROLE

1 cup uncooked rice	1 (10¾-ounce) can cream of chicken soup	1 (10¾-ounce) can cream of celery soup
1 (10¾-ounce) can cream of mushroom soup		4 boneless, skinless chicken breasts

Preheat oven to 350°. Combine rice and soups in prepared casserole. Top with chicken. Bake for 45 minutes to 1 hour or until chicken is no longer pink in center and rice is done.

Yield: 4 servings

Cook chicken and cut into small pieces. Combine with soups and rice and bake at 325° for 45 minutes to 1 hour.

★ MARK F. LINDSAY AND CARLA MORRIS ★

A vice president with UnitedHealth Group in Minnetonka, Minnesota, Mark Lindsay served President Clinton for five years. In his last role as Assistant to the President for the Office of Management and Administration, three offices reported to him: the Military Office, Operations, and the Office of Administration. Among other organizations, he managed Air Force Once, Camp David, Marine Helicopter Squadron One, the President's physicians, and the Photography Office.

 **SOFT DINNER ROLLS**

1 (1.25-ounce) package yeast	1 egg, lightly beaten	¼ cup butter, melted
⅓ cup warm water	4 cups unbleached white flour, divided	1 teaspoon salt
1¼ cups warm milk	¼ cup sugar	Melted butter, for brushing rolls

Dissolve yeast in warm water. Add to warm bowl with milk, egg, and 2 cups flour, stirring until no lumps are present. Add sugar, butter, and salt. Add 1 cup flour, stirring until dough holds together. Sprinkle remaining flour on kneading board; knead dough until smooth and elastic, adding more flour if needed. Place dough in greased bowl, cover with plastic wrap, and leave in warm place about 1 hour or until doubled in size. Punch dough down. Roll out dough and cut with cutter or top of glass. Place rolls on baking sheet, cover, and let rise 25 minutes. Brush with melted butter. Preheat oven to 425°. Bake for 10 minutes or until golden brown, being careful not to overbake.

Yield: 36 rolls

We make these every Christmas! Carla's sister first got the recipe from a National Academy of Public Administration colleague.

★ MARK F. LINDSAY AND CARLA MORRIS ★

 ## EXTRA SPECIAL LINGUINI AND CLAM SAUCE

Olive oil
2-5 garlic cloves, minced
2 celery stalks, thinly sliced
2 zucchini, thinly sliced

2 tomatoes, coarsely chopped
2-3 (6.5-ounce) cans minced clams
1 cup white wine

1 (16-ounce) package linguine, cooked al dente
Shredded Pecorino Romano cheese

Cover bottom of large saucepan with olive oil. Sauté garlic over medium-high heat, being careful not to overcook. Add celery, zucchini, and tomatoes. Reduce heat and simmer 10 minutes. Drain clams, reserving juice. Set clams aside. Add clam juice and wine to vegetables; continue simmering. Add clams and remove from heat. Place pasta in serving bowl, adding just enough clam sauce to keep moist. Transfer remaining clam sauce to soup tureen and serve at the table with shredded cheese.

Yield: 2 to 3 servings

Friends of ours treated us to this feast one night when we first moved to Minnesota. It's an awesome dish! We've tried it since with great success. We serve it with salad and garlic bread. It's the type of dish you can easily prepare while your guests are there, and even if everyone is hovering in the kitchen, this recipe won't stress you out as the hosts!

★ LIZ CLINTON LITTLE ★

Liz Clinton Little is the daughter of Janet and the late Roy Clinton, Sr., and lives with her husband Gene in Hot Springs Village. As a child, her family and the Roger and Raymond Clinton families spent a great deal of time together, many times in the evenings playing while their parents played dominoes. Liz and Gene have two children-Stacy, married to Eric Briggs, and Clint Burks, who is married to Romi. Liz also became a grandmother in January 2003 with the birth of Janet Elizabeth Briggs.

 ## BACON AND CHEESE STUFFED MUSHROOMS

6 cups fresh mushrooms, stemmed	½ onion, finely chopped	Seasoned salt to taste
10 bacon slices, cooked and crumbled	¾ cup mayonnaise	1 cup shredded Cheddar cheese

Preheat oven to 325°. Wash mushrooms in salted water. Drain on paper towels. In small bowl, combine bacon and remaining ingredients, blending thoroughly. Place mushrooms, cap side up, in prepared glass casserole. Fill each cap with bacon mixture. Bake for 20 minutes and serve immediately.

Yield: 48 appetizer servings

 ## PECAN PIE

4 eggs, well beaten	3 tablespoons butter, melted	1 cup pecan halves
Pinch of salt	1 tablespoon all-purpose flour	1 teaspoon vanilla
1 cup sugar	1½ cups light corn syrup	1 (9-inch) unbaked pie shell

Preheat oven to 350°. In large mixing bowl, combine eggs and next 5 ingredients. Add pecans and vanilla, mixing well. Pour into pie shell. Cover edges of pie shell with aluminum foil to keep from browning too quickly. Bake for 1 hour.

Yield: 8 servings

★ SOPHIA LOREN ★

Italian born actress Sophia Loren is considered one of the most successful international stars in the post-war era. She is a supporter of the William J. Clinton Presidential Foundation.

 ## PENNE ALLA PUTTANESCA

4 anchovy fillets, drained
2 garlic cloves
2 tablespoons extra virgin olive oil
3 tablespoons unsalted butter

2-3 tomatoes, peeled, seeded, and chopped
½ cup pitted black olives, finely chopped

1 tablespoon capers, rinsed and drained
¼ cup minced Italian parsley
1 pound penne, cooked al dente

In mortar, pound anchovies and garlic to a paste with pestle or very finely chop. Heat oil and butter in large saucepan over medium heat. Add anchovy paste and sauté 1 to 2 minutes. Add tomatoes, olives, and capers; cook 15 minutes. Toss with penne, coating well. Sprinkle with parsley and serve immediately.

★ ROBIN WOODS LOUCKS ★

Robin Loucks was a neighbor to the Clintons while they occupied the Arkansas Governor's Mansion. Since then, she has been a supporter of the Clintons and the William J. Clinton Presidential Foundation.

REFRIGERATOR BRAN MUFFINS

1   (15-ounce) package raisin and bran
    cereal
5   cups all-purpose flour
3   cups sugar

5   teaspoons baking soda
1   teaspoon salt
1   teaspoon apple pie spice
1   cup cooking oil

4   eggs, beaten
4   cups buttermilk
1   cup nuts, chopped

Preheat oven to 375°. In large mixing bowl, combine cereal and next 5 ingredients. Add oil, eggs, buttermilk, and nuts; mix well. Pour batter into prepared muffin pans. Bake for 20 to 25 minutes.

These muffins will keep for up to 6 weeks in refrigerator.
A wonderful way to bake at a moment's notice!

HAITIAN WATERMELON SOUP

4   cups chopped fresh watermelon,
    juice reserved
1   cup finely chopped fresh pineapple

1-2 chopped fresh mangoes
    Juice of 1 key lime

Dash of vanilla
Sugar to taste

In large mixing bowl, combine watermelon, pineapple, and mango. Add lime juice, vanilla, and sugar, mixing thoroughly. Chill and serve on a hot summer day!

Other fruits, such as, oranges, bananas, and peaches may also be added.

I learned to make this on a trip to Haiti. It is so good that people come begging for more! Better double or triple the recipe!

★ BRIDGETTE STREETT LYNCH ★

Bridgette Streett Lynch did advance work for both President and Senator Clinton during the 1992 and 1996 campaigns. She and her husband Wally currently reside in Sugarland, Texas, with their two children, Allie and Nick.

 ## MANDARIN SALAD

¼ cup sliced almonds
4 teaspoons sugar
¼ head red leaf lettuce, torn into
   bite-sized pieces

¼ head green leaf lettuce, torn into
   bite-sized pieces
1 cup chopped celery

2 green onions, chopped
1 (11-ounce) can Mandarin oranges,
   drained

In saucepan over low heat, cook almonds and sugar, stirring constantly, until sugar dissolves and almonds are coated. Spoon onto waxed paper and allow to cool. When cool, break almonds apart and set aside. In salad bowl, combine lettuce, celery, onions, and orange segments. When ready to serve, toss with dressing and top with almonds.

DRESSING
¼ cup olive oil
2 tablespoons cider vinegar

1½ tablespoons sugar
1 tablespoon snipped parsley

½ teaspoon salt
Dash of black pepper

Combine dressing ingredients in a jar. Seal tightly with lid and shake well to mix.

Cone and Betty Magie have known the Clintons since Bill Clinton first ran for Congress in 1974. They are publishers of several local newspapers, including the *Cabot Star,* the *Lonoke Democrat,* the *Carlisle Independent,* the *Sherwood Voice,* and the *Jacksonville News.*

 ## POTATO CASSEROLE

1   (2-pound) package frozen hash
    browns
½   cup butter, melted
2   tablespoons minced onion

1   (10¾-ounce) can cream of chicken
    soup
1   cup sour cream
1   teaspoon salt

½   teaspoon pepper
¼   cup milk
2   cups shredded American cheese
2   cups corn flakes
¼   cup butter, melted

Preheat oven to 350°. In large mixing bowl, combine hash browns and next 8 ingredients. Spread potato mixture into prepared 9x13-inch baking dish. Sprinkle with cereal and drizzle with butter. Bake for 50 minutes to 1 hour.

This tasty potato dish can be made ahead and placed in the oven a little over an hour before mealtime. My aunt and cousin thought they should always bring a dish when invited to our home, and this was one of their favorites. Now family members look forward to the dish at gatherings.

DOUBLE CRUST PINEAPPLE PIE

1½ cups sugar	1 (20-ounce) can crushed pineapple	2 pie crusts
½ cup butter, melted	4 tablespoons all-purpose flour	

Preheat oven to 400°. In large mixing bowl, combine sugar, butter, pineapple (with juice), and flour; mix well. Gently press 1 pie crust into pie plate. Pour filling into pie crust. Place remaining pie crust over filling, tightly sealing edges with fork. Wrap aluminum foil around edges to prevent edges from browning too quickly. Make several cuts in top crust. Bake for 15 minutes. Reduce heat to 350° and bake for 35 minutes.

Yield: 8 servings

My mother was a good cook, and though she worked during most of my "growing up years", she managed to cook my favorites often, and especially for my birthday. One of her easiest and best recipes is this pie.

★ BARBARA NORRIS MAILER ★

Barbara Mailer grew up in Arkansas, but left for New York when she met and married Norman Mailer, the widely known author. She met Bill Clinton when he was running for Congress in 1974 and worked in his campaign. She and Norman have remained friends with the Clintons through the years.

CHOCOLATE GRAVY

1 cup whole milk	1 tablespoon cocoa	1 teaspoon vanilla
¾ cup sugar	1 tablespoon all-purpose flour	

In medium saucepan, heat milk over medium heat. Add sugar, cocoa, flour, and vanilla, stirring constantly until thickened. Pour over hot buttered biscuits. Faint with pleasure.

If this dish was ever consumed outside of Atkins, Arkansas, I don't know about it, but it was one of the happiest memories of my childhood-getting up on a cold morning to a big plate of chocolate gravy and hot buttered biscuits.

★ RUBY MAILLIAN ★

Ruby Maillian is currently a resident of Los Angeles. For many years, she has been a delegate to the California Democratic Convention. She is also a volunteer with Congresswoman Maxine Waters, the City Council, and the California State Assembly.

 ## SHRIMP CREOLE

¼ cup cooking oil
¼ cup all-purpose flour
1 onion, chopped
½ bell pepper, seeded and chopped
4-6 cups water

4-5 garlic cloves, minced
2 (8-ounce) cans tomato sauce
6-8 bay leaves
1 tablespoon Creole hot sauce
½ teaspoon salt

½ teaspoon pepper
2 pounds medium or large peeled shrimp
White rice, cooked

In Dutch oven over medium-high heat, brown oil and flour, stirring constantly, to create a roux. Add onion and bell pepper and sauté 5 minutes. Add water and next 6 ingredients. Bring to a boil. Reduce heat, cover, and simmer 1 hour, stirring frequently. Add shrimp and cook additional 30 minutes. Cook rice according to package directions 20 minutes before serving. Serve shrimp over rice with cornbread on the side.

Edwina Mann's father was actively involved in Lonoke County, Arkansas' Democratic politics, so it was natural for her and her sister Sandra Carlisle to follow in his footsteps. She's always been personally interested in Bill Clinton and his public service. That's why she continues to support him by volunteering for the William J. Clinton Presidential Foundation while enjoying her retirement from a thirty-five year career as a medical librarian at the University of Arkansas for Medical Sciences.

 JAM CAKE

CAKE

1 cup shortening	3 cups all-purpose flour	1 cup buttermilk
2 cups sugar	1 teaspoon cinnamon	1 cup strawberry jam
4 eggs	1 teaspoon baking soda	1 teaspoon vanilla

Preheat oven to 325°. In large mixing bowl, cream together shortening and sugar with electric mixer on medium speed, adding sugar gradually. Beat in eggs one at a time, beating well after each addition. Sift together flour and cinnamon and set aside. In small mixing bowl, stir baking soda into buttermilk. Add flour mixture and buttermilk mixture alternately to creamed mixture until well blended. Beat in jam and vanilla. Pour into greased and floured baking pan. Bake for 45 minutes or until cake tester inserted in center comes out clean. Pour Pineapple Topping over cake while warm.

PINEAPPLE TOPPING

1 (20-ounce) can crushed pineapple	2 cups sugar	½ cup all-purpose flour

In medium saucepan over medium-high heat, combine ingredients. Bring to a hard boil, stirring until thickened.

This was a favorite cake recipe that Edwina's mother, Mrs. J. E. Walls from the Tomberlin Community at England, Arkansas, passed down. The family has enjoyed it for over twenty years.

★ CAPRICIA MARSHALL ★

Capricia Penavic Marshall worked on the First Lady's staff during the Clinton Administration. She was Special Assistant to Mrs. Clinton from 1993 to 1997 and then Deputy Assistant to the President and Social Secretary from 1997 to 2001. She is married to Robert James Marshall, MD, and they have a three-year-old son, Robert "Cole" Penavic Marshall. She is presently working for an all-women telecommunications company, Northpoint Technology, in Washington, DC.

 ## COLE'S KIDDIE COOKIES ON A STICK

You will need a Cookie Treat Pan and 8-inch cookie sticks. Both are available at kitchen specialty stores.

1 cup butter	1 large egg	2 teaspoons baking powder
1 cup sugar	1 teaspoon vanilla	3 cups all-purpose flour

Preheat oven to 400°. Spray inside of pan with nonstick cooking spray. In large mixing bowl, cream butter and sugar with electric mixer on medium speed. Beat in egg and vanilla. Add baking powder and flour one cup at a time, mixing well after each addition. (Dough will be stiff.) Dough should be used immediately and not chilled. Press dough into molds to within ⅛-inch of rim. Insert 2 inches of stick cookie stick into dough. Place pan on middle oven rack, being careful not to let cookie sticks touch sides of oven. Bake for 10 to 15 minutes. Cool 5 minutes in pan and remove to wire rack. Decorate as desired.

Cookies may be used in a basket for a great centerpiece or tucked into "goodie bags" for departing guests.

Mr. Cole's third birthday allowed the true inner mom to emerge... maybe psycho mom! I made cookies on a stick. Every child who attended had his name beautifully emblazoned on a cookie which also provided great decor for the room! Best of all, the recipe is simple, and Cole had a great time sticking the sticks in the cookies and licking the bowl!

PENAVIC PALACINKE

1½ cups milk	3 eggs	Syrup (optional)
1½ cups all-purpose flour	3 tablespoons cooking oil	Confectioners' sugar (optional)
⅛ teaspoon salt	Butter	

In large mixing bowl, combine ingredients, mixing well. (The consistency of the batter should be smooth and somewhat thin.) In small skillet over medium heat, melt butter. Pour small amount of batter in center and swirl so as to thinly coat the bottom. Flip like a pancake, but do not let them get crisp. Spread Cheese Filling over palacinke. Roll up and fold ends. Drizzle with syrup to serve for breakfast or sprinkle with confectioners' sugar to serve as dessert. For extra decadence, add a scoop of ice cream on the side.

CHEESE FILLING

1 (8-ounce) package cream cheese, softened	1 (8-ounce) package farmer's cheese	Vanilla to taste
	1 egg	Sugar to taste

In large mixing bowl, combine ingredients, blending well. The mixture should have a chunky texture and be sweet to the taste.

Even though my Mexican bloodline has taken a leading role in my personal identity at times, the food I adore comes from my father's homeland, Croatia-Herzegovina. I have forever loved this recipe. My mother made these for special Sunday breakfasts with crispy bacon. I have also served them as a great appetizer before dinner or as a dessert.

★ THURGOOD MARSHALL, JR. ★

Thurgood Marshall, Jr. served as a member of the White House senior staff, holding the post of Assistant to the President and Cabinet Secretary under President Clinton. Mr. Marshall served as Vice Chair of the White House Olympic Task Force and, in that capacity, coordinated the involvement of the federal government in its preparations for the 2002 Salt Lake Winter Olympics and Paralympic Games. Prior to his appointment as Cabinet Secretary in July 1997, Mr. Marshall was the Director of Legislative Affairs and Deputy Counsel for Vice President Al Gore.

 ## SEAFOOD PIGALLE

1 onion, chopped	1 (28-ounce) can tomatoes, coarsely chopped	1 pound shrimp, shelled and deveined
4 garlic cloves, minced	Salt and pepper to taste	1 pound fish (cod, grouper, or orange roughy)
2-3 tablespoons olive oil	Rosemary sprigs	White rice, steamed
1 (15.8-ounce) can white beans, rinsed and drained	4 (8-ounce) bottles clam juice	½ cup chopped fresh Italian parsley, for garnish

In Dutch oven over medium-high heat, sauté onion and garlic in olive oil until tender. Add beans, tomatoes, salt, pepper, and rosemary. Add clam juice. Bring to a boil. Reduce heat and simmer 15 to 20 minutes. Add seafood and cook 2 to 3 minutes or until seafood is done. Serve over steamed rice and sprinkle with parsley. Serve with crusty French or sourdough bread and lime wedges.

Any good firm fleshed fish works well. Cod, grouper, and orange roughy are good choices.

★ JOANN B. MARTIN ★

A long-time Democratic Party activist, Joann frequently tells people she is a "Professional Volunteer". Politics, theater, and travel are her favorite interests. As a mother of three sons and grandmother of six girls and boys, she is seldom at home to cook.

CARAMEL CHEWS WITH CARAMEL ICING

CARAMEL CHEWS

2 cups butter, melted	1 (16-ounce) package brown sugar	1 teaspoon vanilla
2 eggs, lightly beaten	1¾ cups all-purpose flour	¾ cup chopped pecans

Preheat oven to 350°. In large mixing bowl, combine margarine and remaining ingredients, mixing well. Mixture will be thick. Pour into 9x13-inch baking pan. Bake for 25 minutes and check for doneness. Bake for additional 5 minutes if needed. Allow to cool and spread with Caramel Icing.

CARAMEL ICING

½ cup butter	¼ cup half-and-half or milk	1 teaspoon vanilla
½ cup firmly packed dark brown sugar	1¾-2 cups confectioners' sugar	Pinch of salt

In large saucepan over medium-high heat, melt butter and cook until brown. Add brown sugar, stirring until sugar dissolves. Stir in half-and-half. Remove from heat and allow to cool. Add confectioners' sugar, vanilla, and salt, beating until thick enough to spread.

Yield: 24 servings

Caramel Chews is an old Junior League of Little Rock recipe. I combined that with an icing recipe to make them irresistible and doubly decadent!

★ SYLVIA MATHEWS ★

Sylvia Mathews was the Deputy Director of Economic Policy in the 1992 campaign. Once President Clinton took office, she became Staff Director for the National Economic Council and Special Assistant to Robert E. Rubin, then Assistant to the President for Economic Policy. She followed Secretary Rubin to Treasury and became his Chief of Staff between 1995 and 1997. In October of 1998, Sylvia was confirmed as Deputy Director of OMB by the Senate. She is currently the Executive Director and Chief Operating Officer of the Bill and Melinda Gates Foundation.

 ## SPANAKOPITA

¾	cup melted butter, for brushing	5	eggs, beaten	1	(16-ounce) package frozen phyllo, thawed
1	(12-ounce) block feta cheese	2	tablespoons dill weed		
6	green onions, chopped	1	pound fresh spinach, stemmed, rinsed, and patted dry	2	tablespoons sesame seeds

Preheat oven to 375°. Generously brush bottom and sides of 9x22-inch baking pan with butter. In large mixing bowl, crumble feta into large pieces. Add green onions, eggs, dill weed, and spinach, mixing gently. Place 1 phyllo layer in bottom of pan and coat with butter. (Cover remaining phyllo with a damp cloth to keep from drying out.) Repeat process 6 times. Spread half of cheese mixture over phyllo. Cover with 3 layers of phyllo, brushing each layer with butter. Spread remaining cheese mixture over phyllo. Cover with 7 layers of phyllo, brushing each layer with butter. Trim excess phyllo around edges of pan. Sprinkle with sesame seeds. Bake for 50 minutes to 1 hour or until golden brown.

★ TERRY McAULIFFE ★

Terry McAuliffe was elected Chairman of the Democratic National Committee in February 2001. Mr. McAuliffe also serves on the William J. Clinton Presidential Foundation's Board of Directors. He is married to the former Dorothy Swann, and they have five children: Dori, Jack, Mary, Sally, and Peter. The family lives in McLean, Virginia.

 ## MILLIE McAULIFFE'S APPLE PIE (PREFERABLY WITH NEW YORK APPLES, OF COURSE!)

6-8 tart apples, peeled, cored, and sliced	½ cup all-purpose flour	½ cup butter, cut into pats
1 cup brown sugar	1½ teaspoons apple pie spice	2 pie crusts

Preheat oven to 400°. In large mixing bowl, toss apples with brown sugar, flour, and apple pie spice. Gently press 1 pie crust into pie plate. Pour filling into pie crust. Dot with butter. Place remaining pie crust over filling, tightly sealing edges with fork. Wrap aluminum foil around edges to prevent edges from browning too quickly. Make several cuts in top crust. Bake for 50 minutes to 1 hour, testing tenderness of apples with fork.

Yield: 8 servings

★ DOROTHY McAULIFFE ★

 ## DOROTHY McAULIFFE'S TRASH BAG SALAD

4 cups fresh lettuce or greens
½ cup roasted pine nuts or sunflower seeds

½ cup seedless grapes, halved
1 cucumber, sliced
½ cup crumbled blue cheese

1 cup grape tomatoes, sliced
½ (16-ounce) bottle Italian dressing

Immediately before serving, toss lettuce and next 5 ingredients in unused 13-gallon trash bag. Add dressing, shaking well to coat.

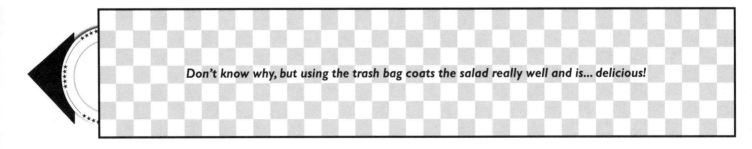

Don't know why, but using the trash bag coats the salad really well and is... delicious!

Peggy McClain served as an Arkansas Traveler in President Clinton's national campaigns. She has been a long-time supporter of the Clintons.

 ## PICKLED CABBAGE SLAW

1 large head green cabbage, finely shredded	1 green bell pepper, seeded and finely chopped	1 yellow bell pepper, seeded and finely chopped
	1 red bell pepper, seeded and finely chopped	1 cup sugar or to taste
		1 cup red cider vinegar or white vinegar or to taste

In large salad bowl, combine cabbage and bell peppers; cover and set aside. In mixing bowl, whisk together sugar and vinegar. Add additional sugar or vinegar to taste if desired. Pour over cabbage mixture, tossing well to coat. Cover and chill overnight.

This is a Pennsylvania Dutch recipe from my grandmother. It goes well with fried catfish, barbeque, or just about anything. It's great to serve at picnics and political potlucks.

24 CARROT CAKE

CAKE

2 cups all-purpose flour	½ teaspoon nutmeg	1½ cups cooking oil
3 teaspoons cinnamon or to taste	½ teaspoon allspice	4 eggs, beaten
1 teaspoon baking soda	½ teaspoon cloves	3 cups shredded carrots
1 teaspoon salt	2 cups sugar	

Preheat oven to 375°. In large mixing bowl, sift together flour and next 6 ingredients. Add sugar, mixing well. Add oil and eggs, beating 2 minutes with electric mixer on medium speed. Fold in carrots, mixing well. Pour into 3 greased and floured 9-inch round cake pans. Bake for 30 minutes or until sides pull away from pans. Cool on wire racks before icing.

CREAM CHEESE ICING

2 (8-ounce) packages cream cheese, softened	4 teaspoons vanilla	2 (16-ounce) packages confectioners' sugar
	1 cup butter, softened	2 cups pecans, coarsely chopped

In large mixing bowl, cream together cream cheese, vanilla, and butter with electric mixer on medium speed. Gradually add sugar and fold in pecans, mixing well.

This cake is in constant demand among my friends. It would be great for a political cake supper.

★ DOLORES McCLARD ★

Dolores Jennings McClard attended high school with President Clinton in Hot Springs. She and her husband Joe have been players in the success of McClard's Bar-B-Q in Hot Springs, Arkansas, which has had a special place in President Clinton's heart since he was a child. The McClard family has many fond memories of the entire Clinton family. J.D. and Lois McClard (Joe's parents) even remember when the Clintons stopped by on their wedding day because they had to have some barbecue before they left for their honeymoon.

 ## McClard's Easy Crock

2	onions, sliced	6	cloves	1	bottle McClard's Bar-B-Q Sauce
1	(5-pound) picnic ham	2	cups water	1	onion, chopped

Place half of sliced onions in bottom of crockpot. Add ham, cloves, water, and remaining onion slices. Cover and cook on low 8 to 10 hours or overnight. Remove bone and fat from ham. Return meat to crockpot. Add McClard's Bar-B-Q Sauce and chopped onion. Cover and cook additional 8 to 12 hours on low, stirring 3 times. Serve on large onion buns.

Yield: 6 servings

★ SCOTT McCLARD ★

Scott McClard helps run the family business. He is the son of Dolores and Joe and the grandson of J.D. and Lois. While he wasn't around to experience the younger Bill Clinton like his grandparents, Scott was able to visit the White House and provide barbecue for Air Force One when it was in Arkansas. Scott fondly remembers entering the Oval Office and being immediately asked by President Clinton, "How are J.D. and Lois?" Scott particularly misses Mrs. Virginia Kelley, who always wanted a hug.

 ## McClard's Hunka Hunka Burning Pork

1	(13 to 14-pound) pork leg (fresh ham)	2	bottles McClard's Bar-B-Q Sauce

Insert meat thermometer into leg of pork, taking care not to touch bone or fat. Grill pork and cover with grill lid. Cook over low heat (250° to 300°) 4 hours, 30 minutes, turning occasionally. Baste often with McClard's Bar-B-Q Sauce. Cover and grill 1 hour, 15 minutes or until thermometer registers 160°. Let stand 10 to 15 minutes before slicing. Place remaining sauce in small saucepan, bring to a low boil, and serve with pork.

If using a gas grill, try using one burner.

Fill the ice chest full of your favorite beverage, and plan on serving this succulent pork to a big and hungry crowd.

★ KEVIN McCLURKAN AND FRIEDA LIM ★

A graduate of Pine Bluff High School and the School of Architecture at the University of Arkansas, Kevin McClurkan lives and works in New York City for the Polshek Partnership. As of late, he is the Project Manager for the Clinton Presidential Center and Park project. The recipe included was perfected by his wife of twelve years, Frieda Lim, a superb cook and fashion designer.

 ## GRILLED FAT CAT STEAK

¼ cup soy sauce	¼ cup fresh oregano	1 teaspoon kosher salt
¼ cup Worcestershire sauce	¼ cup fresh thyme	Zest of 1 lemon
¼ cup ketchup	3-6 garlic cloves, crushed	2 flank steaks of equal size
¼ cup red wine	¼-1 teaspoon red pepper flakes	1 (10-ounce) package frozen chopped spinach, thawed and drained
½ cup chopped green onions	½-1 tablespoon freshly ground black pepper	1 (6-ounce) block feta cheese

In large zip top plastic bag, combine soy sauce and next 11 ingredients, shaking well to mix. Tenderize and pound steaks to ½-inch thickness. Add steaks and marinate overnight. Remove steaks from bag, reserving marinade for basting. Spread spinach over 1 steak, leaving 1-inch perimeter for skewers. Slice feta in half lengthwise and place on top of spinach lengthwise. Top with second steak. Secure and seal steaks together by threading wet bamboo or metal skewers through edges of steaks. Grill over medium-high indirect heat 20 to 30 minutes. Brush steaks with marinade while grilling. Let steaks stand 10 minutes. Remove skewers and slice widthwise.

Governor and Mrs. Clinton asked Ann McCoy to serve as Administrator of the Arkansas Governor's Mansion from 1985 to 1993. Upon their move to the White House, Ann was appointed as Special Assistant to the President and Director of Personal Correspondence from 1993 to 2001.

DIRTY RICE

½ cup butter, cut into pats
2 cups rice

2 (10.75-ounce) cans French onion soup
2 (10.5-ounce) cans beef consommé

1 (4-ounce) can sliced mushrooms, drained
1 (8-ounce) can water chestnuts, drained

Preheat oven to 350°. Place all ingredients in 2-quart casserole. Do not stir. Bake for 1 hour.

Yield: 8 servings

This recipe is from my cousin, Nancy Bridges, at Linden Hall Plantation, Glen Allen, Mississippi. It goes with beef, pork, chicken, and ham. It's quick, easy, and good! Also great for a camping trip.

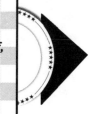

★ ELLEN McCULLOCH-LOVELL ★

Ellen McCulloch-Lovell served as Deputy Assistant to the President and Advisory to the First Lady on the Millennium. She directed the White House Millennium Council, supervising programs such as Save America's Treasures, Millennium Trails, Millennium Communities, and Millennium Evenings at the White House. She worked with Mrs. Clinton on the White House conferences on philanthropy and on cultural diplomacy. Ellen also served the First Lady as Director of the President's Committee on the Arts and the Humanities. Prior to her White House service, she was Senator Patrick Leahy's chief of staff for ten years.

 ## GRAMMA BROWN'S DEVILED CRAB

4 tablespoons butter, melted	1 teaspoon salt or to taste	1 pound crabmeat
2 tablespoons all-purpose flour	1 teaspoon pepper or to taste	2 hard-boiled eggs, finely chopped
1 teaspoon dry mustard	1 tablespoon chopped parsley	½ cup breadcrumbs
1 cup milk	2 teaspoons lemon juice	2 tablespoons butter, cut into pats

In medium mixing bowl, combine melted butter, flour, and mustard. Stir in milk. Add salt, pepper, parsley, and lemon juice, stirring until smooth and thickened. Fold in crabmeat and eggs, gently mixing. Place in shallow casserole or 6 individual ramekins. Sprinkle with breadcrumbs and dot with butter. Bake for 30 minutes or until brown and bubbling.

My mother Sarah Brown McCulloch notes, "Back fin is best quality, but claw meat is sweeter and tastier, I think."

This recipe came from my grandmother, Pauline Huey Brown, who lived until she was 89-years-old on the eastern shore of Maryland in Snow Hill. She was a wonderful cook, and some of my best memories are of sitting around her and Pop Brown's large table eating local specialties—asparagus from Pop's garden and deviled crab! Resist the temptation to add exotic ingredients—this is good, plain cooking!

★ DONNA AND MACK McLARTY ★

Donna McLarty is a long-time advocate for the arts and humanities and has been a leader in international efforts to support women, children, and families. She and her husband Thomas F. "Mack" McLarty were awarded the National Conference of Christians and Jews Humanitarian Award.

Mack McLarty's distinguished record includes advising three Presidents: Bill Clinton, George Bush, and Jimmy Carter. As Chief of Staff under President Clinton, Mack helped enact the historic 1993 deficit reduction package, NAFTA, and the Family and Medical Leave law. He later served the President in the positions of Counselor and Special Envoy to the Americas.

PAO DE QUEIJO (CHEESE BALLS)

4 cups milk	Salt to taste	6 eggs
1 cup cooking oil	2 pounds pure manioc flour	1¼ pounds shredded Monterey Jack cheese

Preheat oven to 350°. In large saucepan over high heat, bring milk and oil to a boil. Remove from heat. Transfer mixture to large mixing bowl. Add salt and flour, mixing well. Allow to cool slightly. Add cheese, mixing well. Add eggs one at a time, beating well after each addition, then knead. Roll dough into 1-inch sized balls. Place baking parchment on baking sheet. Place balls on parchment and bake for 30 minutes or until lightly golden brown.

Yield: 150 to 200 cheese balls

Cheese balls may be frozen before baking. Do not defrost in microwave; thaw to room temperature before baking.
Pure manioc flour can be found in Latino markets.

As we traveled throughout Latin America during the years that Mack served as Special Envoy to the Americas, we were continually delighted by the warmth and generosity of the people we met, the cultural richness of the countries we visited, and the fabulous cuisine we sampled. One special favorite was Pao De Queijo (Portuguese for "cheese balls")—a common offering throughout Brazil, usually served with fresh, hot espresso. I've been told the dish originated in the seventeenth century among African communities in the Brazilian state of Minas Gerais. Today it can be found in every bakery—an apt (and appetizing!) symbol of the vibrant mosaic of colors, cultures, and traditions that makes Brazil so wonderful and unique. This recipe is offered and translated with the compliments of Maria Ignez Barbosa, wife of Brazilian Ambassador Rubens Barbosa.

★ THE HONORABLE SIDNEY S. McMATH ★

Sid McMath served as Arkansas's 34th Governor from 1949 to 1953, where he was recognized for his many progressive achievements including his work in education. After his terms in office, he continued to practice law in Little Rock and served in the United States Marine Corps Reserve. He is still very active in the community today and is the author of a new memoir that is to be released in 2004.

 ## SOUTHERN CORNBREAD

2   cups yellow cornmeal
1   teaspoon baking soda

1   teaspoon salt
2   eggs, well beaten

2   cups buttermilk
¼   cup bacon drippings

Preheat oven to 450°. In large mixing bowl, combine cornmeal, baking soda, and salt. Stir in eggs and buttermilk, mixing well. Heat bacon drippings in iron skillet over medium-high heat until hot. Pour mixture into skillet, stirring well. Bake for 25 to 30 minutes or until golden brown.

Yield: 8 servings

I was the first governor to live in the Arkansas Governor's Mansion in 1950 with my wife and three small boys. We had a chef, John Wright, who prepared the meals during my years there. A simple Southern family meal of fried chicken, boiled new potatoes, and green beans was always accompanied by a bountiful supply of cornbread.

Montine McNulty is the Executive Director of the Arkansas Hospitality Association and is a friend and supporter of the William J. Clinton Presidential Foundation.

 ## Montine's Favorite Macaroni Casserole

5 (15-ounce) packages frozen macaroni and cheese, thawed

1 (10-ounce) package frozen chopped spinach, thawed and drained

1 bunch green onions, chopped
½ teaspoon oregano
Salt to taste
White pepper to taste

1 can French fried onion rings
1 (12-ounce) package shredded sharp Cheddar cheese
Cayenne pepper to taste (optional)

Preheat oven to 350°. In large prepared casserole, combine macaroni and next 5 ingredients. Sprinkle with onion rings, cheese, and cayenne pepper. Bake for 45 to 50 minutes.

Yield: 12 to 16 servings

Wonderful and different! This is a favorite company dish, and the recipe is always requested.

★ BRIAN J. McPARTLIN ★

Brian J. McPartlin did advance work for President and Senator Clinton during the 1992 and 1996 campaigns and went on to be appointed as Associate Director of Presidential Advance during the Clinton Administration. He also served as a Presidential appointee in the U.S. General Services Administration and the U.S. Department of Education. He is currently the Chief of Administration of the Illinois State Toll Highway Authority and resides in the Village of Mount Prospect, Illinois, with his wife Amy and three boys, Michael, Matthew, and Patrick.

 ## OREO COOKIE CAKE

1 (20-ounce) package Oreo cookies, crushed and divided	½ gallon vanilla ice cream	1 (12-ounce) container frozen whipped topping, thawed
½ cup butter	1½ (12-ounce) jars hot fudge sauce, warmed	

Set aside ¼ to ½ cup cookie crumbs for garnish. In medium saucepan over medium heat, combine cookie crumbs and butter, cooking until cookies soften. Press mixture lightly into 9x13-inch glass dish. Freeze 1 hour. Soften ice cream and spread onto frozen crust. Return to freezer. When completely frozen, pour warm hot fudge over top. Return to freezer. When completely frozen, spread with whipped topping and sprinkle with remaining cookie crumbs. Enjoy!

 ## McPARTLIN'S IRISH SODA BREAD

½ teaspoon baking soda	2½ cups all-purpose flour	½ cup yellow raisins
1 cup buttermilk	2 teaspoons baking powder	1 apple, peeled, cored, and chopped
½ cup butter	½ teaspoons salt	½ teaspoon caraway seeds
1 egg, well beaten	⅞ cup sugar	

Preheat oven to 340°. In large saucepan over medium-high heat, combine baking soda, buttermilk, and butter. Remove from heat. Add egg and mix well; set aside. In large mixing bowl, combine flour, baking powder, salt, and sugar. Add to buttermilk mixture, mixing well. Fold in raisins, apple, and caraway seeds. Pour into prepared loaf pan. Bake for 1 hour.

Yield: 1 loaf

This recipe has been in my father's family for many generations.

★ CHERYL MILLS ★

Cheryl Mills, an attorney, was Deputy Counsel to the President at the White House, where she supervised thirty-five attorneys and staff. Her legal experience also includes serving as Associate Counsel to the President, as Deputy General Counsel of the Clinton/Gore Transition Planning Foundation and as an associate at the Washington, DC law firm of Hugan and Hartson. From 1999 to 2001, Mills was Senior Vice President for Corporate Policy and Public Programming at Oxygen Media. Currently, she is Senior Vice President and Counselor for Operations at New York University and serves on the Board of Directors for the William J. Clinton Presidental Foundation.

 **CHERYL'S FAVORITE CHEESECAKE**

CRUST
2	cups graham cracker crumbs	1	tablespoon cinnamon
3	tablespoons sugar	½	cup butter, melted

In mixing bowl, combine crumbs, sugar, and cinnamon. Stir in butter, mixing well. Press mixture in bottom and up sides of prepared springform pan.

FILLING
3	(8-ounce) packages cream cheese, softened	4	eggs	1	tablespoon vanilla
		1	cup sugar		

Preheat oven to 350°. In large mixing bowl, beat cream cheese with electric mixer on medium speed. Add eggs one at a time, beating well after each addition. Gradually add sugar and vanilla, mixing well. Pour into crust and bake for 45 minutes or until center of cheesecake is firm. Remove from oven and cool 10 minutes.

TOPPING
2	cups sour cream	2	tablespoons sugar	1	tablespoon vanilla

In small mixing bowl, combine ingredients, stirring until smooth. Spread over cheesecake. Increase heat to 475°. Return cheesecake to oven and bake for 5 minutes. Cool 1 hour and freeze 2 hours before serving.

★ DEBORAH MOHILE ★

Deborah Mohile worked at the Democratic National Committee, Clinton/Gore 96, and the 1997 Presidential Inauguration Committee. She then served as Associate Director of Public Liaison at the White House where she worked until joining the Gore 2000 campaign. After participating in the Florida recount, she moved to New York City where she currently lives and works.

 ## POTATO LATKES

3-4 large frying potatoes, washed, shredded, and drained
1   large onion, minced

1-2 eggs, beaten
Salt and pepper to taste

5-6 tablespoons all-purpose flour
Cooking oil

In large mixing bowl, combine potatoes, onion, eggs, salt, and pepper. Gradually add flour, stirring until batter sticks together. Preheat oil in skillet. Drop mixture by spoonfuls into oil; flip when brown. The smaller the latke, the crispier it will be. Drain on paper towels after frying. To keep warm, place latkes on baking sheet in 350° oven. Serve with applesauce or sour cream.

 *Potato latkes are a traditional Jewish food. They are most often served on the Jewish festival of Chanukah, which celebrates the rededication of the Jewish Temple in Jerusalem. At this event, the Jews lit an oil lamp with enough oil for just one day, but miraculously, the oil lasted for eight days. As a result, it is a tradition to eat foods prepared with oil, such as potato latkes and donuts. Each year during Chanukah, the Clintons invited local school children to light a menorah that had been loaned to the White House by a variety of contemporary artists and craftspeople. On the other nights, several members of the White House staff would gather to light the menorah in the foyer of the West Wing.*

A native of Lexington, Kentucky, Megan Moloney worked for the Clinton Administration beginning in 1994 as a White House advance volunteer. She subsequently worked for the Department of Transportation, the Clinton/Gore 1996 campaign, the 1997 Presidential Inaugural Committee, and beginning in February 1997, as a member of the White House Press Office staff, serving as Director of Radio and Television Production.

BROCCOLI CASSEROLE

1 (10-ounce) package frozen chopped broccoli, cooked and drained	¼ pound processed cheese loaf, melted	½ cup butter, melted and divided
		12 round buttery crackers, crushed

Preheat oven to 250°. Place broccoli in prepared casserole dish. In small mixing bowl, combine melted cheese and ¼ cup melted butter. Pour over broccoli. Combine remaining ¼ cup melted butter and cracker crumbs, mixing well. Sprinkle over broccoli. Bake for 30 minutes.

During the four years I worked in the White House Press Office, many of my holidays were spent at work, on "duty" with the White House press pool. Thanksgiving 1997 stands out as particularly memorable. President Clinton and his family were at Camp David, which meant that the press pool was on "standby" in Washington, DC. I was up early preparing side dishes for our "Orphan Thanksgiving"-friends and co-workers who weren't able to go home for the holiday. My kitchen was covered with ingredients when the call came that President Clinton was leaving Camp David to play a round of golf and the press pool needed to be there in an hour. I called a fellow Thanksgiving "orphan", Dominique Cano, who took me to work so I could travel with the pool to Camp David and then return to my house to finish the cooking. By the time golf was over and the press pool had returned to DC, I had missed the first serving at dinner. But the food, including my Grandmother's broccoli casserole, made it there in plenty of time.

★ DOROTHY MOORE ★

Dorothy Moore volunteered in then-Governor Clinton's office during legislative sessions. She currently resides in Arkansas City, where she once served as Desha County's sheriff.

 PECAN PIE

3 eggs	⅛ teaspoon salt	Pie crust
½ cup sugar	1 teaspoon vanilla	1 cup pecans
1 cup white corn syrup	¼ cup butter, melted	

Preheat oven to 350°. In large mixing bowl, beat eggs. Add sugar, syrup, salt, vanilla, and butter, mixing well. Line pie plate with pie crust. Arrange a layer of pecans on crust. Pour mixture over pecans. Bake for 50 minutes to 1 hour. The pecans will rise to the top and form a crusted layer.

Yield: 8 servings

MISSISSIPPI RIVER MUD PIE

½ cup butter	3 eggs, well beaten	1 teaspoon vanilla
1 (3-ounce) square unsweetened chocolate	3 tablespoons white corn syrup	1 (9-inch) unbaked pie shell
	1½ cups sugar	

Preheat oven to 350°. In small saucepan over medium-high heat, melt together butter and chocolate. Remove from heat and cool slightly. In large mixing bowl, combine eggs, syrup, sugar, and vanilla, mixing thoroughly. Add to chocolate mixture and mix well. Pour into pie shell and bake for 35 minutes.

Yield: 8 servings

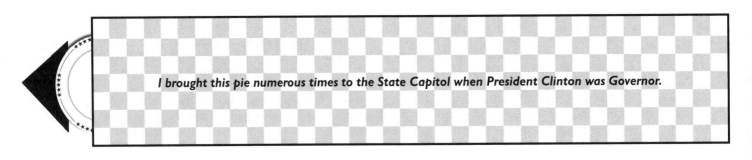

I brought this pie numerous times to the State Capitol when President Clinton was Governor.

Harry Truman Moore has worked in every one of Bill Clinton's campaigns for public office. Harry shot the photographs for Clinton's first brochure and campaign poster. During President Clinton's national campaigns, Harry volunteered as an Arkansas Traveler.

 ## H.T.'s "HOT TODDY" DUCK

1	(3- to 4-pound) Long Island duckling Salt	½	onion, chopped	4	ounces honey
½	large apple, peeled, cored, and chopped	3-4	celery stalks, chopped	2	ounces bourbon
				2	tablespoons lemon juice

Preheat oven to 350°. Remove and discard giblets from duck. Rinse duck and pat dry. Trim off wing tips. Trim part of excess skin from cavity, leaving enough to close later. With sharp knife, prick skin repeatedly all over. Salt generously. In small mixing bowl, combine apple, onion, and celery. Stuff duck cavities with apple mixture. Close cavity on both ends and secure with toothpicks. Place duck on wire rack over roasting pan or large glass dish. Roast about 3 hours or until skin is light brown and crispy. Remove from oven and allow to cool. Split duck along breast bone with heavy, sharp knife and remove stuffing. Split into halves by cutting along both sides of back bone. Remove and discard rib bones from each half. Return duck to oven and cook additional 15 to 20 minutes or to desired doneness. In small mixing bowl, combine honey, bourbon, and lemon juice, mixing well. Serve duck with wild rice. Drizzle with honey sauce immediately before serving.

Yield: 2 servings

The honey sauce may also be used as a glaze during last few minutes of cooking time. If used as a glaze, increase the amount of honey.

To avoid grease splatters, wrap aluminum foil around roasting pan, extending foil above edges of pan.

★ LENA AND BRUCE MOORE ★

Bruce Moore was appointed as City Manager of Little Rock, Arkansas, on December 17, 2002, after having served as Assistant City Manager since April of 1999. He has been the lead city staff person for the development of the William Jefferson Clinton Presidential Center and Park in downtown Little Rock. In addition, his wife Lena sang the national anthem at the groundbreaking of the Clinton Presidential Center and Park on December 5, 2001.

LASAGNA

1½ pounds ground beef	2 tablespoons cooking oil	2 cups cottage cheese
¾ cup chopped bell pepper	2 (26-ounce) jars commercially prepared pasta sauce	1 cup shredded mozzarella cheese
¾ cup chopped onion		1 cup shredded mild Cheddar cheese
1 tablespoon minced garlic	1 (8-ounce) package no boil lasagna noodles	1 (10-ounce) package frozen chopped spinach, cooked and drained
1 tablespoon salt		

Preheat oven to 350°. In large skillet or Dutch oven over medium-high heat, cook ground beef with bell pepper, onion, garlic, and salt until no longer pink. Drain excess grease. Add oil and pasta sauce to beef mixture, mixing well. Spread one-fourth of meat sauce on bottom of 9x13-inch baking pan. Place one-third of uncooked noodles over sauce. Layer half of cottage cheese and spinach and one-third of mozzarella and Cheddar cheeses over noodles. Repeat process. Top with remaining noodles and meat sauce. Cover with aluminum foil and bake for 1 hour. Remove from oven, uncover, and sprinkle with remaining mozzarella and Cheddar cheeses. Bake for additional 5 minutes or until cheese is bubbly. Let stand 15 minutes before cutting and serving. Enjoy!

Mary Morrison worked at the White House during the Clinton Administration from 1995 to 2001. She began as an Oval Office Intern and then served as the Special Assistant to the Director of Scheduling for two years. She later became the Special Assistant to the Director of Oval Office Operations and held this position until the end of the Administration. During 2001, she worked in President Clinton's transition office.

SUPPER CLUB CHILI

1	tablespoon cooking oil	1	pound ground beef	1	tablespoon mustard
¼	teaspoon chili powder	3	(14.5-ounce) cans stewed	2	(15.5-ounce) cans dark kidney
1	tablespoon cumin		tomatoes		beans, rinsed and drained
2	tablespoons cayenne pepper	1	cup ketchup	2	(15-ounce) cans pinto beans,
2	cups chopped onion	½	cup brown sugar		rinsed and drained
2	garlic cloves, minced	¼	cup molasses	1	(15-ounce) can cannelloni beans,
2	bell peppers, seeded and chopped	¼	cup Worcestershire sauce		rinsed and drained

Heat oil in Dutch oven over medium-high heat. Add chili powder, cumin, cayenne pepper. Sauté onion, garlic, and bell pepper 4 minutes. Add ground beef and cook 10 minutes, cooking until onion and bell pepper are tender. Stir in tomatoes one can at a time. Add ketchup, brown sugar, molasses, Worcestershire sauce, and mustard. Reduce heat. Cover and simmer 20 minutes, stirring occasionally. Gently fold beans one can at a time. Cover and simmer 30 minutes, stirring occasionally, to blend flavors. Serve with shredded cheese, chopped chives, sour cream, fresh tomato salsa, cilantro, and corn chips.

To make the chili sweeter, add more brown sugar and molasses. Also, play with recipe by adding more tomatoes or beans if desired.

This chili is best if prepared ahead and kept in refrigerator 24 to 48 hours to bring out the flavors.

Supper Club was a group of Clinton Administration women who gathered monthly at each others' homes and each cooked a new meal. It was a time for us to practice our cooking... as well as get together!

★ PATRICIA MORROW ★

Pat Morrow began volunteering for President Clinton during the 1992 campaign in the Compliance Department and has been volunteering in President Clinton's Little Rock office weekly since the spring of 1994. She and her husband Fred were Arkansas Travelers and made many out-of-state trips during the '92 and '96 campaigns. Their daughter Shari and her husband Jordan met on a trip with the New York City delegation to New Hampshire in '92. Their other daughter Teresa volunteered in the Austin, Texas, campaigns. Fred and Pat like to say that their support of President Clinton is a family affair.

 ## BRIE WITH SUN-DRIED TOMATOES

1	(16-ounce) wheel brie, rind removed	2	tablespoons minced fresh parsley
4	sun-dried tomatoes, packed in oil	2	tablespoons freshly shredded Parmesan cheese
		6	garlic cloves, minced and mashed
		1	teaspoon crushed dried basil

Place brie on serving plate and set aside. Drain sun-dried tomatoes, reserving 1 tablespoon oil. Rinse, pat dry, and mince tomatoes. In small mixing bowl, combine tomatoes, parsley, Parmesan cheese, garlic and basil. Add reserved oil and mix well. Spread mixture over brie. Let stand at room temperature at least 1 hour before serving. Serve with thin slices of fresh French bread.

Bagged sun-dried tomatoes may be used. Add 1 tablespoon of extra-virgin olive oil.

This hors d'oeuvre is for SERIOUS garlic lovers only!

 ## ORANGE CRANBERRY TORTE

2¼	cups all-purpose flour		Zest of 2 oranges	2	eggs, beaten
2	cups sugar, divided	1	cup chopped pecans or walnuts	1	cup buttermilk
1	teaspoon baking powder	1	cup chopped dates	¾	cup cooking oil
1	teaspoon baking soda	1	cup fresh cranberries	1	cup orange juice
¼	teaspoon salt				

Preheat oven to 350°. In large mixing bowl, sift together flour, 1 cup sugar, baking powder, baking soda, and salt together. Stir in zest, nuts, dates, and cranberries. In separate mixing bowl, combine eggs, buttermilk, and oil. Add to flour and fruit mixture, stirring until well blended. Pour into prepared tube pan or Bundt pan. Bake for 1 hour. Let stand in pan until lukewarm. Invert onto wire rack placed over a wide dish. In small mixing bowl, whisk together orange juice and remaining 1 cup sugar, whisking until sugar dissolves. Spoon orange glaze over warm cake until glaze is absorbed. Wrap in aluminum foil and chill 24 hours. Slice and serve with a dollop of whipped topping.

Yield: 16 servings

I always bake this cake for Thanksgiving or Christmas. It makes the house smell great! Our neighbor in New Orleans shared this recipe with me in 1961.

★ LISSA MUSCATINE AND DORIS MUSCATINE ★

Lissa Muscatine was a Presidential speechwriter, Chief Speechwriter for the First Lady, and Director of Communications to the First Lady during the Clinton Administration. She also worked with Senator Clinton on her White House memoir. She lives in Bethesda, Maryland, with her husband and three children. Her mother, Doris, is an avid Clinton supporter and writer who lives in Berkeley, California.

 **POACHED SALMON**

SALMON

8	bacon slices	1	fennel bulb, coarsely chopped	1	tablespoon kosher salt
1	(4-pound) center cut salmon fillet		Pinch of saffron	3	cups white wine
1	leek, coarsely chopped	1	sprig fresh tarragon	2-3	cups fish or chicken stock or clam juice
1	onion, coarsely chopped	2	sprigs fresh thyme		
2	shallots, coarsely chopped	2	fronds fresh dill	1	tablespoon chopped, fresh dill
4	carrots, coarsely chopped		Zest of 1 orange		Salt to taste
2	celery stalks, coarsely chopped	2	bay leaves		White pepper to taste
4	garlic cloves, minced	¼	cup black and red peppercorns		

Remove and discard any fat and pin bones from salmon, leaving skin on. Line bottom of fish poacher or large shallow stockpot with bacon. Wrap fish in 1 yard of cheesecloth and place over bacon. Add leek and next 14 ingredients to poacher. Add wine and stock, adding water if needed, until liquid comes three-fourths up sides of salmon. Bring to a boil. Reduce heat, simmer, and cover. Poach salmon 10 minutes per inch of thickness at thickest part of fillet. Remove poacher from heat and lift salmon from poaching liquid. Skim, strain, and reserve stock for sauce if desired. Sprinkle salmon with chopped dill, salt, and white pepper. Serve warm or at room temperature.

SAUCE

2	tablespoons butter, melted		Reserved stock
2	tablespoons all-purpose flour	1	cup heavy cream

In small mixing bowl, whisk together butter and flour to form a paste. In medium saucepan over medium-high heat, bring reserved stock to a simmer. Slowly whisk in paste and simmer 5 minutes or until sauce has thickened. Add cream to sauce and simmer for additional 5 minutes. Serve warm over poached salmon.

Yield: 8 servings

★ BOB NASH AND JANIS KEARNEY ★

Bob Nash served as President Clinton's Director of Presidential Personnel from 1994 to 2001. Prior to that role, he served as Under Secretary of the Department of Agriculture. He is now Vice-Chair of ShoreBank, an internationally recognized community development bank, the first and largest such bank in the world. Janis F. Kearney served in the Clinton White House as President Clinton's personal diarist from 1995 to 2001. Before that, she was appointed Director of Communications at the U.S. Small Business Administration where she served from 1993 to 1995. Before joining the Clinton Administration, Janis owned and published the Arkansas State Press Newspaper and worked for the State of Arkansas for a number of years. Now a writer and lecturer living in Chicago, she is completing two books, both expected to be published in 2004: *William Jefferson Clinton: From Hope to Harlem* and *Cotton Field of Dreams,* a personal memoir.

 ## MEXICAN-SOUL JALAPEÑO CORNBREAD

1 cup yellow cornmeal	1 purple onion, chopped	1 cup sour cream
1 teaspoon salt	½ cup cooking oil	Cooking oil, for frying
½ teaspoon baking powder	1 (17-ounce) can cream-style corn	½ pound shredded Cheddar cheese,
2 eggs	3 jalapeño peppers, finely chopped	divided

Preheat oven to 400°. In large mixing bowl, combine cornmeal and next 7 ingredients. In iron skillet over medium-high heat, heat small amount of cooking oil. Pour half of batter in skillet, covering bottom. Top with half of cheese. Pour remaining batter in skillet and cover with remaining cheese. Remove from heat. Place skillet in oven and bake for 30 to 40 minutes or until brown. Allow to cool slightly and remove from skillet.

Yield: 12 servings

★ VIC AND FREDDIE NIXON ★

Vic Nixon presided over the Clinton's wedding on October 11, 1975. His wife, Freddie, worked for then-Governor Clinton in 1978 during his first term as governor. Vic and Freddie continue to support the Clintons and the William J. Clinton Presidential Foundation.

 ## LAZY PIE

½ cup butter	1 cup all-purpose flour	¾ cup milk
1 cup sugar	2 teaspoons baking powder	1½ cups sweetened fruit or berries

Preheat oven to 350°. Melt butter in casserole. Combine sugar, flour, baking powder, and milk, mixing well. Pour over butter. Top with fruit; do not stir. Bake for 30 minutes or until brown on top.

Willie Oates, widely known as "the hat lady," may have fun with her large collection of hats, but she is serious about her volunteerism. A former state legislator, an avid Razorback fan, and a former Little Rock Woman of the Year, her contributions to her community are legendary.

 ## DATE NUT BARS

¾ cup sifted all-purpose flour	1 cup firmly packed brown sugar	1 cup dates, chopped
½ teaspoon salt	¼ cup melted shortening	1 cup nuts, chopped
½ teaspoon baking powder	2 eggs, well beaten	Confectioners' sugar for garnish

Preheat oven to 350°. Sift together flour, salt, and baking powder and set aside. Combine brown sugar and shortening in large mixing bowl. Add eggs and flour mixture, mixing well. Fold in dates and nuts. Pour into prepared baking pan. Bake for 25 to 30 minutes. Cut bars while warm and dust with confectioners' sugar.

Yield: 12 servings

HARVEY WALLBANGER CAKE

1 (18-ounce) package yellow cake mix	¾ cup cooking oil	⅓ cup vodka
1 (3-ounce) vanilla flavored instant pudding mix	½ cup orange juice	4 eggs
	⅓ cup Galliano	

Preheat oven to 350°. Combine cake mix and remaining ingredients in large mixing bowl. Beat 5 minutes with an electric mixer on medium speed. Pour into greased and floured 10-inch Bundt pan. Bake for 45 to 55 minutes. Remove from oven and invert onto serving plate immediately.

Yield: 12 to 16 servings

★ THE OSBORNE FAMILY ★

Jennings Osborne is a successful businessman in Arkansas. However, he's probably more remembered for the way he celebrates Christmas. Since 1993, he and his wife Mitzi and daughter Breezy have lit up Walt Disney World with their three million Christmas lights. Thirty-two other sites in Arkansas have been "Osbornetized" with Christmas lights. The Osbornes are also known for their huge barbecues and lavish fireworks displays. The Osborne Family has hosted barbecues following both the Groundbreaking and the Topping Out Ceremony of the Clinton Presidential Center and Park.

 ## FAMOUS OSBORNE FAMILY DINOSAUR RIBS

¼ cup paprika
¼ cup firmly packed dark brown sugar

4 teaspoons garlic powder
4 teaspoons onion powder
2 teaspoons chili powder

2 teaspoons black pepper
5 pounds choice beef back ribs

In small mixing bowl, combine paprika and next 5 ingredients. Rub spice mix into ribs on meaty side. Wrap in heavy aluminum foil and seal tightly. Marinate 2 hours at room temperature (below 75°) or in refrigerator for 72 hours. Preheat grill to 300°. Open foil, but do not remove. Place ribs in open foil on grill with grill lid open and cook until ribs are brown (about 1 hour). Reseal ribs in foil and close grill lid with grill vents open. Cook until tender (about 2 and a half to 3 hours). A meat thermometer inserted in thickest portion of meat should register 185° to 190°. Ribs will be pink inside and charred on outside. Remove from grill, cut into 3 to 4 bone sections, and serve.

Yield: 5 servings

We love to cook ribs for President Clinton, his step-father Dick Kelley, and their many friends.

★ LAZAR PALNICK AND SUSANNE GOLLIN ★

Originally from Little Rock, Lazar Palnick has known President Clinton since he was fourteen. He and his wife Susanne worked in many of Clinton's campaigns in Arkansas. After moving to Pennsylvania in 1988, they were responsible for organizing the '92 and '96 Presidential campaigns in Pennsylvania.

 **NAOMI'S PLUM TORTE**

½-1 cup sugar
½ cup unsalted butter, softened
1 cup all-purpose flour
1 teaspoon baking powder

Pinch of salt
2 eggs
12 pitted plums, halved

Sugar
Lemon juice
Cinnamon

Preheat oven to 350°. In large mixing bowl, cream together sugar and butter and set aside. Sift together flour, baking powder, and salt. Add to creamed mixture and mix well. Add eggs, blending thoroughly. Spoon batter into prepared 9-inch springform pan. Place plum halves skin side up on top of batter. Sprinkle lightly with sugar, lemon juice, and cinnamon. Bake for 1 hour. Remove from oven and place on wire rack. Chill or freeze. Serve lukewarm or at room temperature. To serve frozen torte, thaw and reheat briefly at 300°. Serve with vanilla ice cream or frozen whipped topping.

Yield: 8 servings

Peaches, nectarines, pitted cherries, or other fresh or canned fruit (drained) may be substituted for plums.

This plum torte was always in high demand when campaign workers and officials stayed with Lazar and Susanne.

★ LEON E. PANETTA ★

Leon Panetta served during the Clinton Administration as Chief of Staff and Director or the U.S. Office of Management and Budget. He was a U.S. Representative for sixteen years, including four years as Chairman of the Budget Committee. He currently serves as Director of the Leon & Sylvia Panetta Institute for Public Policy.

 ## GNOCCHI DI MOMMA (MY MOM'S GNOCCHI)

8 medium russet potatoes	2⅓-3 cups all-purpose flour, divided	Butter, olive oil, pesto, or tomato sauce
1 egg yolk	1 tablespoon olive oil	Parmesan cheese
1 tablespoon salt		

Preheat oven to 350°. Puncture potatoes with fork in several places. Bake for 1 hour or until tender. Peel potatoes, discarding skins. Mash hot potatoes through a ricer or food mill into large mixing bowl. Allow to cool slightly. Add egg yolk, salt, and 2 cups flour, mixing until mixture holds together. Place potato mixture on lightly floured flat surface and knead into a ball. Dough should be soft, pliable, and slightly sticky. Add flour if too sticky. Break or cut dough into 3-inch pieces. Roll pieces into 18-inch logs about 1-inch thick. Cut each roll into 1-inch pieces. Arrange dumplings on large flat surface, being careful dumplings do not touch. Sprinkle generously with flour. Place dumplings in cool room and let stand 2 to 3 hours. Fill large saucepan two-thirds full of salted water. Bring water to a boil. Add olive oil and dumplings. When dumplings come to surface, cook 10 to 12 seconds and remove immediately with slotted spoon or strainer, draining against side of saucepan. Place dumplings in warm dish. Toss with butter, olive oil, pesto, or tomato sauce and Parmesan cheese. Enjoy this favorite Panetta dish!

Yield: 8 servings

Italians love their gnocchi, particularly if they melt in your mouth with a great sauce. My mom made the best gnocchi in the world. To the rest of you, these are potato dumplings... but what dumplings! Try them and "buon appetito"!

Jo Parker and her husband Jerry have known the Clintons since Bill Clinton ran for Congress in 1974. They had just opened a restaurant in the Scott County community of Waldron, Arkansas when the campaign was heating up. The Clintons would often stop by for some burgers and fries as they traveled the district well into the night. Since then, the Parkers have been supporters of the Clintons. Jo was an Arkansas Traveler during the Presidential campaigns and volunteered in the White House. She claims to be the only person admitted to the White House using her Sam's membership card for identification.

BEEF STROGANOFF

2 pounds beef, cut into strips	5 tablespoons butter, divided	2 tablespoons tomato juice or paste
Salt and pepper	2 cups beef stock	3 tablespoons very finely chopped
1 tablespoon all-purpose flour	2 tablespoons sour cream	onion

Season beef strips generously with salt and pepper. Let stand 2 hours in a cool place. Make a roux by blending flour with 2 tablespoons butter in large saucepan over low heat until mixture bubbles and is smooth. Gradually stir in beef stock; cook until mixture begins to thicken. Boil 2 minutes; strain into saucepan. Add sour cream alternately with tomato juice, stirring constantly. Simmer on low, but do not boil. Melt remaining 3 tablespoons butter in large skillet. Brown beef strips with onion. Pour meat, onion, and butter into sauce. Season with salt and pepper to taste. Simmer or cook in double boiler over hot water 20 minutes.

Yield: 6 to 8 servings

After Senator Kennedy became President, I used Mrs. Kennedy's Beef Stroganoff recipe for special occasion dinners. I would tell my children, "This is what they are eating at the White House," never dreaming some day we would have the privilege of eating at the White House with President and Mrs. Clinton.

★ JO PARKER ★

 ## PINEAPPLE EGGNOG

1	(46-ounce) can pineapple juice	8 eggs, separated
3	cups whipping cream, divided	1 cup sugar, divided

Nutmeg

Pour pineapple juice in large saucepan and bring to a boil. Remove from heat; gradually add 2 cups cream, stirring constantly, and set aside. In large mixing bowl, beat egg yolks until glossy. Gradually add ¾ cup sugar, beating well. Slowly stir in one-quarter of pineapple mixture into egg yolk mixture. Add remaining pineapple mixture, stirring constantly. Cover and chill. Beat remaining 1 cup whipping cream and ¼ cup sugar until stiff peaks form. Fold into chilled pineapple mixture or dollop on individual servings of eggnog. Sprinkle with nutmeg and serve immediately.

This recipe has been a favorite at our Scott County Democratic Women's Christmas Party for many years.

★ MARK PENN ★

Mark Penn served as President Clinton's pollster and advisor from 1995 through 2000. He is a graduate of Harvard University and attended Columbia Law School before establishing his own polling company, Penn, Schoen and Associates, in 1975. He is married to Nancy Jacobson Penn, one of President Clinton's first fundraisers. The couple has a new baby in addition to three other children ranging in ages from 10 to 15. He cooks frequently when they entertain.

 ### MARK PENN'S POACHED SALMON

2	cups champagne		Fresh tarragon		1	side of salmon
3	cups chicken broth		Fresh basil			Fresh thyme
2	leeks, sliced ¼-inch thick		Dash of salt and pepper			

In fish poacher, combine champagne and next 4 ingredients. Add salt and pepper. Add salmon and cover with thyme. Simmer, covered, 25 to 30 minutes or until thickest part of fish flakes easily with fork. Remove from poacher and chill. Dress serving plate with leeks and herbs and top with salmon. Serve with Sour Cream Dip.

SOUR CREAM DIP

1	cup sour cream		¼	cup honey mustard
¼	cup whipped cream cheese		3	sprigs dill, stemmed and finely chopped

Combine ingredients, mixing well. Chill at least 1 hour.

★ DARREN AND VIVIAN PETERS ★

Darren Peters currently works at Entergy, where he is the manager of System Government Affairs. Darren served on the '92 and '96 Clinton Presidential Campaigns and subsequently went to work at the Democratic National Committee in Washington, DC, soon after Bill Clinton was elected President. While in Washington, Darren worked at the Department of Commerce and the White House. He also served as the Chief of Staff in the International Affairs Office of the Department of Energy. Vivian worked as a political appointee at the U.S. Department of Agriculture in the Office of International Affairs and the White House during the Clinton Administration. They both continue to volunteer their time and support to the William J. Clinton Presidential Foundation.

 ## SEAFOOD CIOPPINO

2   (6.5-ounce) cans chopped clams
¼   cup olive oil
1¼ cups chopped onion
2   tablespoons chopped garlic
4   teaspoons oregano

2   cups crushed tomatoes
1   (8-ounce) can stewed tomatoes
2½ cups bottled clam juice
1   cup white wine

1   pound large shrimp, peeled and deveined
2   (6-ounce) cans crabmeat
½   cup fresh basil
    Salt and pepper to taste

Drain clams, reserving juice, and set aside. Heat oil in large saucepan or Dutch oven over medium heat. Sauté onion, garlic, and oregano about 8 to 10 minutes. Add drained clam juice, bottled clam juice, tomatoes, and white wine. Bring to a boil; cook 15 minutes. Add shrimp and crabmeat. Reduce heat and simmer 2 minutes. Add basil and season with salt and pepper to taste.

This dish is perfect for the winter time. Serve with a green salad, dinner rolls, and a glass of white wine.

Nina Planck grew up on a working farm in Virginia selling vegetables at farmers' markets. In 1999, when Nina was writing speeches for Philip Lader, then President Clinton's ambassador to Britain, she started the first farmers' markets in London. In Washington, DC, she founded the non-profit agency *Local Foods*. She is the author of *The Farmers' Market Cookbook* and director of Greenmarket in New York City.

SHRIMP WITH GARLIC

2-4 tablespoons olive oil	1-2 teaspoons dried red pepper flakes	Salt to taste
8-12 garlic cloves, peeled and cut into slivers	16 peeled shrimp	4 tablespoons sherry

Warm individual ceramic serving bowls in oven. Heat oil in large, heavy skillet over low heat and cook garlic and pepper flakes until garlic is half-cooked. Do not burn garlic. Add shrimp and cook, stirring constantly, until shrimp are no longer pink. Season with salt to taste. Add sherry and increase heat until liquid has reduced somewhat. Bring warm bowls and hot skillet to table immediately and serve hot with crusty bread.

Yield: 2 servings

This one is for garlic lovers. I found this recipe on a trip to the Canary Islands, where it's on every menu. With hot buttered grits and a side of greens, it's a great Southern meal.

MARINATED TUNA WITH FENNEL

½ cup balsamic vinegar
2 tablespoons rice wine vinegar
5 tablespoons olive oil, divided

2-4 garlic cloves, peeled and coarsely chopped
Salt and pepper to taste

2 tuna steaks, rinsed and patted dry
2 medium fennel bulbs, thinly sliced
2 teaspoons balsamic vinegar
Minced fennel leaves

Combine ½ cup balsamic vinegar, rice wine vinegar, 1 tablespoon olive oil, and garlic in shallow dish. Season with salt and pepper to taste. Place tuna in dish and marinate about 2 hours, turning at least once. Sauté fennel in 2 tablespoons olive oil until tender; keep warm and set aside. Combine 2 teaspoons balsamic vinegar and remaining 2 tablespoons olive oil in small bowl, mixing well. Season with salt and pepper to taste. Carefully lift tuna from marinade and sear briefly in hot skillet on both sides. Cook until pink in center if rare is preferred. Slice the tuna against the grain into long, thin strips. Place fennel on serving plate, top with tuna, and drizzle with balsamic vinegar dressing. Do not toss. Top with minced fennel leaves and serve warm.

The longer the tuna marinates, the faster it will cook; the acidic vinegar "cooks" the fish.

Now you know what to do with fennel, that white bulb with the texture of celery and flavor of mild licorice, when you bring it home from the farmers' market.

★ JOHN AND MARY PODESTA ★

John Podesta served as Chief of Staff to President Clinton from October of 1998 until January of 2001. Mr. Podesta first served in the Clinton Administration from January of 1993 to 1995 as Assistant to the President and Staff Secretary. In January of 1997, Mr. Podesta returned to the White House as an Assistant to the President and Deputy Chief of Staff. He is currently Visiting Professor of Law on the faculty of the Georgetown University Law Center. Mary S. Podesta, a Washington, DC, attorney is Senior Counsel in the International Legal Department at the Investment Company Institute, the mutual fund trade association. They have three children, all of whom know their way around the kitchen.

 **FRESH FRUIT WITH GRAPPA SAUCE**

FRUIT

2 grapefruits, peeled and sectioned	1-2 packages frozen raspberries, thawed and drained	1 cup red or green grapes, halved
2 oranges, peeled and sectioned		

In large glass serving bowl, combine fruit. Fruit mixture should equal 4 cups. Pour Grappa Sauce over fruit, tossing gently to coat. Chill 1 to 3 hours.

GRAPPA SAUCE

⅓ cup honey	⅓ cup grappa	1 tablespoon lemon juice

Whisk ingredients together and blend thoroughly.

Grappa is an Italian liquor now available at most liquor stores.

Raspberries may be substituted with 1 pint of stemmed and halved strawberries. Vary the fruits, selecting them for freshness and color.

★ JOHN AND MARY PODESTA ★

 ## Salsa di Noci (Walnut Sauce for Pasta)

¾ pound shelled walnuts
3 tablespoons olive oil
½ teaspoon pepper
1 cup canned tomatoes, drained, peeled, and chopped

½ cup butter
1 chicken bouillon cube
3 tablespoons freshly chopped basil
1 cup water

1 (16-ounce) package pasta, cooked al dente
½ cup Parmesan cheese

Finely chop walnuts in food processor almost to a paste. In large skillet over low heat, cook walnuts in olive oil until lightly browned, stirring occasionally. Add pepper and tomatoes; stir in butter and bouillon cube. Cook until butter melts and sauce has slightly thickened. Add basil and water. Reduce heat and simmer about 10 minutes or until thickened. Toss with pasta and sprinkle with Parmesan cheese.

★ SENATOR DAVID PRYOR AND BARBARA PRYOR ★

David Pryor's life is synonymous with politics, government, and public service. He was a member of the Arkansas State Legislature at 27, a Congressman, Governor, and U.S. Senator until his retirement in 1997. Senator Pryor served as Director of the Institute of Politics at the Kennedy School of Government at Harvard University from 2000 to 2002. He currently serves on the William J. Clinton Presidential Foundation's Board of Directors. His wife, Barbara, has been a strategic partner in his career. They have three sons and three grandchildren.

SCOTCH FUDGE CAKE

1	cup water	2	eggs	2	cups all-purpose flour
3	tablespoons cocoa	1	teaspoon baking soda	½	cup buttermilk
1	cup butter	1	teaspoon vanilla	1	teaspoon cinnamon
2	cups sugar				

In small saucepan over medium heat, combine water, cocoa, and butter, stirring until butter melts. In large mixing bowl, combine sugar and remaining cake ingredients, blending thoroughly. Add cocoa mixture to sugar mixture and beat well. Pour into prepared sheet cake pan and place on top oven rack. Bake for 25 minutes or until cake pulls away from sides.

ICING

½	cup butter	6	tablespoons milk	1	teaspoon vanilla
3	tablespoons cocoa	1	(16-ounce) package confectioners' sugar		Chopped nuts (optional)

In small saucepan over medium heat, combine butter, cocoa, and milk. Bring to a boil. Stir in confectioners' sugar and vanilla. Fold in nuts. Pour warm icing over cake.

This cake is an old family favorite and served on holidays and special occasions. It is included in our family cookbook, Perfectly Delicious, a collection of Susie Pryor's recipes.

★ POLLY RAGON ★

Polly Ragon raised her family in Fort Smith during the 60s and 70s. Utilizing the PTA network, she met Arkansas First Lady Betty Bumpers and assisted her in acquiring the hundreds of volunteers necessary for a statewide inoculation weekend, leading to the full immunization of Arkansas preschool children. Polly then went to Washington to serve on newly elected Senator Bumpers's staff. Even though retired, she continues to volunteer at the Clinton Presidential Foundation's office and enjoys keeping an eye on two gorgeous granddaughters.

CREAMY CARROT SOUP

1 medium onion, chopped	6 carrots, thinly sliced	1 tablespoon tomato paste
1-2 garlic cloves, minced	2 parsnips, thinly sliced	4 dashes hot sauce
1 tablespoon olive oil	½ teaspoon dried thyme	¼ cup nonfat plain yogurt
3 cups chicken broth	1 tablespoon freshly squeezed lemon juice	Salt and pepper to taste

In large saucepan over medium-high heat, sauté onion and garlic in olive oil 5 minutes. Add broth, carrots, parsnips, and thyme. Bring to a boil; reduce heat and simmer 30 minutes. Puree carrot mixture in blender until smooth. Return mixture to saucepan and reheat. Stir in lemon juice and remaining ingredients and serve.

This easy recipe may be prepared a day ahead and is a delicious first course, served hot or cold.

MEXICAN SOUP

½ cup chopped onion	4 cups chicken broth	1 (4.5-ounce) can chopped green chiles
1 garlic clove, minced	2 (8-ounce) cans tomato sauce	1 teaspoon cumin
1 tablespoon olive oil	1 (16-ounce) can diced, stewed tomatoes	½ teaspoon black pepper
3 medium zucchini, cut lengthwise and sliced	1 (12-ounce) can whole kernel corn, undrained	2-3 dashes hot sauce
		4 boneless, skinless chicken breasts, cooked and cubed

In large stockpot over medium-high heat, sauté onion and garlic in olive oil 3 to 5 minutes or until tender. Add zucchini and next 8 ingredients. Bring to a low boil, then add chicken. Cover and simmer 20 minutes. Top individual servings with shredded Cheddar or Monterey Jack cheese and serve with tortilla chips.

If a thicker soup is preferred, stir 4 tablespoons all-purpose flour into ½ cup cold water. Blend thoroughly and add to soup, stirring until soup thickens.

Jon Raney of Beebe, Arkansas, is a landscape architecture student at the University of Arkansas. During the summer months and on breaks from college, he has assisted with the landscaping design and planning for the William J. Clinton Presidential Center and Park.

 ## 30-MINUTE PO BOY MEXICAN CHICKEN

1 (14.5-ounce) can tomatoes with green chiles

1 (10¾-ounce) can cream of chicken soup

1 (10¾-ounce) can cream of mushroom soup

1 (10½-ounce) bag tortilla chips

2 cans chopped chicken, drained

2 cups shredded cheese

Preheat oven to 350°. In large mixing bowl, combine tomatoes and soups; set aside. Layer bottom of prepared casserole with chips. Spread half of chicken over chips. Pour half of soup mixture over chicken, spreading evenly. Sprinkle with half of cheese. Repeat layers. Bake for 20 to 30 minutes or until cheese melts.

★ HANNAH RICHERT ★

After graduating from the University of Kansas in 1992, Colorado native Hannah Richert moved to Washington, DC, to become involved in the Clinton Administration. She worked for Kansas congressman Dan Glickman, and when he became Secretary of Agriculture, she served as his Congressional Liaison. Subsequent work within the Clinton Administration included a position as Director of Special Projects for United States Ambassador to the United Nations, Richard Holbrooke. Hannah currently serves as Personal Assistant to President William J. Clinton in New York.

 ## COLORADO GREEN CHILI

1 onion, chopped	4 cups chicken broth	1 teaspoon dried oregano
1 jalapeño pepper, seeded and minced	2 (8-ounce) cans whole roasted green chilies, drained and cut into strips	Pinch of cayenne pepper
2 garlic cloves, minced		¼ cup cornstarch
1½ tablespoons olive oil, divided		¼ cup water
1 pound coarse ground pork	1 tablespoon cumin seed	Salt

In large, heavy skillet over medium heat, sauté onion, jalapeño, and garlic in 1 tablespoon olive oil until tender. Transfer mixture to stockpot or Dutch oven. In same skillet, sauté pork in remaining ½ tablespoon olive oil, stirring until no longer pink. Transfer pork to stockpot. Add chicken broth and simmer over very low heat about 1 hour, stirring occasionally. Add chilies, cumin seed, oregano, and cayenne pepper. Simmer 15 to 30 minutes. Dissolve cornstarch in water, stirring until smooth. Add slowly to stockpot, stirring to blend. Increase heat and continue to cook, stirring until chili thickens. Add salt to taste and additional spices if desired. Serve hot with flour tortillas and topped with shredded cheese. Colorado Green Chili may also be served over bean burritos.

Yield: 4 servings

Exercise caution when handling jalapeño peppers. Wear rubber gloves to prevent burning the skin and keep hands away from eyes. If thicker chili is preferred, add more cornstarch and water mixture to stockpot.

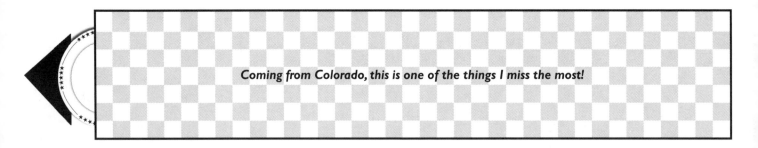

Coming from Colorado, this is one of the things I miss the most!

★ SECRETARY RICHARD RILEY AND TUNKY RILEY ★

Richard W. Riley is the former U.S. Secretary of Education (1993-2001) and former Governor of South Carolina (1979-1987). He is currently a senior partner in the law firm of Nelson Mullins Riley & Scarborough, LLP, with offices throughout South Carolina and North Carolina, as well as in Atlanta. Ann "Tunky" Yarborough Riley is a prolific volunteer and community activist. She and Richard are the proud parents of four children and grandparents of thirteen grandchildren.

 ## ARMENIAN CHICKEN AND LENTIL SOUP WITH DRIED APRICOTS

1 onion, finely chopped	2 teaspoons paprika	12 cups chicken stock
3 garlic cloves, finely chopped	1 teaspoon ground mace	½ cup minced dried apricots
1½ tablespoons sesame seeds	1 teaspoon cayenne pepper	2 cups shredded cooked chicken
2 teaspoons ground coriander	3 tablespoons olive oil	½ cup lemon juice
2 teaspoons cumin	1 cup dried red lentils, sorted and washed	Salt and pepper to taste

In heavy 6-quart saucepan over medium heat, cook onion and next 7 ingredients in olive oil 5 to 7 minutes, stirring frequently. Add lentils, chicken stock, and apricots; increase heat and bring to a boil. Add chicken and lemon juice; cook 5 minutes. Season with salt and pepper to taste. Serve hot with traditional Armenian flatbread.

If you can't find red lentils, try the traditional brown ones—but they'll make the soup a lot heartier.

Yield: 10 servings

★ MR. AND MRS. DOYLE ROGERS ★

Doyle Rogers, Chairman and President of the Doyle Rogers Company, also serves as Chairman of the Board of Metropolitan National Bank. He is one of Arkansas's most prominent business and civic leaders. At his side is Mrs. Raye Rogers, who has developed her own reputation as decorator, humanitarian, and civic activist. She was recently named a Woman of Distinction by Florence Crittendon Services.

 ## SALMON NOODLES ROMANOFF

1 (8-ounce) package medium noodles, cooked and drained	½ cup finely chopped onion	½ teaspoon salt
1½ cups cottage cheese	1 garlic clove, minced	1 (16-ounce) can salmon, drained
1½ cups sour cream	1-2 teaspoons Worcestershire sauce	½ cup shredded sharp Cheddar cheese
	Dash of hot sauce or cayenne pepper	

Preheat oven to 325°. In large mixing bowl, gently combine noodles and next 8 ingredients. Place 1 cup salmon mixture into 6 prepared ramekins. Sprinkle with cheese. Bake uncovered for 20 to 25 minutes. Garnish each serving with a lemon twist.

Yield: 6 servings

This casserole may be baked in a prepared 2-quart casserole. Bake for 40 minutes.
Two (6½-ounce) cans of tuna may be substituted for salmon.
To make a lemon twist garnish, cut slightly more than halfway into a thin lemon slice, then twist.

 ## CHEESE STRAWS

1 cup butter, softened	1 teaspoon salt	1 pound shredded sharp Cheddar cheese
2½ cups sifted all-purpose flour	1-2 teaspoons cayenne pepper	

Preheat oven to 325°. In large mixing bowl, combine butter and remaining ingredients. Knead mixture to blend thoroughly. Squeeze mixture through cookie press in 2-inch strips onto baking sheet covered with waxed paper. Bake 12 to 15 minutes or until straws begin to brown slightly.

★ AVIVA AND DAN ROSENTHAL ★

Dan Rosenthal was Assistant to the President and Director of Advance at the White House and began working for President and Senator Clinton during the 1992 campaign. He worked at USAID and the Department of Commerce before coming to the White House in 1995. Dan now oversees Strategic Alliances and International Business Development for United Online, a leading Internet service provider based in the Los Angeles area. Dan, his wife Aviva, and their daughter Sadie live in Pacific Palisades, California.

Aviva Steinberg Rosenthal was a Special Assistant to the President and Deputy Director of Presidential Scheduling at the White House. She also worked briefly as a scheduler in the Office of the First Lady and was a lead advance person for President Clinton during the 1996 reelection campaign. Aviva now works as an independent consultant and is overseeing the "Declaration of Independence Roadtrip", a three year national tour of one of the original copies of the Declaration of Independence.

 **BABA GHANOUSH**

3 large eggplants	3 tablespoons low fat mayonnaise	Olive oil
1½ tablespoons minced garlic	1 tablespoon freshly squeezed lemon juice	Salt and pepper to taste
1 onion, chopped		Parsley or cilantro
		Paprika

Pierce holes in eggplant skins with fork or knife. Slice eggplant in half lengthwise. Roast on grill, under hot broiler, or over open stove flame about 10 minutes per side or until flesh is soft and skin is charred. Allow to cool. Scoop out pulp with large spoon. Be sure to include charred pulp near skin since it has the best flavor. Transfer pulp to blender or food processor. Add garlic, onion, mayonnaise, and lemon juice. Briefly process. Add small amount of olive oil and season with salt and pepper to taste. Process until semi-smooth. Chill until ready to serve. To serve, spread mixture on small plate in circular pattern. Drizzle with olive oil, sprinkle with parsley or cilantro, and top with a sprinkle of paprika. Serve with warm pita bread.

A traditional Middle Eastern dish, it is usually served as an appetizer or salad course, but it can also be used as a sandwich spread. This recipe substitutes low fat mayonnaise for the tahini (sesame paste) usually used in the delicious Baba Ghanoush found in the Middle East, so we feel less guilty when we can't stop eating it!

★ PHILIP J. ROSS ★

Philip Ross is President of the Bill Clinton Political Items Collectors.

 ## MY MOTHER'S CRANBERRY ORANGE SALAD

1 (3-ounce) package orange flavored gelatin	1½ cups boiling water	½ cup chopped celery
	1 (14-ounce) jar cranberry orange relish	½ cup chopped pecans

In large mixing bowl, combine gelatin and boiling water, stirring until gelatin dissolves. Chill until slightly thickened. Fold in relish, celery, and pecans. Pour into prepared 1-quart gelatin mold and chill until firm.

Wrap a dishtowel soaked in hot water around the bottom of the gelatin mold, and leave it there for several minutes. Invert onto serving platter, and the gelatin should come out of the mold smoothly with just a few taps.

Cranberry orange relish can be a little challenging to find when it's not Thanksgiving, so we buy extra during the holiday and use it throughout the year. This molded salad is an excellent substitute for "straight" cranberry sauce at the Thanksgiving table. In addition, it's an excellent relish to accompany chicken or turkey any time of the year. My mother shared this recipe when my wife had to make her first Thanksgiving dinner. She loves the recipe because it's very forgiving. You may change it in many ways, and it always tastes great. My mother passed away in 1987, but her recipe continues to please family and friends alike.

★ BETTY RUTHERFORD ★

Betty Rutherford of Batesville, Arkansas, celebrated her 105th birthday on May 4, 2003. For most of her adult life, the White River Water Carnival Parade passed her home on Batesville's historic Main Street. Through the years, she has greeted and welcomed numerous Arkansas public figures including Governor Bill Clinton.

 ## APRICOT ICE

2	tablespoons all-purpose flour	4	cups water	2	egg whites, stiffly beaten
3	cups sugar	1	can apricots, drained and chopped		

In large mixing bowl, combine flour and sugar. In large saucepan over high heat, combine flour mixture and water. Bring to a boil and set aside to cool completely. When cool, stir in apricots; fold in egg whites. Pour mixture into glass casserole and freeze.

This recipe originally appeared in a cookbook I edited over 65 years ago. Enjoy! I am honored to be the oldest person in this cookbook.

★ BILLIE AND SKIP RUTHERFORD ★

Billie Rutherford of Little Rock works at Catering To You, a catering, gourmet food, and gift store. Her salad, a very popular item on the menu, has been enjoyed by President Clinton on several occasions. Billie met President Clinton when both worked on Judge Frank Holt's 1966 Arkansas gubernatorial campaign.

Skip Rutherford is the President of the William J. Clinton Presidential Foundation and is coordinating the planning for the Clinton Presidential Center and Park. He is also executive vice president of Cranford Johnson Robinson Woods. In 1992, he was a strategist and senior advisor for the Clinton/Gore Campaign and was one of six Arkansans who cast the state's electoral votes for the Clinton/Gore ticket. The Rutherfords have three children.

 ## BILLIE'S SALAD

Assorted field greens
Leaf Lettuce, torn
Mandarin orange sections
Red bell pepper, seeded and chopped

Purple onion, chopped
Artichoke hearts, quartered and halved
Toasted almonds

Crumbled bacon
Grilled chicken, chopped
Blush Wine Vinaigrette

In large salad bowl, combine greens and next 8 ingredients. Drizzle with vinaigrette, tossing well to coat.
Strawberries, pears, or any other fruit may be substituted for mandarin oranges. Anything else that sounds good may be added!

This is a great main meal or salad. Just add bread and dessert, and you are set!

★ WARWICK SABIN ★

Warwick Sabin is the Director of Special Projects for the William J. Clinton Presidential Foundation in Little Rock, Arkansas. A former Communications Director for U.S. Representative Marion Berry (AR-01) in Washington, DC, he was selected as a 1998 Marshall Scholar, and earned an M.A. (Oxon) in Philosophy, Politics and Economics at Oxford University in 2000. During his time in England, he was the speechwriter to U.S. Ambassador Philip Lader. Before that, he held internships at *Foreign Affairs* magazine in New York City and the White House.

BURGER MADNESS

2 hamburgers	Green bell pepper, seeded and sliced	Hoagie roll
Bacon slices	Red bell pepper, seeded and sliced	Mayonnaise
Onion slices	American cheese slices	Lettuce leaves
		Tomato slices

The folks at Wisemillers would cook the hamburgers, bacon, onions, and peppers on their griddle. When the hamburgers are done, chop them back to the consistency of ground meat. Also chop the bacon into small pieces. Combine the bacon and burger meat and top with cheese, allowing it to melt gently. Toast the hoagie roll lightly and spread with mayonnaise. Place the meat and cheese mixture on the bun along with the onions and peppers. Add lettuce and tomato.

Yield: 1 serving

The owner of Wisemillers would not give me the exact measurements and proportions, but he was kind enough to share the ingredients. The cooking procedure is based on my memory of it.

I spent three summers in Washington, DC, working for the Clinton Administration. After my freshman year of college, I interned at the White House for Deputy Chief of Staff Harold Ickes. In 1996, I was an intern for Craig Smith, who was the Deputy Campaign Manager and Political Director at Clinton/Gore '96 Headquarters. Then I returned to the White House in 1998 to do an internship with Thomas F. "Mack" McLarty, who was Special Envoy to the Americas at the time.

As a White House intern, I remember being extremely busy, and since the position was unpaid, I didn't have a lot of spending money. For both of those reasons, I often never enjoyed a real lunch. Instead, I would periodically walk over to the West Wing Mess and take handfuls of the crackers that were on offer at the take-away window.

Ultimately my culinary experiences as an intern in Washington were limited to the staples of a college student: pizza, sandwiches, and Chinese delivery food. There is one item in particular that always will remind me of those days: Burger Madness. It is the signature sandwich of Wisemillers Grocery & Deli, which was only a short walk from the small Georgetown townhouse I once shared with four other people.

Burger Madness. The name may derive from the fact that because this sandwich tastes so good, it drives you crazy with delight. But it aslo may serve as a health risk. Eat at your own risk.

★ SHIRLEY SAGAWA ★

Shirley Sagawa served as Deputy Chief of Staff to First Lady Hillary Clinton, advising the First Lady on domestic policy and leading the planning for White House Conferences on Philanthropy, Partnerships in Philanthropy, and Teenagers. She was instrumental to the drafting and passage of legislation creating the Corporation for National Service.

photo courtesy of Katherine Lambert

LEMON CHESS PIE

FILLING

½ cup butter, softened	1 tablespoon all-purpose flour	Juice of 4 lemons
2 cups sugar	6 eggs, well beaten	1 tablespoon lemon zest

Preheat oven to 325°. In large mixing bowl, cream together butter and sugar with electric mixer on medium speed. Add flour, mixing well. Add eggs, blending thoroughly. Add lemon juice and zest. Mix well and pour into pie shells. Bake for 30 to 40 minutes or until golden brown and set. Cool and serve with frozen whipped topping.

CRUST

2 cups all-purpose flour	1 cup shortening, softened
1 teaspoon salt	⅓ cup sour milk

Process flour and salt in food processor. Add shortening and pulse until mixture is the consistency of coarse cornmeal. Add sour milk a little at a time, pulsing and checking consistency until it starts to form a ball. Do not overmix. Roll out half of dough and gently press into 9-inch pie plate. Trim excess crust off of edges. Repeat process with remaining dough.

Yield: 2 pies

Carolyn Schaufele met President Clinton through her husband Louis. Louis, a banker, handled the Clintons' personal business and worked with his gubernatorial and presidential campaigns. As governor, Clinton appointed Carolyn to the Governor's Mansion Board, a non-profit group that works to beautify, restore, and improve the Arkansas Governor's Mansion. She continues to serve on it today.

 ## SAUSAGE DRESSING FOR TURKEY

¾	cup chopped onion	1	pound hot pork sausage	1	tablespoon black pepper
¾	cup chopped celery	1	pound mild pork sausage	1	teaspoon salt
2	tablespoons butter	12	slices bread, toasted, buttered, and cubed	¾	cup water

In large skillet over medium-high heat, sauté onion and celery in butter. Add sausages and cook until no longer pink and crumble. Add bread cubes, pepper, and salt; mix well. Stir in water until moist. Stuff inside buttered turkey and bake according to turkey's directions.

Sausage Dressing may also be baked in prepared casserole at 350° for 30 to 45 minutes, or use to stuff fresh mushrooms before baking.

This is an old family recipe that everyone loves—a little hot, but not too spicy.

★ MIKE AND MARTY SCHAUFELE ★

Mike Schaufele met then-Governor Clinton in the early 80s through his wife Marty, who knew him through Senator Clinton. Mike and President Clinton share a love for golf and have enjoyed many rounds together. The Schaufeles have remained friends with the Clintons over the years and were quite honored to visit them in the White House.

HEARTS OF PALM SPREAD

1 (14-ounce) can hearts of palm, drained and chopped	¾ cup mayonnaise or salad dressing	¼ cup sour cream
1 cup shredded mozzarella cheese	½ cup shredded Parmesan cheese	2 tablespoons minced green onion

In large mixing bowl, combine hearts of palm and remaining ingredients. Spoon into lightly greased 9-inch quiche dish. Bake at 350° for 20 minutes or until bubbly. Serve with crackers.

Yield: 2 cups

This is great and so easy if you are in a hurry.

CHICKEN SUZANNE

4-6 chicken breasts	½ cup sour cream	1 (10¾-ounce) can cream of mushroom soup
Salt and pepper to taste	½ cup sherry	Shredded Parmesan cheese
½ cup butter		

Season chicken with salt and pepper to taste. In large skillet over medium-high heat, melt butter and brown chicken on both sides. Transfer chicken to shallow casserole and set aside. Add sour cream, sherry, and soup to skillet and cook over medium heat, mixing well. Pour over chicken. Sprinkle with Parmesan cheese. Cover and bake for 1 hour, 30 minutes or until chicken is done.

Yield: 4 to 6 servings

Sliced mushrooms may be added for a richer entrée.
This is an elegant, easy dish to serve when company shows up. They'll think you've been cooking all day.

★ ARTHUR AND JOYCE SCHECHTER ★

Arthur Schechter served President Clinton as Ambassador to the Commonwealth of the Bahamas from 1998 until 2001. He was the Texas Finance Chair in the 1996 campaign and the Co-Chair in 1992. He and his wife Joyce participate in many philanthropic events in the Houston area. They have two adult daughters and five grandchildren.

 **CHOPPED LIVER PÂTÉ**

1	pound calf liver	1	teaspoon garlic powder	2	tablespoons mayonnaise
1	onion, sliced		Salt and pepper to taste		Paprika
	Butter	3	hard-cooked eggs		Freshly chopped parsley

In large skillet over medium-high heat, sauté liver and onion in butter. Add garlic powder; season with salt and pepper to taste. Transfer liver and onion to food processor. Add eggs and mayonnaise; process until smooth. Pour mixture into decorative mold and chill. Invert mold onto serving platter and sprinkle pâté with paprika and parsley. Serve with rye bread. *Delicious!*

★ DEBRA SCHIFF ★

In the Clinton Administration, Debra Schiff served as the Assistant Chief of Protocol in the Department of State. Prior to that, she worked in the West Wing as a member of the Oval Office Operations staff. She is currently the Vice President of Development at Ovations, a special event production firm.

 ## HALIBUT PUTTANESCA

1 onion, chopped	3 tablespoons capers, rinsed and drained	4 (6 to 8-ounce) halibut filets
2 garlic cloves, minced		Kosher salt to taste
Olive oil	1 teaspoon fresh rosemary, chopped	Freshly ground black pepper
1 (28-ounce) can diced tomatoes	1 teaspoon fresh oregano, chopped	3 anchovy filets, minced
½ cup black olives, pitted and sliced	Pinch of red pepper flakes	2 tablespoons flat leaf parsley, chopped

In large saucepan over medium-high heat, sauté onion and garlic in olive oil until tender. Add tomatoes and next 5 ingredients. Sauté 5 minutes or until liquid reduces slightly. Remove from heat and set aside. Preheat grill. Season halibut with salt and pepper to taste. Grill halibut skin side down 8 to 10 minutes; turn and cook additional 5 to 8 minutes or until done. Transfer halibut to individual serving plates. Reheat sauce and simmer. Stir in anchovies and parsley. Spoon sauce over each halibut and serve immediately.

Yield: 4 servings

Anchovy filets may be substituted with 1 teaspoon anchovy paste.
The halibut may also be prepared in a well-oiled nonstick skillet over medium-high heat, cooking 5 minutes per side.

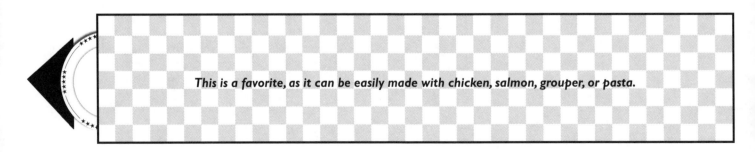

This is a favorite, as it can be easily made with chicken, salmon, grouper, or pasta.

★ KARLA CLINTON SEARCY ★

Karla Clinton Searcy was born and raised in Hot Springs and is one of President Clinton's first cousins. She is the daughter of the late Raymond and Mary Selma Clinton. Karla moved to Portland, Oregon, with husband Larry and daughters Sandy and Mary Karla ("Muffin") in 1972. She was proud to work in her cousin's campaigns in Hot Springs and throughout Oregon. Karla enjoys cooking and sharing recipes with daughter Sandy, who just started *"Tray Chic"*, a catering business, in Portland. Although she lives in Oregon, Karla's heart will always be in Hot Springs. Karla is a proud grandmother of four.

 ## PORK AND PEPPERS WITH FETTUCCINI

2   pork tenderloins
    All-purpose flour
1   cup butter, divided
6   yellow onions, peeled and quartered

6   bell peppers, seeded and cut into squares
1   (10½-ounce) can chicken broth
¾   cup dry sherry
2   tablespoons cornstarch or arrowroot

1   cup water
    Freshly shredded Parmesan cheese
1   (12-ounce) package fettuccini noodles, cooked and drained
    Garlic salt

Rinse tenderloins and wrap separately in plastic wrap. Freeze until just hard enough to slice. Slice tenderloins thinly. Place flour in shallow dish. Dredge pork slices in flour and set aside. Melt ⅓ cup butter in large skillet over medium-high heat. Add onion and bell pepper, sautéing until tender. Drain, transfer onion and bell pepper to mixing bowl, and set aside. Place pork slices in single layer in same skillet. Brown each side then set aside, continuing process until all pork slices are browned. Place pork in Dutch oven. Pour chicken broth and sherry over pork. Simmer and stir occasionally as liquid reduces. Stir in onion and bell pepper. In small mixing bowl, dissolve cornstarch or arrowroot in water and stir until smooth. Add to pork, stirring gently, until thickened. Transfer to prepared 9x13-inch baking pan. Sprinkle with Parmesan. Bake at 350° for 20 to 30 minutes or until bubbly. Gently toss noodles with remaining butter and sprinkle with garlic salt. Serve with pork and sauce on the side.

Serve with a salad and garlic-Parmesan bread.

BARBARA NICHOLS'S BLUE CHEESE DIP AND SPREAD

1 (8-ounce) bottle blue cheese dressing
1 (8-ounce) package cream cheese, softened
1 teaspoon creamy horseradish
1 teaspoon Worcestershire sauce
1 teaspoon lemon juice
2 cups mayonnaise-style salad dressing
6 ounces blue cheese, crumbled and divided

In large mixing bowl, combine dressing and next 5 ingredients; add half of blue cheese. Beat with electric mixer on medium speed until thoroughly blended. Fold in remaining blue cheese. Cover tightly and chill. Serve with crackers or use as a spread for burgers and sandwiches.

This dip may also be used as a salad dressing.

Barbara Nichols had to quit making this for my granddad-he'd eat so much of it, he'd make himself sick!

Jonathan Semans is the Program Manager for the William J. Clinton Presidential Center and Park.

 ## Mom's Family Favorite or Ragoût of Veal or Pork

2	pounds boneless veal or pork stew meat	1 onion, minced
¼	teaspoon thyme	3-4 parsley sprigs
5-6	black peppercorns	1 bay leaf
1	garlic clove	½ cup dry white wine

2 pounds boneless veal or pork stew meat
¼ teaspoon thyme
5-6 black peppercorns
1 garlic clove

1 onion, minced
3-4 parsley sprigs
1 bay leaf
½ cup dry white wine
1 (14-ounce) can chicken broth

6-12 small boiling onions (optional)
1 cup crème fraîche or whipping cream
Salt to taste
Lemon juice

In 3 or 4-quart saucepan over medium heat, combine meat and next 6 ingredients. Cover and cook 30 minutes, stirring occasionally. Add wine and broth. Cover, reduce heat, and simmer gently about 1 hour or until meat is tender when pierced. Add boiling onions after 30 minutes if desired. With slotted spoon, remove meat and boiling onions and set aside. Remove and discard peppercorns, garlic, parsley, and bay leaf. Add crème fraîche to saucepan and bring to a rapid boil or until large bubbles form and sauce thickens (about 7 to 10 minutes). Return meat and boiling onions to saucepan. Season to taste with salt and lemon juice.

Yield: 6 servings

This dish may be prepared ahead up to 2 days and refrigerated. To reheat, add broth if needed.

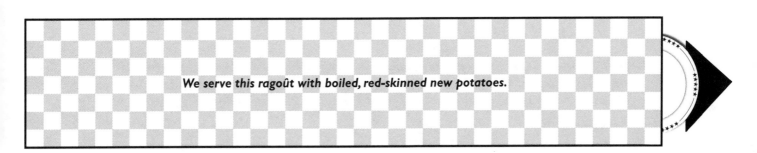

We serve this ragout with boiled, red-skinned new potatoes.

★ LOTTIE SHACKELFORD ★

Lottie Shackelford was appointed to the Board of Directors of the Overseas Private Investment Corporation by President Clinton in 1993 after having held positions in his Presidential campaign and the Democratic Party. She was elected to the Little Rock Board of Directors in 1978 and was the first woman to be elected Mayor of Little Rock in 1987. Currently, she is the Vice Chair of the Democratic National Committee. Lottie has three adult children and six grandchildren.

 ## SQUASH CASSEROLE

2 pounds yellow squash, sliced
1 onion, sliced
½ cup butter

2 eggs, beaten
1 cup breadcrumbs
1½ cups shredded cheese, divided

Salt and pepper to taste
1 cup crushed round buttery crackers

Preheat oven to 350°. In large saucepan over medium-high heat, cook squash and onion in small amount of water until tender. Stir in butter and eggs. Stir in breadcrumbs and 1 cup cheese. Season with salt and pepper to taste. Transfer squash mixture to ungreased casserole and bake for 30 minutes. Remove from oven and sprinkle with cracker crumbs and remaining cheese. Bake for additional 10 minutes or until brown on top.

This dish is even good for those who are not big squash lovers. The cheese and crackers give great flavor to the otherwise bland taste of the squash. Bright yellow crooked neck squash is recommended, but any type of squash may be used. A quick and easy vegetable-your grandchildren will ask for seconds!

★ SECRETARY DONNA E. SHALALA ★

President Clinton appointed Donna E. Shalala as Secretary of Health and Human Services, where she served for eight years, becoming the longest serving HHS Secretary in U.S. History. A distinguished scholar of public policies, she is currently the President of the University of Miami. She has a host of honorary degrees and honors, including the Boys and Girls Club Person of the Year (2002), the 1992 National Public Service Award, and the 1994 Glamour magazine Woman of the Year Award.

 ## TABBOULEH À LA SHALALA

1   cup fine cracked wheat
    Juice of 5 to 6 lemons (about 1 cup)
2   cups freshly chopped Italian
    parsley leaves, patted dry

1½ cups freshly chopped mint leaves,
    patted dry
1   cup seeded, chopped tomato, well
    drained

3   bunches green onions, trimmed
    and sliced
1   tablespoon extra virgin olive oil
    Salt to taste
    Freshly ground pepper to taste

Soak wheat in lemon juice overnight. Squeeze all liquid from soaked wheat and place in serving bowl; discard juice. Add parsley, mint, tomato, and green onions. Drizzle with oil and toss well. Season with salt and pepper to taste.

Yield: 4 to 6 servings

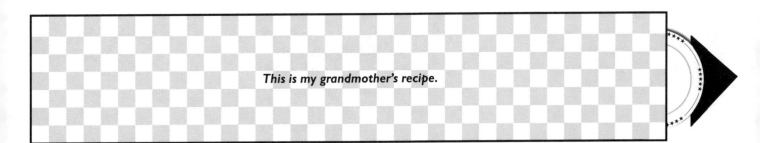

This is my grandmother's recipe.

★ STANLEY SHUMAN ★

Stanley S. Shuman is a Managing Director of Allen & Company LLC. He served on President Clinton's Foreign Intelligence Advisory Board from 1995 until 2001. He is married to Sydney Roberts Shuman, and they each have two sons, David and Michael Shuman, and Gordon and Howard Gould. They reside in New York City. Shuman is a supporter of The William J. Clinton Presidental Foundation.

MR. AND MRS. STANLEY S. SHUMAN'S PRALINE SOUFFLÉ WITH RASPBERRY SAUCE FROM GLORIOUS FOOD OF NEW YORK

PRALINE POWDER

Cooking oil
½ cup sugar
¼ cup water
½ cup chopped walnuts or pecans

Brush baking sheet with cooking oil, wiping excess with paper towel. In heavy saucepan over medium heat, combine sugar and water, stirring with wooden spoon until sugar dissolves. When sugar begins to turn golden, rotate saucepan to ensure uniform color. (Caramel burns quickly, so watch carefully.) When sugar mixture begins to turn amber, fold in nuts and immediately pour a thin layer of mixture onto baking sheet. Cool completely. Break up praline and place in batches in food processor. Process until praline becomes a fine powder. (There should be about 1¼ cups.) Reserve ½ cup Praline Powder. Store remaining powder in tightly sealed container for later use.

SOUFFLÉ

Unsalted butter for greasing
Sugar for dusting
1¼ cups egg whites at room temperature (about 8 egg whites)
Pinch of salt
⅓ cup superfine sugar
⅛ teaspoon cream of tartar
½ cup Praline Powder
2 cups heavy cream, whipped
1½ cups raspberry sauce
1 cup fresh raspberries

Preheat oven to 350°. Butter and sugar 2-quart soufflé dish. In large mixing bowl, beat egg whites with a pinch of salt until frothy. Gradually beat in superfine sugar until stiff peaks form, then add cream of tartar. Fold in reserved Praline Powder. Pour mixture into soufflé dish. Place dish in roasting pan on center rack of oven. Pour boiling water into pan until it reaches half way up sides of soufflé dish. Bake for 40 minutes. Remove soufflé from water bath and transfer to cooling rack. Run a sharp paring knife carefully around sides of soufflé to loosen outside edges. Soufflé will collapse as it cools. When soufflé cools, place serving platter upside down over dish and invert soufflé. Leave alone until ready to assemble dessert. Spoon whipping cream into pastry bag fitted with star tube. Remove dish and pipe cream around sides of soufflé to form a border high enough to hold a light coating of raspberry sauce on top. Pour raspberry sauce over soufflé. Garnish with fresh raspberries.

Linda Sinoway worked on the National Health Care Campaign in 1993-1994 and in the political and interactive media divisions of the Democratic National Committee from 1995 to 1999. In early 2000, Ms. Sinoway joined the Office of Communications at the White House as the Manager of Internet Communications. She lives on Capitol Hill with her husband Doug Kelly and son Jack, where she is a full-time mom and part-time real estate agent.

 ## THE BEST NOODLE KUGEL EVER

½ cup butter, melted	4 eggs	2 tablespoons butter
1 (8-ounced) package cream cheese, softened	2 cups milk	2 cups corn flakes
½-1 cup sugar	1 teaspoon vanilla	Sugar
	1 (12-ounce) package broad noodles, cooked and drained	Cinnamon

In large mixing bowl, beat together melted butter and cream cheese with electric mixer on medium-high speed. Add sugar, eggs, milk, and vanilla. Beat until smooth. Fold in noodles and chill overnight. Preheat oven to 350°. Melt and spread 2 tablespoons butter in 9x13-inch baking dish. Place noodle mixture in dish and top with corn flakes. Sprinkle with sugar and cinnamon. Bake for 1 hour, 15 minutes. Allow to cool and firm at least 15 minutes. Cut into squares and enjoy!

This recipe is the perfect side dish for dinner or brunch. Don't count on having leftovers!

★ CRAIG SMITH ★

Craig Smith is currently the Senior Vice President at mCaptiol Management. Smith served as Assistant to President Clinton and White House Political Director, coordinating the political activities of the President and First Lady. Smith previously served as Deputy Director of White House Personnel, where he developed and oversaw employment placement programs for political appointees. He later served as Deputy White House Political Director, coordinating state-by-state political activities on behalf of the President. Mr. Smith also served as Co-Executive Director of the 53rd Presidential Inaugural.

 ## CRAIG'S ARKANSAS SALSA

1 (32-ounce) can whole peeled tomatoes	1 dash lemon juice	1 teaspoon pepper
½-1 jalapeño pepper, seeded	1 tablespoon salt	½ garlic clove
	1 small onion	

Place ingredients in blender or food processor. Process until liquefied and chill. Serve with tortilla chips.

During the early days of the 1992 campaign, I would have staff parties at my house to provide staff, especially those not from Arkansas, a form of entertainment outside of work. Generally, by the time people arrived, everyone was tired and hungry and therefore, I had very little time to prepare. I used this recipe often when various campaign vagabonds would show up on short notice.

Mary Smith worked on the Clinton/Gore 1996 campaign and the Inaugural Committee. From 1997 to 2000, Ms. Smith was Associate Director of Policy Planning in the White House Domestic Policy Council. From 2000 to 2001, she was Associate Counsel to the President in the Office of White House Counsel. Currently, Ms. Smith is practicing law at Skadden, Arps, Slat, Meagher & Flom LLP in Washington, DC.

 **ARANCINI**

1 onion, thinly sliced	½ cup raisins, plumped in hot water and drained	½ cup Parmesan cheese
3 pounds ground beef		½ cup butter
1 (6-ounce) can tomato paste	¼ teaspoon cinnamon	All-purpose flour
1½ cups water	¼ cup pistachio nuts	4 eggs, well beaten
½ teaspoon pepper, divided	2 tablespoons cooking oil	Breadcrumbs
1 teaspoon salt	1 (2-pound) package rice	Cooking oil

In large skillet over medium-high heat, brown onion and ground beef until done. Add tomato paste and cook 5 additional minutes. Add water, ¼ teaspoon pepper, and next 5 ingredients. Taste and adjust seasonings if necessary. Mix well and remove from heat. Allow to cool 15 minutes. Cook rice in salted boiling water until almost done. Drain well and mix in cheese, butter, and pepper. Form rice mixture into balls the size of an orange, placing 1 tablespoon meat mixture in center of each rice ball. (There will be meat mixture left over.) Roll balls in the following order: flour, beaten eggs, and breadcrumbs. Heat cooking oil in deep fryer. Place rice balls in fryer and cook until brown. Heat remaining meat mixture and serve as gravy over rice balls.

My grandmother, "Nana" as we called her, used to make these arancini, or rice balls, for the Feast of St. Joseph on March 19-a kind of Italian St. Patrick's Day. The tradition of St. Joseph's Day began when there was a drought in Sicily in the Middle Ages. The people prayed to St. Joseph for rain and promised to prepare a big feast in his honor if he would intervene. According to tradition, the rains came, and the people prepared a big public banquet in gratitude. Poor people were invited to come and eat as much as they wanted. Today, many churches hold St. Joseph's banquets, and arancini is one of the traditional foods served on these "St. Joseph's tables".

★ MARTHA SNELLBACK ★

Martha "Marty" Snellback volunteers her time for the William J. Clinton Presidential Foundation. She resides in Lonsdale, Arkansas, with her husband, Steve, and her two daughters, Taylor and Alana.

 ## REALLY, REALLY GOOD LASAGNA

1	pound ground beef	1	bell pepper, seeded and finely chopped	¼	cup butter
1	jar chunky garden style spaghetti sauce	1	onion, finely chopped	1	(16-ounce) container cottage cheese
2	cans roasted garlic spaghetti sauce	1	can mushrooms, drained	2	pounds shredded mozzarella cheese
				1	package lasagna noodles, cooked al dente

In large skillet over medium-high heat, brown beef. Drain beef and transfer to large saucepan or Dutch oven. Add spaghetti sauces. In same skillet, sauté bell pepper, onion, and mushrooms in butter until tender. Add to sauce. Simmer 1 hour, stirring frequently. In mixing bowl, combine cheeses. Layer ⅓ noodles, ⅓ sauce, and ⅓ cheese in prepared baking dish. Repeat process twice. Bake at 350° for 45 minutes or until golden brown.

Sean Sonta, from Sayreville, New Jersey, served as an intern in the Little Rock office of the William J. Clinton Presidential Foundation during the summer of 2003. He is a senior political science major with a pre-law concentration at Lyon College in Batesville, Arkansas. Sean had the honor of writing his way into history by signing over 5,000 names, all supporters of President Clinton, to the last steel beam which completed the internal skeleton of the Presidential Library. The beam was lifted into place at the Topping Out Ceremony held on May 23, 2003, with over 2,500 people in attendance. Sean plans to attend law school and enter politics.

 SEAN'S SIGNATURE RIGATONI

Extra virgin olive oil	Salt	1 (28-ounce) can tomato puree
Garlic powder	Black pepper	1-2 packages hot Italian sausage
Onion powder	Crushed red pepper	2 tablespoons salt
Onion salt	3 garlic cloves, thinly sliced and divided	2 packages rigatoni
Basil	2 (28-ounce) cans crushed tomatoes	4 cups shredded mozzarella cheese, divided
Oregano	1 (28-ounce) can diced tomatoes	2 small containers ricotta cheese

Cover bottom of Dutch oven with olive oil. Season with garlic powder and next 7 ingredients. Sauté half of garlic in seasoned oil over medium-high heat about 30 to 45 seconds. Add tomatoes and puree and season with additional spices to taste. Cover, reduce heat to medium-low, and cook 10 minutes, stirring occasionally. Reduce heat and simmer until ready to serve. Cover bottom of skillet with olive oil. Season with spices and sauté remaining garlic over medium-high heat about 30 to 45 seconds. Fill skillet halfway with water. Place sausage links in skillet and lightly season with additional spices. Cover and cook until water reduces. Fill skillet halfway with water and cook until water reduces. Repeat once more. Split sausages lengthwise and turn over. Fill skillet halfway with water and cook until water reduces. Repeat twice. Cut two sausages in half. Place cut sausages and pan juices in tomato sauce. Set remaining sausages aside until ready to serve. Preheat oven to 350°. Fill large saucepan halfway with water and add salt. Bring to a boil; add pasta and cook 2 minutes. About 30 seconds before draining pasta, cover bottom of 16⅝x11⅞x2⅝-inch baking pan with tomato sauce. Drain pasta and transfer to baking pan. Sprinkle 2½ cups mozzarella cheese evenly over pasta. Pour ⅓ of tomato sauce over mozzarella cheese. Cover sauce with dollops of ricotta cheese. Pour ⅓ of tomato sauce over ricotta cheese. Cover with aluminum foil and bake for 15 minutes. Remove from oven and stir ingredients well. Pour remaining ⅓ of tomato sauce over pasta and sprinkle with remaining 1½ cups mozzarella cheese. Return to oven, uncovered, and broil until cheese lightly browns. Serve with sausage on the side.

★ MARY STEENBURGEN ★

A native of Little Rock, Arkansas, Mary Steenburgen is an Academy Award and Golden Globe winning actress. She and her husband, actor Ted Danson, are long-time supporters of the Clintons.

 ## GARLIC CHEESE GRITS

1 teaspoon salt	1 (6-ounce) tube garlic cheese, cut
4 cups water	into pieces
1 cup uncooked grits	¼ cup butter
1 (6-ounce) tube jalapeño cheese, cut into pieces	

Preheat oven to 350°. In large saucepan over high heat, bring salted water to a boil. Slowly add grits and bring to a second boil. Reduce heat and cook over medium heat 4 to 5 minutes, stirring often. Add cheeses and butter, stirring until melted and thoroughly blended. Pour into ungreased 1½-quart casserole. Bake, uncovered, for 30 minutes.

Yield: 6 servings

We have great difficulty locating tubes of cheese. We have substituted processed cheese and added a small amount of freshly minced garlic and fresh or canned chopped jalapeños.

★ IDA MARGARET STONE ★

A fifth generation Arkansan and true southern Yellow Dog Democrat, Ida Margaret Stone was one of the original Friends of Bill, having been introduced to him in 1974 during his run for U.S. Congress. Ida Margaret was well known in Arkansas political circles, especially Southwest Arkansas, with few candidates ever making it out of the gate without her support. Her devotion to the Clintons became extremely apparent when a friend of hers called posing as a sales representative for her cable television company. The "rep" offered her the "Bill and Hillary Channel" for $39.95 a month, to which she immediately replied, "Yes!"

 ## IDA'S GERMAN CHOCOLATE TORTE

CAKE

2 cups sugar	½ cup boiling water	1 teaspoon vanilla
1 cup shortening	1 teaspoon baking soda	Pinch of salt
6 egg yolks	1 cup buttermilk	6 egg whites, stiffly beaten
1 (4-ounce) bar German sweet chocolate	2¼ cups all-purpose flour	

Preheat oven to 350°. In large mixing bowl, cream together sugar and shortening with electric mixer on medium speed. Add egg yolks, one at a time. Melt chocolate in boiling water and add to creamed mixture. In small bowl, dissolve baking soda in buttermilk. Add flour to creamed mixture alternately with buttermilk mixture. Add vanilla and salt; fold in egg whites. Pour batter into six 9-inch cake pans. Bake for 30 minutes. Allow to cool. Spread frosting between each layer and on top of torte.

FROSTING

2 cups sugar	6 egg yolks, beaten	2 cups chopped pecans
2 cups evaporated milk	1 (14-ounce) package flaked coconut	2 teaspoons vanilla
1 cup butter		

In double boiler over medium-high heat, cook sugar, milk, butter, and egg yolks, stirring constantly. Cook until thickened. Fold in coconut, pecans, and vanilla and mix well.

★ MARCIA STRAUSS ★

Marcia Strauss and her husband Neil have been long-time supporters of the Clintons. In addition to hosting President Clinton at their home, they have also attended several dinners and events with the former First Family. They currently reside in Houston, Texas, where they enjoy their retirement and watching over their granddaughter Lexie Rose.

 ## CHILI CHEESE SQUARES

4 (4½-ounce) cans chopped green chile peppers, drained

2 cups shredded Cheddar cheese

2 cups shredded Monterey Jack cheese

2 eggs, lightly beaten

Garlic salt to taste

Black pepper to taste

Preheat oven to 375°. Place chiles in 9x9-inch glass casserole. Sprinkle with combine cheeses. Pour beaten eggs over cheeses. Sprinkle with garlic salt and black pepper to taste. Bake for 30 minutes or until brown on top. Allow to cool 10 minutes. Cut into squares and serve atop shredded wheat crackers.

During her tenure at the White House, Carrie Street worked in the Comment Line and Greetings Office as Deputy Director and in the Scheduling Office as Director of Presidential Scheduling Correspondence. At the end of the Adminstration, she worked in President Clinton's transition office in Washington, DC. She currently resides in DC and works for the Prince of Wales Foundation.

 **BROCCOLI SALAD**

3	bunches broccoli, stalks trimmed	½	cup raisins
10	bacon slices, cooked and crumbled	¼	cup finely chopped onions

In large salad bowl, combine broccoli, bacon, raisins, and onions. One hour before serving, pour dressing over salad, tossing well to coat.

DRESSING

1	cup mayonnaise	⅔	tablespoon vinegar	½	cup sugar

In small mixing bowl, combine ingredients, mixing well. Chill until ready to toss.

Yield: 6 to 8 servings

Leftovers will keep in refrigerator about 24 hours.

I received this recipe from a volunteer at the White House. It brings back fond memories of the wonderful "potluck parties" we had in the Greetings and Comment Line Office!

★ GRAHAM STREETT AND JIMMY STREETT ★

Jimmy Streett did advance for President and Senator Clinton during the Clinton Administration and Vice President Gore during the 2000 campaign. He also served as an intern in the White House Office of Speechwriting. He currently resides in Nashville, Tennessee, where he is a law student at Vanderbilt University.

Graham Streett did advance during the 1992 and 1996 campaigns for both President and Senator Clinton. During the Clinton Administration, he was a Deputy Chief of Staff at the Department of Commerce. He currently resides in Fayetteville, Arkansas, and is the CEO of Washington County Financial Management.

 ## SOUTHERN BOURBON SLUSH

1 cup bourbon whiskey	1 (12-ounce) can frozen lemonade	2 cups strong tea
¾ cup sugar	1 (6-ounce) can frozen orange juice	6 cups water

Combine ingredients and freeze overnight. Thaw slightly to slush and serve in individual glasses.

Mary Streett did advance in the 1992 and 1996 campaigns for both President and Senator Clinton. She was the Deputy General Counsel at the Department of Commerce. She currently resides in Chicago and is an attorney with Mayor, Brown, Rowe & Maw.

 **CRAB CROUSTADES**

1 loaf white bread, unsliced	1 egg yolk
½ cup butter, melted	1 (6-ounce) can crabmeat, drained and flaked
1 (5-ounce) jar pasteurized sharp cheese spread	1 teaspoon Worcestershire sauce
	¼ teaspoon onion powder
	⅛ teaspoon pepper

Cut bread into 1-inch slices; trim and discard crust. Cut slices into 1-inch cubes. Hollow out each cube, leaving ⅛-inch thickness on bottom. Brush top and sides with melted butter. Place on baking sheet. Bake at 400° for 10 minutes or until crisp and brown. Transfer to wire rack and cool. In large mixing bowl, beat together cheese and egg yolk. Add crabmeat, Worcestershire sauce, onion powder, and pepper. Mix well. Fill croustades with crab mixture. Bake at 400° for 10 minutes or until filling begins to brown. Serve hot.

After filling croustades with crab mixture, they may be frozen. Place in foil or a covered plastic container. To serve, place frozen croustades on baking sheet. Heat at 400° for 10 minutes.

★ STEPHANIE STREETT ★

Stephanie Streett worked as a scheduler in the 1992 campaign and Presidential transition and went on to become Assistant to the President and Director of Presidential Scheduling at the White House. She is currently the Executive Director of the William J. Clinton Presidential Foundation. She and her husband, Don Erbach, reside in Little Rock, Arkansas, with their children, Olivia and Katherine.

 ## HOT ARTICHOKE DIP

1 (14-ounce) can artichoke hearts, drained and chopped	1 cup mayonnaise
	1 cup Parmesan cheese

In mixing bowl, combine ingredients and mix well. Pour into ramekins or small casserole. Bake at 350° for 20 to 25 minutes. Serve with bagel chips or toasted pita chips.

FOR A SPICIER DIP, YOU MAY ADD THE FOLLOWING INGREDIENTS AND SERVE WITH CORN CHIPS:

1 (4-ounce) can chopped green chiles, drained	1 teaspoon cumin	¾ teaspoon garlic powder
	1 teaspoon cayenne pepper	

I served this tasty dip for our Scheduling and Advance Holiday party each year. It was always a favorite and so easy to make!

226

Sue H. Streett is the mother of Stephanie, Bridgette, Mary, Graham, and Jimmy, who all worked in the 1992 campaign or in various positions in the Clinton Administration. She and her husband Alex reside in Russellville, Arkansas, where she is a Registered Dietician.

 **FROZEN LEMON CREAM**

1	cup whole milk		Juice and zest of 3 lemons		Mint leaves for garnish
1	cup whipping cream	6	large lemons		Lemon slices for garnish
1	cup sugar				

In large mixing bowl, combine milk, cream, and sugar, stirring until sugar dissolves. Pour into 8x8-inch dish and freeze until slushy. Add lemon juice and zest, beating thoroughly with electric mixer. Return to freezer for 2 hours. Beat mixture again with electric mixer. Return to freezer and freeze until solid. Slice off tops of lemons; with grapefruit knife and spoon, remove all pulp. Cut thin slice from bottom of each lemon so that it will stand upright. Fill lemon shells with frozen cream, piling it high. Serve on individual plates; garnish with mint leaf and lemon slice.

Yield: 6 servings

★ BARBRA STREISAND ★

Barbra Streisand has established a record of extraordinary "firsts" and achieved an array of distinguised awards as an actress, singer, composer, producer and motion picture director. She has poured similar passion and talent into her work as a civil rights and environmental activist and has been a bold and powerful participant in the political process of this country. She is a supporter and friend of President William J. Clinton and was a dear friend of his late mother, Virginia Kelley, in whose memory she dedicated her album of songs of faith, "Higher Ground."

 ## SOUTHERN LEMON ICE BOX PIE

PIE
Juice of 3 lemons
3 egg yolks, beaten
1 teaspoon vanilla
1 (14-ounce) can sweetened condensed milk
1 teaspoon cornstarch
1 graham cracker pie crust

In large mixing bowl, combine lemon juice and next 4 ingredients. Pour into pie crust. Spread with Meringue Topping, forming peaks with the back of a spoon. If desired, place pie under broiler very briefly to brown meringue. Remove from oven and chill 4 hours or overnight.

MERINGUE TOPPING
3 egg whites
½ cup sugar

In mixing bowl, beat egg whites with electric mixer on medium-high speed, adding sugar 1 tablespoon at a time.

Yield: 8 to 10 servings

This dessert was made for a luncheon on August 13, 2000, that we had on our front yard for President Clinton.

Tammy Sun worked in Vice President Al Gore's West Wing office during the Clinton Administration. She is now the Associate Director of Communications and Research at the Office of William J. Clinton in Harlem.

 ## LINGUINE WITH TOFU, TOMATOES, AND ONIONS

4 teaspoons olive oil
1 small package firm tofu, cubed
2 onions, finely sliced
1 tablespoon sugar
1-2 garlic cloves, crushed

6 large peeled tomatoes, seeded and chopped
¼ cup freshly chopped basil
1 tablespoon freshly chopped oregano
Salt and pepper to taste

1 tablespoon butter
1 (12-ounce) package linguine, cooked al dente
½ cup Parmesan cheese, divided
Extra virgin olive oil

In large nonstick skillet over medium-high heat, heat olive oil. Brown tofu cubes on all sides; set aside. In same skillet, sauté onions and sprinkle with sugar. Add garlic and stir frequently. Add tomatoes, basil, and oregano. Season with salt and pepper to taste. Reduce heat and simmer about 5 minutes. Return tofu to skillet and sauté 1 minute. Remove tofu and set aside. In large saucepan over medium-high heat, melt butter. Add linguine and stir in ¼ cup Parmesan cheese. (Add boiling water if needed.) Add tomato mixture and tofu, tossing well. Sprinkle with remaining Parmesan cheese. Serve on 4 individual plates and drizzle with olive oil.

Yield: 4 servings

★ LAURIE AND JOHN SYKES ★

John Sykes is the former President of VH-1. He and his wife, Laurie, are both activists for music education. In 1996, Skyes founded the VH-1 Save the Music Foundation to help restore music education programs in America's public schools and to raise awareness of the positive impact music participation has on students. President Clinton was an early supporter of the Save the Music Foundation and since leaving office, the former President has continued to work with the organization to bring music education back to public schools in Harlem, New York.

 ## TOMATO PIE

PASTRY

1¾ cups all-purpose flour	1 tablespoon sugar	4 tablespoons ice water
½ teaspoon salt	¾ cup cold butter, cut into pats	

Combine flour, salt, and sugar in food processor; add butter and process until coarse and crumbly. Run processor and add water; process until ball forms. Cover and chill 30 minutes. Spread pastry on bottom and up sides of round pie plate.

FILLING

⅓ cup Dijon mustard	6-8 firm, ripe tomatoes, thinly sliced	Salt and pepper to taste
1 pound shredded Gruyère cheese, divided	1 tablespoon chopped garlic	2 tablespoons olive oil
	1 teaspoon dried oregano	

Preheat oven to 400°. Brush pastry with mustard. Sprinkle with most of cheese and tomato slices. Sprinkle top evenly with garlic and oregano. Season with salt and pepper to taste. Drizzle with olive oil. Sprinkle with remaining cheese. Bake for 25 to 30 minutes.

Yield: 8 servings

Our dear friend Linda made this for her first date with her husband... he flipped for it... and her! She passed it onto us—we've never had any leftovers!

Elizabeth Taylor is an Oscar winning actress who has used her success to raise funds and awareness for the fight against HIV/AIDS in the United States and around the world. In 1992, she received the Jean Hersholt Humanitarian Award from the Academy of Motion Picture Arts and Science recognizing her tireless efforts. She has also been a friend and supporter of the William J. Clinton Presidential Foundation.

 ## SPICY CHICKEN

2 teaspoons curry powder	½ teaspoon turmeric	1 teaspoon fresh ginger, grated
1 teaspoon cumin	½ garlic clove, crushed	1 medium chicken, cut into pieces and skinned
½ teaspoon ground ginger	1 onion, chopped	

In shallow dish, combine curry and next 6 ingredients. Coat chicken with seasoning and chill at least 2 hours. Place on moderately hot grill or broil in oven for 30 minutes or until chicken is done, turning once.

Yield: 4 servings

★ THECIA TAYLOR ★

Thecia Taylor has volunteered at the William J. Clinton Presidential Foundation since July of 2001. Prior to this, she worked in the 1996 Presidential campaign and in several gubernatorial campaigns. Thecia and her son Kelly Power have supported the Clintons throughout all of their endeavors.

BOURBON BALLS

30 vanilla wafers, crushed
2 tablespoons cocoa

2 tablespoons light corn syrup
⅓ cup crushed pecans

4 tablespoons bourbon
Confectioners' sugar

In mixing bowl, combine crushed wafers, cocoa, and corn syrup, mixing well. Add pecans and bourbon. Shape into balls and roll in confectioners' sugar. Store in airtight container.

HOLIDAY VEGETABLES

1 (10¾-ounce) can cream of mushroom soup
¾ cup water
1 (16-ounce) can diagonally cut wax beans, drained

1 (16-ounce) can small onions, drained
2 tablespoons chopped pimiento
¼ cup finely crushed breadcrumbs or cracker crumbs

¼ cup Parmesan cheese
2 tablespoons butter, melted

Preheat oven to 325°. In 1 ½-quart casserole, dilute soup with water, mixing well. Add beans, onions, and pimiento. In mixing bowl, combine crumbs, cheese, and butter. Sprinkle over casserole. Bake for 35 to 40 minutes.

Yield: 6 to 8 servings

Pat Torvestad worked with Bill Clinton on his first gubernatorial inaugural gala "Diamonds and Denim". She then went to work for the Governor's Office as Director of Volunteers. She recently held the position of Director of Planning and Development for the University of Arkansas System, allowing her to develop the academic program for the new Clinton School of Public Service. She is now the Vice Chancellor for Communications and Marketing at the University of Arkansas for Medical Sciences and resides in Little Rock with her dog Beans and her husband Bob, who served as Executive Officer of AmeriCorps during the Clinton Administration.

 ## SANTA FE CHEESE GRITS

1 teaspoon salt
4 cups water
1 cup uncooked grits
1 (6-ounce) tube jalapeño cheese, cut into pieces

1 (6-ounce) tube garlic cheese, cut into pieces
¼ cup butter
1-2 tablespoons cumin

2 tablespoons red chili (NOT chili powder)
2 tablespoons chopped green chilies

Preheat oven to 350°. In large saucepan over high heat, bring salted water to a boil. Slowly add grits and bring to a second boil. Reduce heat and cook over medium heat 4 to 5 minutes, stirring often. Add cheeses and butter, stirring until melted and thoroughly blended. Stir in cumin, red chili, and green chilies. Pour into ungreased 1½-quart casserole. Bake, uncovered, for 30 minutes.

Yield: 6 servings

Available for purchase at specialty stores or over the internet, red or green chili is from New Mexico and is required for taste.

This is a spicy, southwestern version of the more bland traditional Southern cheese grits. It goes great with peppered ham and curried or sweet fruit for brunch. It may be prepared ahead, frozen, and reheated. The difference is the real red chili, cumin, and chopped green chilies.

★ JUNE GAYLE TURNER ★

June Gayle Turner worked for Sylvia Matthews, Deputy Chief of Staff, from January of 1997 until June of 1998. From June 1998 to January 2001, she served as the West Wing Receptionist. During her last two years at the White House, she was on several advance teams for the President's trips.

 ## FIVE FLAVOR POUND CAKE

1 cup butter	3 cups all-purpose flour	1 teaspoon butter flavoring
½ cup shortening	1 cup buttermilk	1 teaspoon rum flavoring
3 cups sugar	½ teaspoon baking powder	1 teaspoon coconut flavoring
5 eggs, well beaten	1 teaspoon vanilla	1 teaspoon lemon flavoring

Preheat oven to 325°. In large mixing bowl, cream together butter, shortening, and sugar with electric mixer on high speed. Beat in eggs. Add flour alternately with buttermilk. Add baking powder and remaining ingredients, mixing well. Pour into prepared Bundt pan or tube pan. Bake for 1 hour, 20 minutes.

Yield: 12 to 16 servings

June was responsible for baking many of the cakes and treats served at birthday parties and showers in the White House during the Clinton Administration. This recipe is just one example.

★ LORETTA UCELLI ★

Loretta Ucelli served as White House Communications Director for the last two years of the Clinton presidency. She now lives in New York City, where she counsels corporate and organization leaders on image, positioning, and crisis management.

 ## BROCCOLI WITH OLIVE OIL AND LEMON

1	head broccoli, cut into florets		Juice of ½ lemon		Salt and freshly ground black
1	garlic clove, halved lengthwise	¼	cup extra virgin olive oil		pepper

Place broccoli florets in large saucepan of salted boiling water. Return to boil; cook 1 minute. Drain immediately and dry on paper towels. Rub garlic halves on bottom and sides of serving bowl. Arrange broccoli in serving bowl. Drizzle with lemon juice and olive oil, tossing well to coat. Season with salt and pepper to taste. Serve warm or at room temperature.

Yield: 4 servings

 ## PORCINI RISOTTO

½	ounce dried porcini mushrooms	4	tablespoons extra virgin olive oil, divided	½	pound cremini mushrooms
½	cup water			2	tablespoons extra virgin olive oil
8	cups chicken stock	1	(12-ounce) package arborio rice	2	tablespoons unsalted butter
2	garlic cloves, crushed	¼	cup white wine	2	tablespoons chopped Italian parsley
				4	tablespoons mascarpone cheese

Soak porcini mushrooms in water. Rinse, drain, chop, and set aside. In large saucepan over high heat, bring chicken stock to a boil. In heavy saucepan over medium heat, sauté garlic in 2 tablespoons olive oil 3 minutes. Add porcini mushrooms and stir. Add rice to mixture and sear about 1 minute. Add white wine, cooking 2 to 3 minutes, or until wine reduces somewhat. Add heated chicken stock ½ cup at a time as needed, stirring constantly, about 15 to 20 minutes or until rice softens and mixture thickens. In small skillet over medium-high heat, sauté cremini mushrooms in 2 tablespoons olive oil until tender. Add cremimi mushrooms to rice mixture and cook additional 10 minutes or until rice is done, stirring constantly. Remove from heat; stir in butter, parsley, and cheese. Serve immediately.

Yield: 4 servings

★ MARY LYNN VAN WYCK AND BRONSON VAN WYCK ★

Mary Lynn van Wyck is a lifelong resident of Tuckerman, Arkansas. Her son Bronson served as Mrs. Clinton's photographer and worked in her correspondence office in 1992, traveling with her during the Presidential campaign of that year.

 ARROWHEAD FARMS FRIED CHICKEN

1	fryer chicken	1	cup mayonnaise	4	cups all-purpose flour
	Salt to taste	4	eggs, lightly beaten	2	teaspoons paprika
4	cups buttermilk	½	bunch fresh basil, chopped		Pepper to taste
½	(12-ounce) bottle dark ale	2	tablespoons Italian seasoning	5	cups peanut oil

Cut up chicken and wash and pat dry. Season chicken generously with salt, cover, and set aside for 20 minutes. In large glass bowl, combine buttermilk and next 5 ingredients, whisking together to form a thick batter. Add chicken one piece at a time, making sure each piece is thoroughly coated. Place bowl in refrigerator 1 hour, 30 minutes. In shallow dish, combine flour, paprika, salt, and pepper. In deep skillet over medium-high heat, heat peanut oil. Oil level should be high enough to almost cover chicken pieces. If oil smokes, heat should be reduced. Thoroughly coat each piece of chicken with flour mixture. Carefully drop each piece of chicken into hot oil. Brown 8 to 10 minutes; turn pieces over. Immediately reduce heat to medium-low and cover skillet. Cook 10 minutes or until uniformly brown. Increase heat to medium-high and uncover. Cook additional 3 to 4 minutes and turn, cooking 5 more minutes. Remove chicken from skillet and drain on paper towels.

Originally from the Mid-South, Dwight Vick began his political interests sitting in his grandfather's screened-in porch and his grandmother's kitchen. It was during his doctoral studies that Dwight worked as an intern for Congressman Ed Pastor and later, the Domestic Policy Council during the Clinton White House. Dwight recently accepted an assistant professor's position in the Department of Political Science at the University of South Dakota.

 ## MAPLE PECAN PIE

1 cup pure maple syrup	¼ cup sugar	1 teaspoon vanilla
¾ cup firm packed light brown sugar	3 tablespoons butter, melted	1 (9-inch) frozen deep-dish pie crust
3 eggs	1 tablespoon all-purpose flour	1½ cups coarsely chopped pecans

Preheat oven to 350°. In large mixing bowl, combine syrup and next 6 ingredients, whisking well to blend. Place pie crust on baking sheet. Sprinkle bottom evenly with nuts. Pour syrup mixture into crust. Bake for 1 hour or until filling is set and slightly puffed. Transfer pie to wire rack and cool completely before serving.

Yield: 8 servings

This pie is really good. I like the flavor the maple syrup gives the pie. I do encourage those who make the pie to get a local or New England-made syrup-nothing but the best will do!

★ LISA WALDEN ★

A native New Yorker, Lisa Walden is currently the Executive Assistant to the Chief of Staff for President Clinton. Before politics, she was an award winning songwriter and former blues club owner.

POTATO SALAD

8	white potatoes	3	small sweet gherkins, chopped	¾	cup mayonnaise
2	eggs	1	teaspoon prepared mustard	1½	teaspoons salt
4	celery stalks, chopped	2	teaspoons French dressing		

Boil potatoes and eggs one day ahead. Chill overnight. Peel and dice potatoes and eggs. In large salad bowl, combine potatoes, eggs, and remaining ingredients; mix thoroughly. Chill until ready to serve.

Mark Walsh is Managing Partner at Ruxton Ventures LLC, a private investment entity, with stakes in a number of technology companies and venture funds. He is the Democratic National Committee's Chief Technology Advisor. A voluntary position, its goal is to reach out to core and fringe voters using interactive techniques and tactics, and to help create a more nimble DNC. He was also named Man of the Year by the Maryland State Democratic Party in 2001.

SHERRIED PUMPKIN CHIFFON PIE

1 (¼-ounce) package plain gelatin	½ cup sherry	¼ teaspoon nutmeg
¼ cup cold water	1 cup sugar, divided	¼ teaspoon ginger
3 eggs, separated	¼ teaspoon salt	1 (9-inch) baked pastry or graham cracker pie crust
1 cup canned pumpkin	½ teaspoon cinnamon	Frozen whipped topping

In small mixing bowl, soften gelatin in cold water and set aside. In double boiler over medium-high heat, beat egg yolks lightly. Stir in pumpkin, sherry, ½ cup sugar, and next 4 ingredients. Cook in double boiler 5 minutes, stirring constantly. Remove from heat, add softened gelatin. Stir until gelatin dissolves and chill. When mixture begins to thicken, beat egg whites with remaining ½ cup sugar until stiff. Fold into pumpkin mixture. Pour into pie crust and chill several hours. Top individual servings with frozen whipped topping and serve.

Yield: 8 to 10 servings

This is my mother's favorite dessert recipe. It's very good at any time of year, but particularly at Thanksgiving and Christmas. It's also my son Jack's favorite pie. When this pie is prepared for a family gathering, there's one for Jack and one for the rest of the family!

★ PARKER WESTBROOK ★

Parker Westbrook met Bill Clinton in the 1960s when Clinton was an intern in Senator Fulbright's Washington, DC, office. Parker is known throughout Arkansas as "Mr. Preservation" and currently serves as the President on the Board of the Pioneer Washington Restoration Foundation.

PARKER WESTBROOK'S FAMOUS MUSCADINE WINE

1	gallon boiling water	1	package baker's yeast
8	cups mashed muscadines	3	pounds sugar

Pour boiling water over muscadines in large crockpot and steep several hours. When water is lukewarm, add yeast and sugar, mixing well until dissolved. Cover with cheesecloth and let stand 7 days, stirring once or twice. Strain wine, bottle, and cover with cheesecloth until bubbles stop. Cap and chill to stop action. Do not let wine stand in sunshine after corking-it's been known to explode!

Parker Westbrook's Famous Muscadine Wine is pleasantly sweet, thus may be served as a dessert wine with fruits and cheese.

This wine recipe is an old one known in Howard and Pike counties, Arkansas, by my mother's family, and influenced by a recipe I discussed with friends in Waterford, Virginia, in the 1960s. At the time, Bill Clinton used to ride with me from Senator Fulbright's office to Georgetown in my black 1958 Thunderbird, which I still have and drive in Nashville. The wine became so famous as an entry in auctions at Historic Arkansas Museum fundraisers that the word "Famous" was added to the title when two bottles brought five hundred dollars at an auction in the 1980s.

★ MARGARET AND CARL WHILLOCK ★

Margaret and Carl Whillock volunteered for most of Bill Clinton's campaigns while he was in Arkansas. In 1993, Margaret was appointed as a commissioner and served all 8 years on the White House Presidential Scholars Committee. For the last 3 years of the administration, she served as the Deputy Director of the White House Visitor's Office. Her husband Carl served as the Special Assistant for Agriculture and Trade. They currently reside in Little Rock, Arkansas, and continue to volunteer and support the William J. Clinton Presidential Foundation.

 ## HOMEMADE HOT ROLLS

¾ cup sugar	1 cup water	2 eggs, well beaten
1 cup butter	2 (¼-ounce) packages yeast	6 cup unsifted all-purpose flour
2 teaspoons salt	1 cup lukewarm water	

In saucepan over medium heat, combine sugar, butter, salt, and water, stirring until butter melts. Remove from heat, transfer to large mixing bowl, and cool to lukewarm. Dissolve yeast in lukewarm water. Add to sugar mixture. Add eggs and mix well. Stir in flour gradually. Cover with waxed paper and chill several hours or overnight. Roll out on lightly floured flat surface. Cut with biscuit cutter and place one inch apart on greased baking sheet. Let rise in warm place about 2 hours. Bake at 375° for 15 minutes or until light golden brown.

The dough will keep several days in refrigerator.

★ ANNIE WHITWORTH ★

Annie Whitworth worked in the Office of Presidential Scheduling and Political Affairs in the White House. In addition, she worked at the Department of Commerce for Secretary Daley. She currently resides in Washington, DC, and is working at ABC News for Cokie Roberts as a researcher for Cokie's next book due to be released in May 2004.

 ## O'BRIEN POTATOES BY ALICE WHITWORTH

1 (8-ounce) package shredded Cheddar cheese, divided	1 (27-ounce) package frozen O'Brien style potatoes	1 (10¾-ounce) cream of chicken soup
		1 cup sour cream
		2 tablespoons butter, melted

Preheat oven to 350°. In large mixing bowl, combine half of cheese and remaining ingredients and mix well. Transfer mixture to prepared 9x11-inch glass casserole. Sprinkle with remaining cheese. Bake for 45 minutes or until hot and bubbly.

This is a very simple and yummy recipe that my mom used to make all of the time. It's great for breakfast and as a side dish!

★ HUBERT AND CONSTANCE WILHELM ★

Hubert and Constance's son David served as the Campaign Manager in the 1992 race. They currently reside in Athens, Ohio.

 ## HAM LOAF

I	pound smoked ham	¼	cup catsup	I	cup small white bread cubes
I	pound lean pork	I	egg, well beaten	½	cup milk

Have ham and pork ground together at butcher's counter. In large mixing bowl, combine all ingredients, blending thoroughly. Shape mixture into loaf and bake at 350° for I hour, 30 minutes to 2 hours.

In January 1993, we received a call from Lynda Dixon, scheduler for Mrs. Virginia Kelley, President Clinton's mother. Ms. Dixon informed us that Mrs. Kelley and her husband would be attending a conference at the Ohio University Inn in our hometown of Athens, Ohio. Our son, David Wilhelm, had been President Clinton's campaign manager and at that time was Chairman of the Demoratic National Committee.

We were delighted and immediately invited them for dinner along with a couple of our best friends. We had Ham Loaf, Potatoes Au Gratin, and all the Midwest trimmings. What fun we had-much laughter and eating!

Although Mrs. Kelley was ill at the time, she left our house saying that she'd be at the horse races tomorrow back in Arkansas. A Barbra Streisand concert was next on her agenda. How fortunate we were that we had this time together.

★ JAMES LEE WITT ★

James Lee Witt served as the Director of the Federal Emergency Management Administration from 1993 to 2001; in 1996, James became the first head of FEMA to be elevated to a Cabinet position. He is widely recognized for re-organizing and re-energizing FEMA into an effective agency with an emphasis on customer relations and mitigation. James is a native of Arkansas; he previously served as the County Judge of Yell County for five terms and as the Director of the Arkansas Office of Emergency Services. Currently, he is the President of James Lee Witt Associates and the CEO of the International Code Council. He and his wife Lea Ellen divide their time between Washington, DC, and Arkansas.

 **BISCUITS AND CHOCOLATE GRAVY**

BISCUITS
2 cups self-rising flour	Dash of salt	1 teaspoon sugar
⅔ cup milk	¼ cup shortening	Bacon drippings or milk

Preheat oven to 450°. In large mixing bowl, combine ingredients and lightly knead. Roll out dough on floured surface to ¼-inch thickness. Cut with biscuit cutter and place on baking sheet. Brush tops with bacon drippings or milk. Bake for 12 to 15 minutes.

CHOCOLATE GRAVY
3 tablespoons cocoa	⅔ cup all-purpose flour
1 cup sugar	3⅔ cups milk

In large skillet over medium heat, combine ingredients, mixing well until thickened.
Serve over hot buttered biscuits.

★ BRIAN L. WOLFF AND SUE McLAUGHLIN ★

Brian Wolff did advance work for President and Senator Clinton in the '92 and '96 campaigns as well as assisted Senator Clinton in her election to the Senate in 2000. He was the Northwest Finance Director for Al Gore in 2000. He currently resides in Washington, DC, and is the National Finance Director for the Democratic Congressional Campaign Committee and the Campaign Director for the House Democratic Leader, Nancy Pelosi. Sue McLaughlin is Brian's mother.

 ## THE **PERFECT** CHOCOLATE CHIP COOKIE

1 cup butter flavored shortening, softened	2 eggs	1 teaspoon salt
¾ cup sugar	2 teaspoons Mexican vanilla	Pinch of cinnamon
¾ cup brown sugar	2¼ cups all-purpose flour	2 cups milk chocolate chips
	1 teaspoon baking soda	1 cup pecans, chopped

Preheat oven to 350°. In large mixing bowl, cream together shortening and sugars with electric mixer on medium speed until light and fluffy. Add eggs one at a time, beating well after each addition. Stir in vanilla. In separate mixing bowl, combine flour, baking soda, salt, and cinnamon. Gradually stir into creamed mixture. Fold in chocolate chips and pecans. Drop by heaping tablespoonfuls onto prepared baking sheets. Bake for 8 to 10 minutes or until light brown. Allow to cool on baking sheet 5 minutes before transferring to wire racks to cool completely.

Mexican vanilla can be found in Mexican markets. Feel free to substitute regular vanilla.

Dina Wood joined her Arkansas friends during the 1992 and 1996 Clinton/Gore campaigns by traveling, advancing campaign events, and managing special events and national convention activities. In 1993, she worked in the Clinton Administration as a Special Assistant in the U.S. Department of Veterans Affairs. Following the 1996 transition period, she was appointed a staff assistant in the White House Office of Presidential Personnel. Dina then resumed her term as an administration appointee as Executive Assistant to the Secretary of Veterans Affairs and, later, Director of Intergovernmental Affairs for the Overseas Private Investment Corporation. Dina is also an attorney and is currently the Director of Development for the J. William Fulbright College of Arts and Sciences at the University of Arkansas in Fayetteville.

 **MOLTEN CHOCOLATE BABYCAKES**

Butter
1 (12-ounce) package bittersweet chocolate

¼ cup unsalted butter, softened
½ cup superfine sugar
4 eggs, at room temperature

Pinch of salt
1 teaspoon vanilla
⅓ cup all-purpose flour

Preheat oven to 400°. Place baking sheet in oven. Butter six (6-ounce) custard cups. Place small rounds of buttered parchment into bottoms of cups. In double boiler over medium-high heat, melt chocolate. Remove from heat and set aside to slightly cool. In large mixing bowl, cream unsalted butter and sugar with electric mixer on medium speed. In small bowl, beat eggs and salt. Gradually beat eggs into creamed mixture. Stir in vanilla and flour, mixing until smooth. Fold in cooled, melted chocolate, stirring until thoroughly combined. Divide batter among custard cups. Place cups on hot baking sheet. Bake for 10 to 12 minutes, being careful not to overbake. (The outer portion of cupcake will appear baked, but the center must remain very soft.) Remove immediately from oven and carefully invert custard cup onto serving dish. Serve piping hot with sweetened cream.

Yield: 6 servings

For intense chocolate lovers, the outside has the look of a cupcake and in the inside is a powerful chocolate sauce. This is a quick and memorable dessert that must be combined and baked in the same time frame.

★ SHELBY AND DIANNE WOODS ★

Shelby Woods is directly involved in the day-to-day management of CJRW as the Chairman of the Board and Chairman of the Executive Committee. He is a former chairman of the Little Rock Regional Chamber of Commerce and has served on numerous tourism-related taskforces and committees. He and his wife Dianne spend their free time touring the state and nation on their Harley Davidsons.

 ## ENGLISH PEA SALAD

1 (15-ounce) can English peas, drained
1 (11-ounce) can white shoepeg corn, drained
1 (8-ounce) can sliced water chestnuts, drained
1 cup chopped celery
1 green bell pepper, seeded and chopped
2 bunches green onions, chopped
1 (2-ounce) jar sliced pimientos, drained
   Marinade Mix

Combine peas and next 6 ingredients in large salad bowl. Pour Marinade Mix over salad, tossing well to coat. Marinate at least 4 hours before serving.

MARINADE MIX
½ cup sugar
½ cup cooking oil
½ cup vinegar
1 teaspoon salt
¼ teaspoon pepper

In mixing bowl, whisk marinade ingredients together until thoroughly combined.

This is light and tasty and can be doubled to take to any reunion, picnic, or church luncheon... a potluck pleaser!

★ WOODY AND BETTY— "THE CATERERS OF BLUE JEANS BASH" ★

Woody and Betty, who are widely known for their delicious barbecue, owned Woody's Sherwood Forest for a number of years. While Governor, President Clinton attended many events held there. One of the more memorable events was a get-together of the campaign and governor's staffs in 1992. President Clinton, Mrs. Clinton, and Chelsea arrived in Bill's Ford Mustang convertible at the 1950s-themed party.

 ## BUTTERMILK FLAVORED FRIED CATFISH

4 cups cornmeal
1 cup all-purpose flour
1 tablespoon pepper
1 tablespoon salt
1 tablespoon sugar
Catfish filets
4 cups buttermilk
Cooking oil for frying

In shallow dish, combine cornmeal and next 4 ingredients. Dip catfish in buttermilk and gently dredge in cornmeal mixture. Heat cooking oil to 375° in deep fryer or skillet. Fry filets until thickest portion of fish is done.

This was served high on a rooftop in New York City in August of 1992 before Governor Bill Clinton's acceptance speech. Arkansas catfish was introduced at a very prestigious party with many influential people. A comment to Woody from a famous Massachusetts senator was that he "didn't eat catfish" because it was a scavenger fish. Moments later he was seen feasting on the fish along with Senator David Pryor and was enjoying it very much.

★ WOODY AND BETTY—
"THE CATERERS OF BLUE JEANS BASH" ★

 BBQ Dry Rub for Ribs

1	pound ground chili pepper	½	cup sugar
2	tablespoons salt	4	tablespoons pepper

Combine ingredients, including your own favorite spices to taste, and rub on spare ribs just before baking. Store remaining Rub in air tight container for later use.

Served at the most talked about Inaugural Party, "The Blue Jeans Bash" in January 1993, Woody's ribs were the "talk of the town". The "Bash" was so popular that it was repeated twice.

Carolyn Wu worked in the White House form May 1997 until January 2001. She worked in Management and Administration and the Chief of Staff's office under Erskine Bowles and John Podesta. Carolyn also did advance work on trips to China, Japan, Nigeria, Russia, India, and Northern Ireland. She lives in New York City and is Global Issues Manager for Nike, Inc.

PEPPERMINT SNOWBALL COOKIES

½ cup finely crushed peppermint candies (about 24), divided

¼ cup confectioners' sugar

1 cup butter, softened

⅓ cup confectioners' sugar

1 teaspoon vanilla

2¼ cups all-purpose flour

¼ teaspoon salt

Preheat oven to 325°. In mixing bowl, combine ¼ cup peppermint and ¼ cup confectioners' sugar and set aside. In large mixing bowl, combine butter, ⅓ cup confectioners' sugar, and vanilla. Stir in flour and salt, mixing well. Shape dough into 1-inch balls and place two inches apart on ungreased baking sheet. Bake 12 to 15 minutes or until set, but not brown. Immediately remove from oven and roll in reserved candy mixture. Cool completely on wire rack and roll again in candy mixture.

'Tis the season for cookie making! Get in the spirit with these festive peppermint cookies that look like mint snowballs! These are great holiday cookies and always a hit! Enjoy!

★ KATSU YOSHIDA ★

Katsu Yoshida is the CEO of Global Artists, Inc. Global Artists, Inc. is an international company located in Japan that focuses on the development of intellectual property rights of entertainers.

 ## FOIE GRAS AND TRUFFLE OMELETTE

OMELETTE
1 medium Autumn truffle	1 cup heavy cream	Salt and to taste
1½ tablespoons olive oil, divided	1 cup long grain rice, uncooked	Butter
7 ounces foie gras terrine, chopped	2 cups chicken stock	4 eggs

Slice truffle and sauté in ½ tablespoon oil until fragrant; add foie gras. Stir in cream and remove from heat; set aside. Pour 1 tablespoon oil into large saucepan and heat. Stir in rice and heat just until it begins to turn white. Add stock a little at a time. Stir constantly as stock reduces, taking care not to overcook rice. Season with salt to taste. Stir rice mixture into truffle cream sauce and mix well. Mix eggs for omelette two at a time and pour into heated, buttered skillet. When eggs begin to set, spoon half of rice mixture over half of omelette. Fold over and continue to cook until eggs are completely set. Repeat process for second omelette. If desired, spoon Omelette Sauce over dish and serve immediately.

OMELETTE SAUCE
2 tablespoons ketchup	1½ tablespoons white wine	1½ tablespoons oyster sauce
2 tablespoons Worcestershire sauce	1½ tablespoons soy sauce	Black pepper to taste
1½ tablespoons sugar		

In small saucepan over medium heat, whisk ketchup and next 5 ingredients together. When mixture begins to reduce and thicken, remove from heat and stir in pepper to taste.

Yield: 4 servings

 *This special omelette was prepared for President Clinton by Chef Koshimizu of Kun restaurant in Tokyo after a speech and discussion in late November of 2002.*

★ INDEX ★

DIPS AND SPREADS

POTATOES

POULTRY

PUDDINGS (see Desserts)

PUMPKIN

★ R ★

RASPBERRIES

RECIPE CONTRIBUTORS

RICE

★ S ★

SALADS

★ T ★

★ V ★

★ W ★

★ Y ★